WORLD WAR TWO IN ALASKA AND NORTHWEST CANADA 1941 – 1945

I0802738

A COMPANION TO THE FORGOTTEN WAR SERIES

BY STAN COHEN

RESEARCH ASSISTANT Blaine Cornelison

Copyright © 2019 Stan Cohen

First Printing, May 2019

FRONT COVER

An AD Wire photo from the US Army. (September 3) Yanks in Alaska on the alert–from foxholes dug along the fringes of their encampment, two US soldiers stationed at an outpost in Alaska scan the skies for Jap raiders during an "alert."

PHOTO ACKNOWLEGEMENTS

NA – National Archives

KHS – Kodiak Historial Society

USN – United States Navy

ASL – Alaska State Library

AM – Anchrage Museum at Rasmuson Center

USAF – United States Air Force

Photos not credited are from Pictorial History Publishing Company's archives or credited to their sources.

Library of Congress Cataloging-in-Publication Data

Names: Cohen, Stan, author. | Cornelison, Blaine, research assistant.
Title: World War Two in Alaska and Northwest Canada 1941-1945 : a companion to the forgotten war series / by Stan Cohen ; research assistant, Blaine Cornelison.
Other titles: World War II in Alaska and Northwest Canada 1941-1945 | WWII in Alaska and Northwest Canada 1941-1945
Description: Missoula, Montana : Pictorial Histories Publishing Company, an imprint of Mountain Press Publishing Company, [2019] | Series: Forgotten war series | Includes bibliographical references.
Identifiers: LCCN 2019004967 | ISBN 9780878426935 (pbk. : alk. paper)
Subjects: LCSH: World War, 1939-1945–Campaigns–Alaska. | World War, 1939-1945–Alaska. | World War, 1939-1945–Northwest, Canadian. | World War, 1939-1945–Alaska–Personal narratives. | World War, 1939-1945–Northwest, Canadian–Personal narratives. | Alaska–History–1867-1959.
Classification: LCC D769.87.A4 C64 2019 | DDC 940.53/798–dc23
LC record available at https://lccn.loc.gov/2019004967

PRINTED IN INDIA

PICTORIAL HISTORIES PUBLISHING COMPANY
AN IMPRINT OF MOUNTAIN PRESS PUBLISHING COMPANY

Mountain Press Publishing Company
P.O. Box 2399 • Missoula, MT 59806 • 406-728-1900
800-234-5308 • info@mtnpress.com
www.mountain-press.com

INTRODUCTION

When I started researching World War Two activities in the Territory of Alaska and Northwestern Canada (Yukon, Northwest Territories, British Columbia and Alberta) back in 1980 I had plenty of photos and articles for my first volume of my Forgotten War series. As it got into circulation, many people contacted me with their own photos and stories of their time in the North or families of veterans would do the same. I also started attending reunions of Air Force and Army veterans in Alaska and around the country. I was lucky that there were still a great number of veterans around when I started my research.

Through the years, all of this information kept coming in, plus I poured through thousands of photos in archives in Alaska and Canada and even in Washington, DC. This allowed me to write and publish three more volumes. By the time of Volume Four, published in 1993, I thought I had pretty much covered every aspect of the conflict in the area. But in the next few years more and more photos, items and personal accounts surfaced along with books published, including some on the subject I published for other authors.

I discovered in the Canadian Forces Archives a treasure trove of photos and information on the Royal Canadian Army and the Royal Canadian Air Force (RCAF) in Alaska and the Kiska invasion. Some other very detailed information was sent to me on the Russian Lend-Lease program in the Yukon and Alaska and other aspects of the war and what was left behind. In 1989 I was very fortunate to be included, as a historian, on an expedition to Kiska sponsored by the US Navy, The National Park Service and The US Fish and Wildlife Service to document undersea and land remains left when the Japanese evacuated the island. I participated in the 75th anniversary ceremonies in June 2017 of the bombing of Dutch Harbor, where I met veterans of Attu and natives who were evacuated from the islands during the war. It has been a great honor in the past 38 years to have been with individuals who lived through history in the years 1941-45. I have also been able to visit many of the islands in the Aleutians including St. Paul in the Priblofs, to give me a better insight into the subject and area that I have written about.

New monuments have been erected and museums opened, such as the National Park Services' World War Two museum in Dutch Harbor. The reunions are over now but the legacy of participants in this remote theater of war will live on, and I hope my volumes will contribute to this.

Many, many people have contributed to this series through the years and I must give a lot of credit to my good friend and research assistant, Blaine Cornelison of Wasilla, Alaska for taking me "under his wing" when I visited Alaska and for all the photos and stories he contributed. This volume could not have been done without him. All the photos not acknowledged are from my own collection and the rest are acknowledged to the person or organization where I obtained them. The staffs of the Kodiak Historical Society, the Alaska State Library and the Canadian Forces Archives were very helpful. Also Jann Sherill, Charles Robison, Patrick Durand, Mark Stumsky, Karen Abel, Steve Harding, Suellyn Wright Novak, Anne Millbrooke, Ed Storey, and David Foster.

So ends a long journey in history and I hope that this book, and my other volumes will keep the legacy alive for many years to come.

STAN COHEN
January 2019

TABLE OF CONTENTS

Chapter One: North Country at War 1

Chapter Two: Recreation in the USO 57

Chapter Three: The ALCAN and CANOL Construction Projects 79

Chapter Four: Civilian Contractors 107

Chapter Five: Dutch Harbor 119

Chapter Six: Transportation Systems 133

Chapter Seven: Russian Lend-Lease 145

Chapter Eight: Aviation 161

Chapter Nine: Naval Activity 185

Chapter Ten: The Invasion and Battle of Attu 199

Chapter Eleven: Amphibious Task Force 9, The Invasion of Kiska 221

Chapter Twelve: The Kurile Islands Operation 261

Chapter Thirteen: Legacy of the War 269

Appendix 288

Bibliography 289

About the Authors 291

A P-61 night fighter over the Juneau Airport.

— CHAPTER ONE —

NORTH COUNTRY AT WAR

Countries involved in the Northland War—US, Canada, and the Soviet Union.

Supposedly the first person in North America to hear of the attack on Pearl Harbor on the radio was "Augie" Hiebert, who heard it on his ham radio in Fairbanks and alerted the local military. Hiebert was called the "Father of Alaskan Television." In 1939 he and his friend, "Cap" Lathrop moved to Fairbanks and operated the city's first radio station, KFAR. In 1953 Hiebert's company started KTVA, Alaska's first television station in Anchorage and two years later KTVF in Fairbanks. He also helped to establish KENI radio in Anchorage in 1948, and later Alaska's first FM radio station, KNIK in 1960. "Augie" Hiebert died on September 13, 2007

LIFE MAGAZINE

The March 2, 1942 issue of *Life Magazine* had an article entitled, "Six Ways to Invade U.S., Axis Powers can try it if they combine fleets to win sea superiority." As shown on Plan One. It calls for Japanese hop-skip-and –jump across the northern Pacific in great force. It involves war with Russia, hard-pressed by Germany. Opening shot is a surprise attack on the U.S. base at Dutch Harbor with all Japanese aircraft carriers and the fleet reinforced by German battleships, presumably giving superiority. The Japanese captured air bases along the way, then their land-based planes help the carrier planes to protect the next sea advance down the West Coast. An American fleet flings itself into the fight. U.S. fifth column, heretofore held in reserve, creates havoc along the coast. The Japanese take the aviation industry, shipyards and oil wells. Then the Germans stab at the East Coast.

While this scenario sounds very far-fetched today, in March 1942 the U.S. Pacific fleet had been partially disabled at Pearl Harbor and most of the U.S. and British possessions in the Pacific had either been overrun or soon would be by Japanese forces. German U-boats were roaming the Atlantic Ocean, threatening the life-line to Britain and the German forces were still advancing into the interior of Russia.

Obviously the only part of this plan that came true was the bombing of Dutch Harbor and occupation of several islands in the western Aleutian chain. Both sides soon found out that this part of the world was a terrible place to conduct war by land, sea and air.

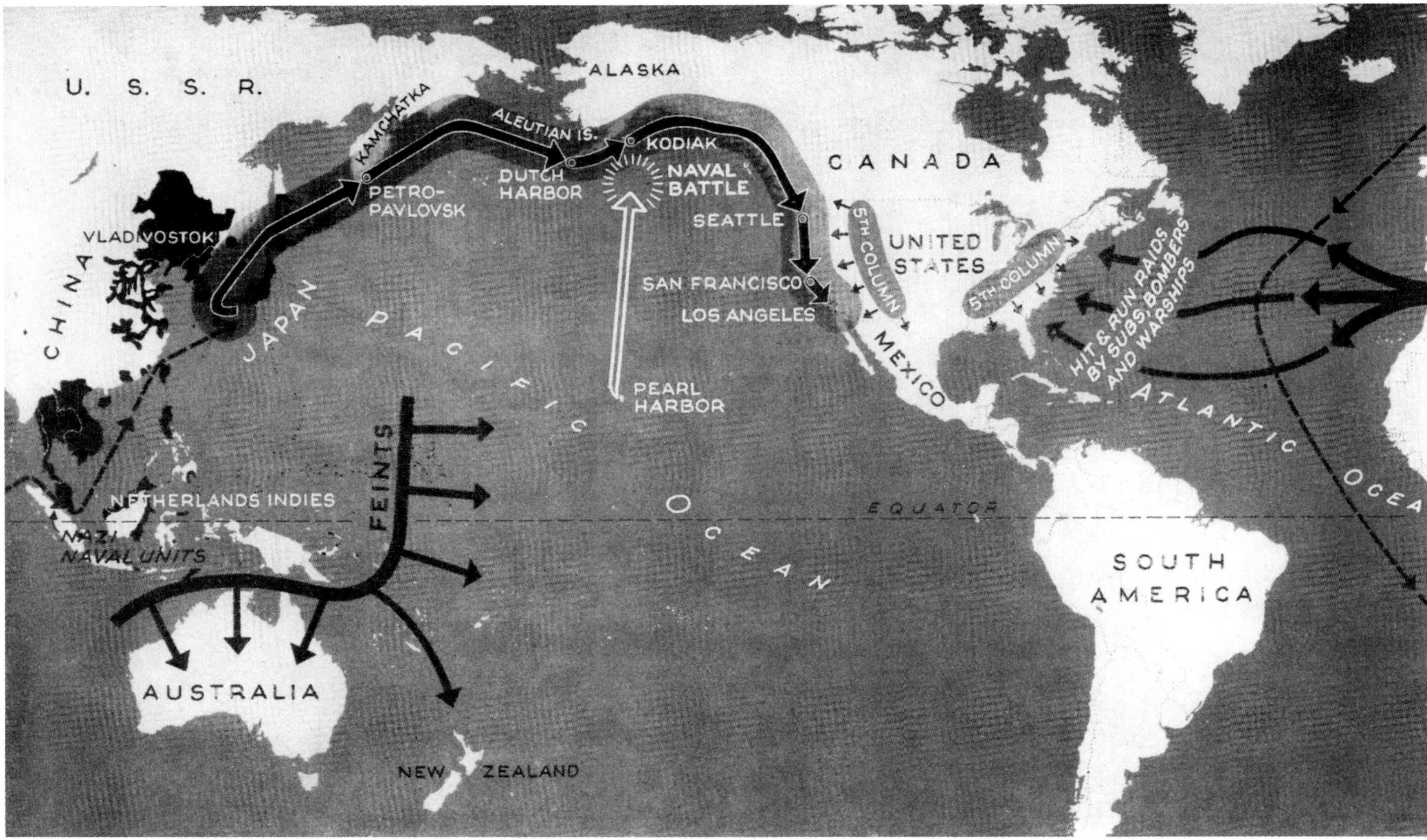
U. S. S. R.
ALASKA
KAMCHATKA
ALEUTIAN IS.
KODIAK
CANADA
VLADIVOSTOK
PETRO-
PAVLOVSK
DUTCH
HARBOR
NAVAL
BATTLE
SEATTLE
5TH COLUMN
UNITED
STATES
5TH COLUMN
HIT & RUN RAIDS
BY SUBS, BOMBERS
AND WARSHIPS
CHINA
SAN FRANCISCO
LOS ANGELES
JAPAN
PACIFIC
MEXICO
PEARL
HARBOR
ATLANTIC
FEINTS
NETHERLANDS INDIES
OCEAN
EQUATOR
NAZI
NAVAL UNITS
SOUTH
AMERICA
AUSTRALIA
NEW ZEALAND

Plan One.

GREATEST USED CAR DISPLAY IN THE WEST
Always in EXAMINER WANT ADS

CHARACTER · QUALITY · AMERICA FIRST! · ENTERPRISE · ACCURACY

Los Angeles Examiner

AN AMERICAN PAPER FOR THE AMERICAN PEOPLE · THE GREAT NEWSPAPER OF THE GREAT SOUTHWEST

Examiner Telephone Richmond 1212 · Giant of Journalism · Examiner Building, 1111 S. Broadway

VOL. XXXIX—NO. 234 · LOS ANGELES, SUNDAY, AUGUST 2, 1942 · Seven Sections—Part 1

Remember PEARL HARBOR

JAP PLAN TO INVADE ALASKA AND U. S. BARED 7 YEARS AGO

6 SQUARE MILES OF DUSSELDORF BLOWN TO BITS

600 R. A. F. Bombers Drop 150 Two-Ton Missiles in Surprise Attack on Industrial Center

By Larry Meier
Staff Correspondent International News Service

LONDON, Aug. 1.—Immense fires enveloped Germany's Rhineland metropolis of Dusseldorf tonight after a raid of record-breaking intensity by 600 or more big British bombers that smashed the heart of the important industrial city with more than 150 two-ton, block-demolishing bombs and hundreds of thousands of incendiaries.

Within the brief space of 50 minutes, the R. A. F. bombing fleet converted four to six square miles of Dusseldorf's industrial area—about 50 per cent of the city proper—into a blazing shambles, participating airmen related upon their return. Munitions plants, steel works, railway yards, motor factories, oil depots and river docks were shattered.

GREATEST IN HISTORY

Never before in the history of aerial operations had such tremendous weight of explosive and fire-kindling metal been loosed upon any single center in such a short time, aviation experts said.

The British air ministry, with characteristic official conservativeness, described the mammoth assault as "probably the most concentrated attack ever made by the bomber command," revealing that a "ceaseless" cloudburst of explosives of all calibers up to the 4000-pound "block-levellers," as well as fire bombs, struck every part of the city.

But the authoritative British Press Association indicated that the raid, executed early Saturday, surpassed any previous air attack in its sudden destructiveness. It characterized the blow as "the most concentrated bombardment in aerial warfare."

The raid struck Dusseldorf by surprise, with explosions ripping up entire buildings and streets and fires breaking out before the city's Nazi defenders could get into action.

Spreading fires, from which

(Continued on Page 10, Cols. 3-5)

U. S. Boy in Raid Sees Great Fires

'Had Perfect Target at Bend of Rhine' to Level War Plants

By Larry Meier
Staff Correspondent International News Service

A BRITISH BOMBER BASE, Aug. 1.—The devastating British raid on Dusseldorf in the pre-dawn hours of this morning left the heart of the Rhineland city a "vast mass of flames," an American R. A. F. volunteer told this correspondent tonight.

A rear gunner on one of the four-motored Lancaster bombers that partook in the 600-plane attack, Sergeant Eugene Choumiere, 19, of Waterford, N. Y., gave a vivid account of the blazing devastation he saw spread out below him.

"It was one of the best shows I have ever seen," said this young veteran of previous 1000-bomber attacks on Cologne and other Nazi cities.

Describing the raid as "the nearest approach to Cologne" he had yet witnessed, Sergeant Choumiere, a bespectacled youth who worked as a machinist in Troy, N. Y., before he joined the R. A. F., related:

"We had a perfect target at the bend of the Rhine River.

"We couldn't distinguish the many individual fires which merged into a single vast mass. When we left there was one tremendous fire leaping high and visible from the Dutch coast (about 150 miles away) as we returned.

"We hit factories for planes, guns, torpedoes, motors—plants whose output goes to practically every branch of the German services.

"Under a bright moonlight we struck the target area as a constant stream of R. A. F. traffic soared across Dusseldorf. It appears that we cut deep into the heart of the Rhineland industrial district."

Choulolere, whose plane was one of the last to leave the scene, said that the first of the bombers arriving over Dusseldorf met with little opposition from anti-aircraft guns and Nazi night fighters. Later, however, the resistance became heavier, with shellbursts puffing all around the R. A. F. planes and enemy fighters spewing machine gun fire.

Nevertheless, all of the Lancasters which took off from this particular airdrome somewhere in England to carry destruction to Dusseldorf returned, with only one of them damaged. I watched the huge bombers depart and saw them come back, their big bomb bays emptied.

Choumiere and all the other participating R. A. F. airmen with whom this writer talked after the raid agreed that, although an estimated 600 bombers were used, the attack equaled in destructive intensity the 1000-plane blows previously dealt such Reich cities as Cologne, Essen and Bremen.

'Twas a Real 'Cologner,' Dusseldorf 'Pranged'!

By Drew Middleton

WITH THE R. A. F. BOMBER COMMAND, Aug. 1.—(AP)—This is a bad moment. Outside in the moonlight you can hear bombers a long way away. But you don't know whether they are units of this squadron returning from the attack on Dusseldorf or Jerry on the prowl. The throbbing silence is oppressive.

Inside the control tower they are waiting for the first radio signal from the homing planes. No one says very much. The squadron leader's pipe sputters. Then a crisp young voice speaks from the receiver:

"D for Donald, D for Donald . . ."

Everyone listens and grins. *Then a red-headed girl gives D for Donald instructions for landing.*

The huge wings of the Lancaster bomber that is D for Donald are moonlit as the plane thunders across the field and glides majestically to a perfect landing. A few moments later, the blond pilot assures you:

"This was a big one for Dusseldorf, a regular *'Cologner.'* We just went in there and pranged 'em and got away. There is a lot of future in a raid like that."

"A lot of future" is the highest praise in the R. A. F. for a well done bombing job.

The station commander looked at his watch.

"Those chaps were just one minute late on their return after a 600-mile flight and a heavy attack," he said. "Here come some other chaps now."

In they come—F for Freddy, B for Beer . . . that's the way the R. A. F. identifies their planes. They are big black planes manned by grinning youngsters who fly into the teeth of the German defenses—tonight, tomorrow, any night.

Every plane in the squadron except H for Harry landed within an hour. The group captain walks to the receiver and stands looking at it. The silence is broken by the happy voice of H for Harry. The captain's shoulders rise a little and he says:

"No casualties, thank God."

3 Surviving Irish Quints Given Civic Welcome in Dublin

DUBLIN, Aug. 1.—(AP)—Given a civic welcome by the Lord Mayor, the three survivors of the Leydon quintuplets were doing well tonight in a special incubator at the National Maternity Hospital after a 200-mile ambulance ride from County Sligo.

The two boys and a girl weighed between two and three and one-half pounds. They were born to Mr. and Mrs. Thomas Leydon, on the Leydon's modest 20-acre potato farm at Breagkwy. Their two sisters died shortly after birth.

The birth of the five babies was the first such authenticated event since the Dionne girls were born May 28, 1934, in Callandar, Ontario.

Leydon and his wife, each 36, formerly lived in New York City, but returned to Ireland six years ago.

The babies have been named Joseph, Thomas and Teresa.

The Leydons have three other children.

1-B's TAKEN INTO SERVICE

New Inductees Release Men for Combat

WASHINGTON, Aug. 1.—(AP)—The first of an estimated 1,000,000 men holding a deferred 1-B classification in the draft because of minor physical defects were accepted today for limited military service.

Undisclosed quotas to be filled by men with faulty eyesight, teeth and other defects which disqualified them from many combat duties, went out July 3 to local boards, to become effective today, August 1.

Those accepted under the relaxed standards will be assigned to duty with Corps Area Service commands and the War Department overhead, it was announced.

By calling each month a number of men who are physically capable of performing limited military service, it will be possible to release almost an equal number of fully qualified soldiers for duty with task forces, the War Department said in announcing the new policy.

NAZIS 100 MI. IN CAUCASUS BELOW ROSTOV

German Drive on Stalingrad Being Fought to Standstill; Kuban Cossacks Join Battle

LONDON, Aug. 2 (Sunday).—(INS)—The Teheran radio reported today the Russians had launched a great counteroffensive along the entire front from Voronezh to Tsimlyansk.

By James E. Brown
Staff Correspondent International News Service

MOSCOW, Aug. 2 (Sunday).—Two reinforced armored columns of a twin-pronged German offensive have plunged some 55 and 100 miles into the northwest Caucasus below Rostov, it was acknowledged officialy today, but the Nazi eastward push on Stalingrad was still being fought to a standstill.

Despite enormous casualties inflicted by bitterly resisting Soviet units, including saber-wielding Kuban Cossacks, German tank and infantry legions, swollen by fresh reserves, managed to pound their way to the vicinity of Kushchevsk and Salsk in the Caucasus.

MAIN RAILWAY PERILED

Endangering the main railway into the oil-producing isthmus from Stalingrad to Novorossisk via Krasnodar, the westerly Nazi column broke through Soviet defenses south of Bataisk to reach the Kuschevsk area for an advance of some 40 miles. Kuschevsk, mention for the first time in the Soviet midnight communique as a scene of fighting, lies on the Rostov-Tikhoretsk Railway, 35 miles south of captured Rostov.

The eastern arm of the Nazi drive into the Caucasus meanwhile was acknowledged to have smashed its way down a branch railway to reach the neighborhood of Salsk, 100 miles southeast of Rostov. Salsk is situated directly on the Stalingrad-Krasnodar-Novorossisk Railway. It, too, was mentioned for the first time by the Soviet information bureau in the midnight war bulletin.

(The German high command announced Saturday the capture of Salsk, saying that Nazi forces had crossed the dontwise Stalingrad-Krasnodar railway on a broad front and that large Soviet contingents were surrounded and faced annihilation.)

The German advance of about 40 miles to the Kushchevsk area from Bataisk, 15 miles below Rostov, was achieved only at a steep price. In the initial stages of the

(Continued on Page 12, Cols. 2-4)

Yellow Air Alert Lasts 37 Minutes in Los Angeles

The Fourth Fighter Command ordered a preliminary "yellow" air raid alert and a radio silence in the Los Angeles area last night when "unidentified targets were reported approaching offshore."

The alert was ordered at 9:34 p. m., and the radio silence at 9:36 p. m. The all clear was given at 10:11 p. m.

No blackout was ordered.

General Mitchell's Warning: Could Bomb Eastern Cities

Senator Johnson of Colorado: 10,000 Japs in Aleutians—That's 10,000 Too Many

WASHINGTON, Aug. 1.—(AP)—Navy report that possibly 10,000 Japanese were in or near the western Aleutian Islands brought the comment from Senator Johnson (Democrat), Colorado, today:

"THAT'S 10,000 TOO MANY."

Senator Thomas (Democrat), Utah, said he regarded with grave misgivings the fact that the Japanese had been permitted to establish themselves anywhere in the Aleutians. He remarked, however, that global strategy might be such that no move would be made to oust the invaders until more favorable conditions prevailed elsewhere.

Delegate Dimond of Alaska said that he "assumed that the Navy knows what it is talking about" in estimating the size of the Japanese force at 10,000, but added that his own information indicated there was a larger number there late in June, "perhaps 25,000."

"BUT 10,000 IS STILL TOO MANY," HE DECLARED.

Northern Frontier Called Key to World Rule; Plea Unheeded

EXCLUSIVE!

There was tense drama in the air on the morning of February 13, 1935.

The great Army dirigible Macon had crashed; Bruno Richard Hauptmann was convicted of the kidnap-killing of the Lindbergh baby; and all Americans were avidly reading those sensational stories.

BUT THE BIGGEST STORY OF ALL PASSED ALMOST WITHOUT NOTICE BEFORE A SESSION OF THE HOUSE MILITARY AFFAIRS COMMITTEE. THAT FELLOW BILLY MITCHELL WAS TALKING.

He was telling a story of grim realism; one filled with foreboding prophecy for the future. Today the Los Angeles Examiner is able to reveal for the first time what he said there. The testimony is preserved in the Congressional Library.

Japan, he was saying, was our dangerous enemy in the Pacific. He was assuming—coldly and calmly—that in the not too far distant future we should have to fight Japan.

He was saying that ALASKA WOULD BE THE STRATEGIC KEY IN THAT WAR; THAT HE WHO HELD ALASKA MIGHT RULE THE WORLD. He was saying that, if Japan should wrest Alaska from our grasp, she could bomb Chicago, Philadelphia, Washington and New York; that she could paralyze our industry, that SHE COULD CONQUER AMERICA AND OCCUPY NEW YORK.

As Alaska was the key to world domination, he said the Aleutian Islands were the key to Alaska. And Brigadier General William (Billy) Mitchell was saying more than that.

He was warning that, unless Alaska's defenses were made impregnable, Japan would seize those vital outposts. He was saying:

"THEY WOULD COME IN THE NIGHT, PROBABLY OUT OF A FOG."

It was a fantastic story—then.

Billy Mitchell was not listened to. Five years later, the Aleutian Islands had not even been adequately surveyed. W. L. Goldsborough, addressing the U. S. Naval Institute, in June, 1941, said, **"At this time (December, 1940) no charts exist on the great majority of Aleutian indentations, and many of those that do exist cannot be trusted."**

No charts? THE JAPS HAD CHARTS—carefully prepared by Jap "fishermen" who infested the region. And the Japs came—as Billy Mitchell predicted, IN THE NIGHT, OUT OF A FOG.

The Jap stroke that General Mitchell foresaw has begun. And so it is of vital interest to Americans to consider the facts that Billy Mitchell laid before the House Military Affairs Commission that morning in 1935.

His warnings were similar to those coming today from Prime Minister Hepburn of Ontario, Anthony J. Dimond, congressional delegate from Alaska and others; his fears were those which spur the Senate military affairs subcommittee, now on its way to Alaska to investigate the situation.

Billy Mitchell was speaking out of a keen, personal knowledge of Alaska. And he was speaking, too, out of a keen appreciation of a new type of warfare—war in the air.

Other men who appeared before the committee in 1935—highranking members of the general staff—spoke of peace; of peacetime development of aviation, of peacetime training.

But Billy Mitchell was talking of Japan. He was saying:

"On account of the earthquakes a great deal of her construction is paper and wood and she is very vulnerable.

"If anybody had any sense in this country, and would prepare for it we could put them out of it in two weeks. There are no two ways about it."

He said:

"Alaska is the most central place in the world for aircraft and that is true either of Europe, Asia or North America. I BELIEVE IN THE FUTURE HE WHO HOLDS ALASKA WILL HOLD THE WORLD. AND I THINK IT IS THE MOST STRATEGIC PLACE IN THE WORLD."

What did he mean by that? Billy Mitchell was blunt:

"If Japan seizes Alaska she can take New York."

If America did not appreciate the strategic truth of Alaska he said the Japanese did. He predicted:

"They won't attack Panama. They will come right here to Alaska."

He spoke with the aid of maps and a blackboard, tracing the strategy of the new, aerial warfare over the vast sweep of the whole North Pacific.

With a sweep of his hand, he showed the air routes from Alaska to Chicago, New York, Boston and Washing-

87 Foe Aliens Seized; Jap Has Coast Maps

NEW YORK, Aug. 1.—(INS)—The FBI today revealed the arrest of 87 dangerous enemy aliens, including a Japanese who was found in possession of two dozen strategic maps of the Pacific Ocean area. Some of the maps contained detailed naval data on the Aleutian and Pribilof Island areas next door to Alaska.

Altogether there were six Japanese among those arrested in the roundup, which took place during the past 24 hours. Three of them had entered the country illegally.

The most important of the Japanese seized, the one found with the maps, was identified by FBI officials as a leader of the Hokoku-Dan, a Japanese imperial service group. He was quoted as telling Federal agents:

"I want to see Japan win the war. My Emperor Hirohito is my ruler and I must obey him to the end."

ALASKA WATERS MAPPED

Among other things, his maps of the Pacific area included depths of the waters surrounding Alaska and listed air and sea distances between the Aleutians and the United States. Several of the other Japanese arrested were also discovered to be members of the Hokoku-Dan society.

Sixty-six Germans and 15 Italians were included in the sweeping roundup of aliens in the New York area. Meanwhile, in Philadelphia the FBI announced a series of simultaneous raids in which 100 aliens were picked up.

Virtually all of those seized in the New York raids were found to be associated with organizations in their native countries. A majority of the Germans arrested were found to be working in or near war production plants.

One of the Germans had a photograph of an American submarine tender and 10 U. S. submarines, snapped while they were at San Diego harbor.

A number of cameras, flares, propaganda leaflets and some ammunition were also found by the FBI operatives.

Seven of the Germans admitted entering the country illegally and 15 admitted having registered at the Nazi consulate here for military service with the Nazi armed forces. The flares were found on one of the Germans, living close to the sea. They were of a type that burns brightly for five minutes and could be used as a guiding signal, the FBI said.

Some of the aliens arrested had elaborate charts in their possession detailing the number of men in New York's armed forces, as well as other information related to national defense.

EASTERN JAPS LISTED

Among the effects of the Japanese, the FBI found a complete census of Japanese residents in the eastern United States which had been compiled by the Hokoku-Dan Society, apparently for purposes of mobilizing agents.

The maps and charts taken from the principal Japanese were well worn, indicating they had been used for repeated study. Some of them were of Japanese origin; others of American origin.

Two of the Germans admitted having ignored travel restrictions on aliens. One told the FBI "If you put me in the American Army, I would surrender to the enemy at the first opportunity." He boasted that his uncle is a Nazi air corps lieutenant colonel and that 16 of his cousins are fighting for Hitler.

'HAPPY' CHANDLER LEADING

Far Ahead in Kentucky Primary

LOUISVILLE, Ky., Aug. 1.—(AP)—Senator A. B. "Happy" Chandler's lead over his opponent, John Young Brown of Lexington, in today's Democratic primary continued to climb tonight as unofficial returns were reported.

With more than half of Kentucky's 4373 precincts tabulated, Chandler continued to add to the lead which he has held since the first precinct was reported.

Voting throughout the state was unusually light.

Returns from 3466 of Kentucky's precincts gave Chandler 165,123 votes to 45,356 for Brown.

Chief issue of the campaign was Brown's charge that Chandler accepted a swimming pool as a gift from Ben Collings, wealthy Louisville war contractor.

The Democratic contest overshadowed the Republican senatorial primary in which four candidates sought the nomination.

Interest in the primary was so low in the Colmar precinct of Bell County in southeastern Kentucky that Clerk Martin Green reported not a single ballot was cast. In last November's general election 49 votes were cast at Colmar.

From Alaska Vital Cities Could Be Bombed

In 1935 General William Mitchell warned of the danger of a Japanese attack on the United States mainland from Alaska. Was the danger solely to our west coast? Congressmen were surprised when he told them: "Our vulnerable area is the triangle of Chicago, Boston and Washington." At about the same time he wrote: "Japan has studied with great care the strategical situation in the Pacific. She knows Alaska is the key point because it is the apex of the Pacific triangle.

"From it New York, Philadelphia, Pittsburgh, Washington, Cleveland, Chicago and Detroit, and all the cities in our decisive area could be bombed directly.

"Alaska is of much more ultimate importance than the Panama Canal."

MITCHELL SAID: 'HIT JAPS FIRST'

'Build Underground Hangars in Alaska,' Was His Advice

ton. He indicated the air line distances—some 3000 miles—and said:

"Of course our vulnerable area is the triangle of Boston, Chicago and Washington."

It is there, he did not need to say, that America's great industrial heart lies. He continued:

"If you put out about seven or eight towns in there, it will greatly hamper us. If you put out 14 power plants in that section south of Sandusky, Ohio, it would paralyze us, and there is no doubt of that."

Are the Japs ready to take advantage of such a strategic advantage? Yes, said General Mitchell:

"Of course, they are organized for that purpose. They study these things and they go after them. They all work together. They really have a department of national defense."

Billy Mitchell realized the attitude of mind he had to overcome. To the average American, Alaska lies far to the north—far out of the way. The average man thinks of the straight line from San Francisco to Tokyo as lying straight out to sea — past Honolulu and Midway.

But the world is a globe—and the "Great Circle Course"—the shortest line around the globe from America to Japan RUNS THROUGH THE ALEUTIAN ISLANDS, intersecting them twice.

Billy Mitchell pointed that out—that the Aleutians are on the direct course to Tokyo.

Having pointed out the danger, Mitchell showed how to guard against it.

Moving swiftly to his great map, he showed how the Pacific, from the Panama Canal to the seacoast of Asia, formed a great triangle with its apex in the Bering Strait. He pointed out the Diomede Islands—one Russian, one American—in the center of the Bering Strait.

Stepping Stones for Japan's Invasion

The distance between the continents at the Panama Canal baseline, he said, was some 7500 to 8000 miles; at the apex in Bering Strait this narrows to 52 miles. He asked the committee to notice the Hawaiian Islands near the center of the triangle, more than 2000 miles from our mainland. He pointed to Guam and Midway lying between Hawaii and Japan, and advocated strong air bases for both.

Guam was never fortified and today we know the result—it is in Japanese hands. But on that day, seven years ago, General Mitchell showed how it might have been held and used for a crushing offensive against Japan.

". . . I think we could hold Guam with a proper air force there, but that will require no half-way protection.

"Guam has a series of islands running up to the great Japanese naval base on the Bonin Islands. That is the great Japanese naval base. We still have that island. (Indicating Guam) and we could put an air fortress on it and hold it."

Then he paused a moment in his rapid, incisive speech. He ran his finger along the curve of the Aleutian Islands. In a series of quick stabs, he picked out this place and that—rocky, barren mounds rising out of the North Pacific—bordering the Great Circle route to Japan, to Tokyo and Yokohama.

He said:

"If we go here to Alaska we have a tongue (the Alaskan Peninsula) ending in Akun Island. Akun Island is about 50 or 60 miles from these islands."

General Mitchell merely indicated this latter group on the map. He did not name it. If he did it is not included in the record. But Dutch Harbor, site of our present military base, is about that distance from Akun.

Here, and here, and here, he continued, are the stepping stones to Japan. Build "air fortresses" here, he urged. Construct underground hangars all along the short route to Japan; equip them with fleets of long-distance bombers and fleets of protective fighter planes; lay in stores of fuel and other supplies. Do the same for Midway. Do the same for Guam. Then in event of war, you have a bracket on Japan. You can strike instantly and decisively at the heart of the Japanese Empire.

Much of what General Mitchell said that day was considered of such important military significance that it was not even made a part of the record. The places, for instance, in the Aleutian Islands where he wished to see air bases established. All the same it is easy to know exactly what he meant. Even earlier he had written in a national magazine:

"Japan has studied with great care the strategical situation in the Pacific. She knows Alaska is the key point because it is at the apex of the Pacific triangle. FROM IT NEW YORK, PHILADELPHIA, PITTSBURGH, WASHINGTON, CLEVELAND, CHICAGO AND DETROIT AND ALL THE CITIES IN OUR DECISIVE AREA COULD BE BOMBED DIRECTLY.

"ALASKA IS OF MUCH MORE ULTIMATE IMPORTANCE THAN THE PANAMA CANAL.

"The distance from the most westerly point of Alaska, Attu Island to Tokyo is less than 2000 miles. An air offensive against Japan from Alaska could be decisive. They know this full well, and they also know that we are preparing in no way whatsoever. THEY ARE MISLEADING US WITH NAVAL PREPARATION, WHILE WITH THE GREATEST SECRECY THEY ARE DEVELOPING LONG RANGE BOMBERS FOR AN ATTACK ON THE UNITED STATES."

Within a few days of the time he testified before the committee on military affairs, he appeared before the committee on patent pools, and again discussed Japan, saying:

"Our only defense is a vigorous offensive—to have the drop on the other fellow. The only defense is to attack the other man, in his own cities and the places where he lives."

He said further that we must have far-flung air bases, *"subterranean places where your airplanes may be put to prevent bombardment, to get out quickly, where you have deposits of fuel and facilities for making repairs."*

To guard against his opinions being considered fanciful, General Mitchell included in his statement much detail of the Alaskan and Aleutian climates. He said:

"Now as to operating ability up there. I spent two years there building the Alaskan telegraph lines and I have traveled all over it. . . . You have a condition in Alaska which is somewhat similar to that in the Atlantic, but it is often worse."

General Mitchell described his experiences while serving in Alaska in the early years of the century and told of the pioneer New York-to-Alaska flight made under his direction by four Army planes 22 years ago. He said:

"We went straight up there in 1920. That was one of the greatest flights ever made in the world. We organized that in a short time, and flew up there and back without the loss of a plane or a man. Those are some of the conditions that exist. We are now able to fly in any kind of weather, and you can fly all through this here. We have got to develop suits where you can cut your ice and snow and buck your winds, which we can do. There is no insurmountable obstacle to it whatsoever. . . . I am speaking from the standpoint of national defense. Either you should prepare against something that you think is going to be there, or else not prepare at all.

Look Ahead Ten Years, His Warning

"YOU HAVE TO SEE WHAT IS GOING TO HAPPEN 10 YEARS FROM NOW; AND IF YOU DO NOT PREPARE FOR IT NOW, YOU WILL BE ABSOLUTELY LEFT."

As for fog (a condition which has made it difficult for the Navy at the present time to drive the Japanese from their landing places in the Aleutians) General Mitchell had this to say:

"If we have to go to Japan and back through the weather we will have to encounter in Alaska and other places, we will have to develop an entirely new outfit of people to handle these machines.

"Navigation through the air is more accurate than navigation in any other way. In the case of fog, if the fog is so thick you cannot see the field from the airship, then the ships can rise above it and use superchargers, which will carry us above any moisture-laden atmosphere, except in certain cases; I mean in the case of heads of thunder clouds around 50,000 feet up. You can always get up, and if you can get a sight on two heavenly bodies at night, you can locate yourself anywhere in the world, even up to 10 miles, absolutely.

"Navigation in the air under those conditions is an exact science. If you want to go from here to a certain place, you can go across the clouds and get where you want to go."

'Japan Is Our Dangerous Enemy'

Every contention made to the committee by General Mitchell as to what the Japanese could and would do to the United States was based on his ideas of what the air power of the near future would be.

Those ideas were not visionary generalizations. General Mitchell was clear and precise about the planes of the future and the uses to which they could be put. Events have proved him accurate to an incredible degree.

Telling of carrying the war to Japan he said:

". . . [illegible] COUNT OF THE EARTHQUAKES A GREAT DEAL OF HER (JAPAN'S). CONSTRUCTION IS OF PAPER AND WOOD, AND SHE IS VERY VULNERABLE.

". . . JAPAN IS OUR DANGEROUS ENEMY IN THE PACIFIC. THERE ARE SIX CENTERS THERE, IF I REMEMBER IT. IF THEY ARE PUT OUT OF BUSINESS THEY WILL BE IN A PRETTY BAD WAY."

All that General Mitchell told the Military Affairs Committee on that February day back in 1935 of the strategy, tactics and mechanics of air power in our coming war with Japan has proved right under every test that has yet been made of it.

The Japanese have already made good his prediction that they would head for Alaska. The delegate from Alaska, Mr. Dimond, in reiterating his demand that the Army and Navy move in and clear the Japanese out of the Aleutians says:

"Billy Mitchell was right in so much else, any sane man must take seriously his estimate of the dominant strategic position of Alaska and what could be done against the United States itself from that base.

"He was a man of remarkable vision. With his terrible prophecy before us, we do not dare assume that the Japanese landings in the Aleutians are merely a face-saving gesture. Or that they are directed solely against the Russians in Siberia. With Mitchell's own words to guide us, we cannot fail to realize what the landings may mean.

"We cannot act on the theory that if we leave them there long enough they will die of old age."

Dimond points out that from Attu to Kiska is 200 miles; from Kiska to Dutch Harbor, U. S. Army base, is 600 and that the Navy and Army base at Kodiak is only 600 miles further. He said:

"If the Japanese should get to Kodiak, they could ignore all the northern part of Alaska and head for Sitka.

"Southeastern Alaska is only 750 miles from Seattle."

From his first-hand knowledge of the Aleutians, Dimond is convinced that good landing fields can be constructed there. He is also convinced that the Japanese are engaged in constructing them now.

Kiska, he says, has a very fine harbor, THREE TIMES THE SIZE OF PEARL HARBOR, and adds:

"It is almost landlocked naturally. The building of a jetty out just a little way would make it completely so. The seas along the Aleutians are free of ice the year round.

"Situated as they are now, the Japanese have three unsinkable aircraft carriers. You cannot sink Kiska, you cannot sink Attu, you cannot sink Agattu. And the planes you can base on them are far superior to anything it is possible to have on a carrier, however large.

"It is my opinion that the Japanese intend to hold these islands, develop them and exploit them eastward. They want Alaska. They want it for its strategic value as pointed out so clearly by General Mitchell.

"WE STILL HAVE TIME TO FORESTALL THEM. IF WE DECIDE TO STRIKE IN FORCE WE CAN DRIVE THEM BACK. IT'S ALL A QUESTION OF BRINGING UP ENOUGH POWER TO DO THE JOB."

AS GENERAL MITCHELL demonstrated in 1935, the "direct" line to Japan lies not due west but actually to the north, touching on the highly vital Aleutian Islands. Hence the strategic value of Alaska, standing as it does, in the words of Mitchell, "at the apex of the Pacific triangle." Owing to the curved surface of the earth, the base of that triangle is here represented as an arc.

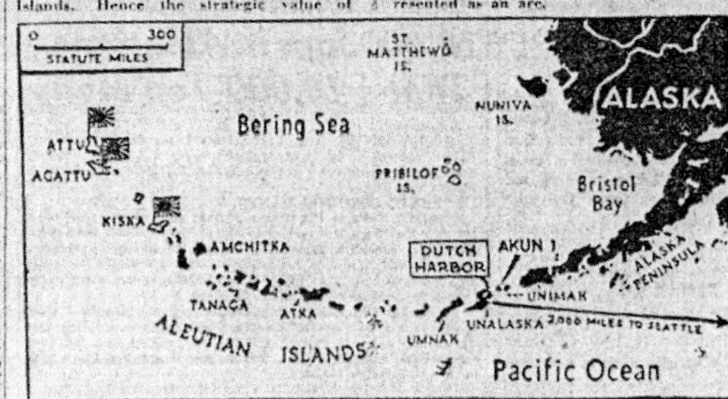

THE CRUCIAL ALEUTIANS on which General Mitchell urged Congress in 1935 to erect a series of strong bases as "stepping stones" to the quick conquest of Japan. Today, 1942, Japan is attempting to use these same stepping stones herself. Jap flags indicate islands held by her.

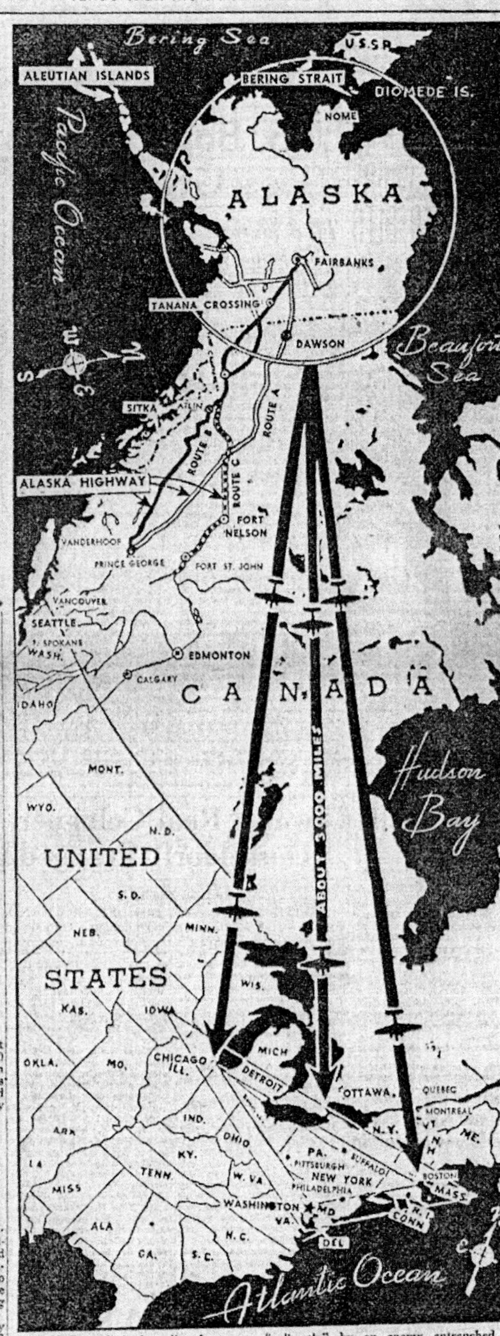

THIS MAP, so devised to allow for curvature of the earth's surface, illustrates graphically the warning of General William Mitchell in 1935, that America's "decisive area," an industrial heart contained within the "triangle" between Chicago, Boston and Washington, "could be bombed directly" by an enemy entrenched in Alaska. Within this triangle, besides the three cities named, lie New York, Philadelphia, Pittsburgh, Cleveland, Detroit, Buffalo and many others. Shown at upper left are the various routes of the U. S.-to-Alaska highway, belatedly under construction.

CONGRESS STARTS ALASKAN PROBE

Special Investigator Sent to Learn Real 'Facts Behind Fogs'

By George Rothwell Brown

(Special to the Los Angeles Examiner)

WASHINGTON, Aug. 1.—Congress took into ts own hands today the business of finding out for tself just what has happened in western Alaska, nd precisely what actions are eing taken by the Army and Navy to blast the Japanese forces ut of the Aleutian Islands.

The House naval affairs committee started an expert investi-ator to the scene of war on the merican continent, where conitions, shrouded in mystery as mpenetrable as the fog banks ver Attu and Kiska, have cre-ted an increasing apprehension n the capital.

Representative Warren G. Magnuson of Washington, a Democratic member of the naval ffairs committee, is the investi-ator selected to go to Alaska nd conduct an exhaustive in-uiry to ascertain the truth.

Magnuson is especially equipped or the task. He is a lieutenant ommander in the Navy and only ecently returned from active uty with the Pacific Fleet, here he participated in some of he recent engagements which ave been making history.

He left Washington today for eattle. There he will confer with anking officers of the 13th Naval District, which has juris-iction over the Alaskan area.

Taking Navy Plane For Dutch Harbor

Magnuson will then leave for laska by Navy aircraft, first roceeding to Dutch Harbor, ith investigative stops on the ay at Sitka and Kodiak.

Meanwhile today a subcom-ittee of the Senate military af-airs committee, headed by Sen-tor Albert B. Chandler of Ken-ucky, was converging on Spo-ane, whence in a few days it ill fly to Alaska, going as far orth as Fairbanks and Nome y the inland route. This com-ittee also will go to Dutch arbor.

Both committees of Congress re determined to get at the facts ehind the fogs. Magnuson will emain in Alaska nearly a month. he Chandler subcommittee hopes o complete its work in about hree weeks.

Complete reports will be ready or both Senate and House when ongress resumes full time sit-ings after the present recess eriod ends early in September.

While West Coast Senators and Representatives are very apprehensive over the situation in Alaska, they are but little more so than nearly the whole of Congress.

Not Satisfied With Command Setup

Members of Congress are not satisfied with the extent to which the Army and Navy have worked out a system of unified command. The recent announcement of unity of command by the Navy indicates clearly that this unity embraces only the air forces of the two services.

There is a growing sentiment in Congress in favor of a complete unified command between the Army and Navy embracing land forces, as well as sea and air forces.

Members of congressional committees, who have sought information on the whole situation in Alaska, have been unable to obtain information from witnesses. It is for this reason the two committees have in effect gone over the heads of the Army and Navy high command and sent their own investigators directly to the scene.

This reflects the gravity which Congress attaches to the presence of an enemy army on American soil.

Feared Japs Given Time To Entrench

It is feared that the Japanese in the Aleutians are being given time to entrench themselves so securely as to be able to launch a major attack on the Alaskan mainland.

"I have no information that the Japanese have landed on the Pribilof Islands," said Senator Robert R. Reynolds of North Carolina, chairman of the Senate military affairs committee. "I am fearful that they have. We want to find out the truth.

"From the Pribilofs Japanese land-based planes could blast Nome off the map, after only a three-hour flight. We cannot risk the danger of a Japanese landing force obtaining a footing on the Alaskan mainland, which would open the whole West Coast to attack."

No new information was forthcoming today from the Navy Department as to the reported presence of Japanese on the Pribilof Islands. The Navy does not deny that such a landing has been made, but it has no information so far as revealed to confirm such reports.

"I am still convinced that the Japanese have got the Pribilofs," said Representative John M. Coffee of Washington, who has been following the Alaskan developments with the closest scrutiny. The Navy says their aerial observers have not sighted any.

"My information, however, coincides with that of Alaskan delegate, Anthony Dimond, that seal fishermen sailing in the Pribilof area of the Bering Sea have observed Japanese vessels in those waters, in sufficient quantity and occasions as to clearly indicate a military force was being landed on the islands.

Hopeful Mystery Will Be Cleared Up

"The Navy is planning to do something about that situation and I am hopeful that within the next two or three weeks the mystery will begin to clear up and we will know just what is going on up there."

Delegate Dimond stuck to his belief that the Japanese have moved into the Pribilof region, pointing out that the Navy does not say they are not there, but that they don't know that they are. Mr. Dimond called attention to the vulnerability of the Pribilofs, exposed as they are to attack from three sides, north, south and west.

Told Anti-Aircraft Guns Being Installed

Nor was Mr. Dimond ready to accept as definite the Navy's report that the Japanese in the Aleutians do not exceed 10,000, as against his information from sources in Alaska that they ranged from 20,000 to 25,000. He pointed out, however, that his reports were as of late June and early July, and there might have been a reduction of the forces in the meantime. Nevertheless he was dubious of the Japs having taken any of their landing parties out of the Aleutians.

Dimond said information had reached him that the Japanese already had begun installing anti-aircraft guns and defenses, and building air and submarine bases on Kiska, adding:

"We must defend all of our territory, every inch of it. We are under a continuous handicap in defending Alaska and the Pacific Coast as long as the Japs hold Kiska. We must get them out of there to protect our mainland territory, and our shipping lanes across the northern Pacific to Siberia.

"If the Japs start any move to invade Siberia, the presence of Jap troops on Kiska and the other occupied islands of the Aleu chain will put them in position to seriously interfere and perhaps cut our direct route to get munitions and supplies to aid Russia in the Siberian defense."

Tokyo Picture of Jap Landing in Aleutians

THE CAPTION accompanying this picture, received in New York from neutral Portugal, describes it as one sent by radio from Tokyo to Berlin showing Japanese troops with their Rising Sun flag after their landing in the Aleutian Islands. —Associated Press wirephoto.

YANK PILOTS IN CHINA DOWN 17 JAP PLANES

CHUNGKING, Aug. 1—(AP)—United States fighte pilots shot down nine Japanese planes over Hengyan yesterday, raising the Japanese losses over that Hunan Provinc air base to at least 17 in tw days, General Joseph W. Stilwe announced today as the Chines reported a new Japanese landin on the coast of Chekiang Province.

In a determined but thwarte attempt to wipe out the American air forces in China, the Japanese sent 29 of their vaunte Zero fighters against Hengyan yesterday, but were broken u by the American fighters, wh include veterans of the AV "Flying Tigers." Besides th nine Japanese destroyed, a 10t probably was shot down.

Three American planes wer lost, one of them while being re paired on the ground, but all th pilots were safe.

Only the day before the Japanese twice tried to raid Hengyang Airport, with disastrous re sults to themselves. Of the fir nine bombers which came ove before dawn, four were destroye

Then by day 27 of the newl improved Zero type fighters trie to clear a way for 34 bomber The Americans destroyed fo of the fighters, probably g three others, and completely di persed the formation, said Stil well's announcement.

The bombers, meeting the fighter vanguard fleeing in di tress, turned back 30 miles sho of Hengyang.

The communique stressed th these Zeros were of the ne type.

In ground combat, the Chines meanwhile reported new Japan ese incursions. After bei beaten off July 27, the Japanes came back later with reinforce ments and landed at the mout of the Ao river 30 miles belo Wenchow, in Chekiang provinc a Chinese communique said.

At the same time other Japanese forces moving west fro Wenchow and east from Lish recaptured Tsingtien, 22 miles i land in Chekiang.

Nazis Hold 'Second Front' Practice

BERLIN, Aug. 1.—(By Official German Wireless.)—(INS)—The Paris radio reported today that German naval units, army and air force have carried out maneuvers against any attempted invasion along the Channel coast.

The Paris report said that a trial alarm was sounded on Thursday night at a German base on the Channel coast and that fire of coastal batteries "prevented any ship from entering the base."

Examiner News Summary - - August 2

WAR

S. boy, witness to Dusseldorf raid, tells of industries on Rhine being "perfect target." Page 1

usseldorf plants razed by surprise raid of 600 R. A. F. bombers. Page 1

azis 100 miles in Caucasus below Rostov. Page 1

usseldorf "pranged" like Cologne, R. A. F. bomber pilots report. Page 1

merican flyers shoot down 17 Jap planes raiding China base. Page 2

ank pilots in China bag 17 Jap raiders. Page 3

llied bombers batter Tobruk. Page 10

ne killed, eight hurt in Paris food riots. Page 7

S. flyer hits U-boat leaving victim. Another ship sunk along East coast. Page 11

aps lose 20 planes in Darwin raid. Page 13

WASHINGTON

erdict being readied for President Roosevelt's approval in Nazi spies case. Page 5

enate group studies Treasury plan for income tax payments being made year in advance. Page 5

amily men still being called in draft to meet quotas. Page 14

oosevelt may get power to assign men to jobs where skill most needed. Page 15

amb price ceiling set by Henderson. Page 15

NATIONAL

ighty-seven foe aliens seized by FBI; Aleutian maps found on Jap. Page 1

STATE

ilk drivers in two counties halt deliveries to enforce wage demands. Page 15

CITY

dward Judson, ex-husband of Rita Hayworth, named in marital row of Jergens heir. Page 4

iss Marion Davis war hospital benefit slated August 9. Page 13

outh Gate honors 500 men in armed forces at Heroes Day ceremony. Page 19

rmy-sponsored defense school opens at Occidental tomorrow. Page 18

FINANCIAL

ailroad shares continue to rise. Page 5-II

inancial writers. Page 5-II

l news. Page 5-II

heat and cotton markets. Page 5-II

SMART SET MAGAZINE

Naval Aid Auxiliary busy at work in their various activities. Page 1-VI

Altadena women rally nearly 100% strong for war work; Cholly Angeleno Observes; Women's Clubs; Hollywood Parade; Ask Cholly. Page 2-VI

U. S. O. runs popular entertainment center in Biltmore Hotel; Personalities; Round About. Page 3-VI

Society; Travel News; Horoscope; The Open Door. Page 4-VI

Fashions; Last Week in Brief. Page 6-VI

SPECIAL FEATURES

Crossword Puzzle. Page 17
Classified Ads. Section VII
Medical News. Page 4-II
Radio. Page 22
Real Estate. Page 8-II
Squads Right. Page 18
Vital Statistics. Page 6-II
Stamps and Covers. Page 22

PICTORIAL REVIEW

Mexico on the Alert. Pages 1-2-3-V
Movie-Go-Round. Page 4-V
Louella O. Parsons on Hollywood. Pages 4-5-V
Harriet Parsons' Keyhole Portrait. Page 5-V
Stage and Music. Page 6-V
Mark Hellinger. Page 7-V
Benjamin De Casseres About Books. Page 7-V
Damon Runyon. Page 7-V
Walter Winchell. Page 7-V
Elsie Robinson. Page 8-V
Arthur "Bugs" Baer. Page 8-V
E. V. Durling. Page 8-V

EVERYBODY EVERY PAYDAY 10% IN WAR BONDS

VOL. XXXIX. SUNDAY, AUG. 2. No. 234

Los Angeles Examiner

Daily and Sunday. Reg. U. S. Pat. Office. Examiner Bldg., Broadway at 11 St. Published by Hearst Publications, Inc.

Entered as second-class matter December 12, 1903, at the postoffice at Los Angeles, Calif., under the Act of March 3, 1879.

The Los Angeles Examiner is Not Responsible for Unsolicited Manuscripts or Photographs. None will be returned unless sender incloses return postage.

MAIL RATES PAYABLE IN ADVANCE California, Utah, Arizona and Nevada.

MEMBER OF THE ASSOCIATED PRESS The Associated Press is exclusively entitled to the use for publication of all news and dispatches credited to it or not otherwise credited in this paper and also the local news published therein.

All rights of publication of special dispatches are also reserved.

NEW REFRIGERATOR INCLUDED

De Luxe 5-Room Outfit 246.50

New Modern Furniture of Style and Quality

An exceptionally complete outfit at a real saving! Includes Living Room Suite, Lamps, Tables, Dinette with upholstered seats. Real Walnut Veneer Bedroom Set, Philco Radio, Kitchen Range and new Refrigerator. Buffet slightly extra.

Up To 12 Months To Pay

OPEN SUNDAY *Everything for Your* LIVING ROOM, BEDROOM DINING ROOM, KITCHEN AND BREAKFAST ROOM

10 Piece 'CALIFORNIAN' LIVING ROOM

3 Lamps Included

Consists of BED DIVAN, CLUB CHAIR to MATCH; OCCASIONAL CHAIR, SMOKERS' STAND, END TABLE, COCKTAIL TABLE, FLOOR LAMP, BRIDGE LAMP, TABLE LAMP and Mexicano Throw Rug. Easy Terms. 10 Pieces, Complete $88

National Furniture Co. 6200 SO. BROADWAY (CORNER 62nd ST.)

OPEN SUNDAYS - OPEN EVENINGS

INVEST IN WAR SAVINGS BONDS AND STAMPS

Dr. Lionel Lewis OPTOMETRIST

Do You Need GLASSES?

12 Months To Pay

No Interest • No Extra Charges

OPEN EVENINGS

Open Every Evening Until 9 p.m.

★ 633 S. Broadway

OFFICES (at lessee) ON MAIN FLOOR LeRoy's Bldg.

Gardens, Auctions, Schools

The activities of the real estate market; homebuilding and gardening news; what's going on at the auction galleries, and the new opportunities opening in our private business, vocational, cultural, professional and dancing schools—all these constitute part of the varied fare offered every Sunday in the Examiner.

HOMES AND GARDENS

with Real Estate and Building News

On Pages 7 and 8, Section II

AUCTIONS

Page 19, Section I

SCHOOLS AND COLLEGES

Summer Schools and Camps, Music and Dancing Schools

Page 7, Pictorial Review Section

NEWCOMERS TO LOS ANGELES

Your Home Town Credit Is Good At LeRoy's

★ Aircraft workers, shipbuilders, war industry workers and other newcomers to Los Angeles are invited to leisurely visit LeRoy's ... friendly, courteous salespeople will show you the West's largest displays of fine jewelry. *Remember*, your home town credit *is good at LeRoy's.*

★ Buy on LeRoy's easier terms: no down payment required on a convenient charge account, or, up to 12 months to pay with a minimum down payment.

★ LeRoy's are open every evening until 9 P.M. for the convenience of War Workers . . . and others too busy to shop daytimes. Park free at any system auto park. If you live out of town, use LeRoy's *"order-by-mail-on-approval"* service. Any merchandise sent, all charges prepaid, for your inspection: Diamonds, Watches, Jewelry, Silverware, Radios, Appliances, Cameras, Luggage, Sporting Goods, Pottery, Dishes and Homewares.

★ We suggest — laying away Christmas presents NOW . . . it's not a bit too soon to assure ample selection.

BUY U. S. WAR STAMPS AND BONDS

LeRoy's Jewelers

633 S. BROADWAY

It's The Examiner for Want Ad Results

HOWARD HANDLEMAN

Handleman was born in Los Angeles in 1913 and attended the University of Redlands. He started his journalism career in San Bernadino, CA with the *Orange Belt Daily News*. In 1935 he joined INS (International News Service) for 20 years, the first eight in Boston, New York, Detroit, Chicago and Los Angeles.

In 1943 he was stationed in Alaska and then sent to the Pacific (Leyte Gulf, Luzon and finally Okinawa) At the end of the war he became the Far East director for INS and established bureaus in Tokyo, Manila, Seoul and Taipei. In 1952 he was bureau chief for INS in San Francisco, diplomatic correspondent in Washington, DC in 1954, then in 1956 he went to Paris as European correspondent and stayed until INS merged with United Press in 1958. Then back to DC working for the office of Civil Defense until finishing his career with US *News & World Report*.

He wrote two books: Bridge to Victory: The Story of the *Reconquest of the Aleutians* (1943) and *Leyte Calling* (1945). He died in Virginia in 1994.

Correspondents recall Aleutians

By ROBERTA GRAHAM
Daily News reporter

Before the battle of Dutch Harbor, before the battle of Attu and Kiska Islands, few Americans realized there existed a stepping-stone chain of islands between Alaska and Japan called the Aleutians.

That area of the Pacific Theater was to become an important segment of World War II history.

Howard Handleman, veteran war correspondent of the Aleutian campaign and now with the book division of U.S. News and World Report, says that before his tenure in the Aleutians, he was just as unaware.

"When I was a college freshman, I wrote a paper in which I referred to them as the Illusion Islands. That's how much we knew about them," he said.

Interviewed by telephone, Handleman said that when he left his Los Angeles typewriter in 1943 to cover the war for the now-defunct International News Service he knew he was going to Alaska.

"But I thought I'd be covering the war from Juneau. I expected to sit in a bar in Juneau and get my stories second hand through the War Department," he said.

Handleman never made it to the state's capital, and spent less than three weeks in Anchorage and Kodiak before being shipped out to Dutch Harbor for his first assignment. From there he recorded action on Amchitka, Attu and Kiska, mostly maneuvering through mud and over tundra on fog-shrouded days.

"Cold and wet. That's what I remember about the Aleutian Islands is that it was god-awful cold and wet," he said. "We had obscene songs about them . . . said obscene things.

Between bombing runs and filing stories, there were poker games.

"I remember on Amchitka we use to play poker every night. And we'd play a few hands and then would shift to the right so we could all share the heat from the one heater."

Handleman said it was on Amchitka that he met Keith Wheeler, war correspondent for the Chicago Times — later renamed the Chicago Sun Times — and now retired from Life Magazine.

Wheeler had been covering the Aleutians for nearly 18 months before Handleman entered the theater.

"I had been covering the war in the Coral Sea, when we were called back into Pearl (Harbor). We knew something big was about to happen, and many suspected Midway," Wheeler said.

Citing security reasons, Waldo Drake, head censor for the commander in chief for the Pacific Command (CINCPAC) would not tell the journalists were they were headed.

Wheeler said he boarded the U.S.S. Indianapolis. All the other reporters were put on another ship.

"They went to Midway," he said. "I went to the Aleutians. That was in 1941 when generally most people thought about the Aleutians as a sideshow to the main event.

"I was very resentful when they finally told me where I was headed. But as it turned out, it was the best area to be in."

On May 5, 1942, Japanese general headquarters ordered the invasion of Midway Islands and key points in the western Aleutian Islands.

But the U.S. had broken the Japanese code, and planned for the main staging to be done at Midway.

Roughly two-thirds of all casualties resulted from trench foot, Wheeler said.

But the most poignant struggle Wheeler and Handleman recall, aside from the constant wind and fog, was the battle waged by the Japanese against themselves.

During the 19 days of fighting on Attus, more than 500 Japanese soldiers died, blowing themselves up with their own hand grenades.

"It was either victory or death," Handleman said. "That was the samurai code. And they just went until they knew they were defeated.

"We learned to live with eating our lunch amidst Japanese soldiers who had blown their heads off with other body parts scattered all over the battlefield," he said. "I had nightmares about it for a while, but the effects just wore off. I know it would bother me now. But that was war."

How to Fight in Alaska

By Corey Ford and Alastair MacBain

The Alaska Clipper, Seattle to Juneau, is pioneering a possible emergency route for Army air transport

Freight sleds are an important part of the winter equipment of the Alaska defense force. Army blacksmith, above, is building a training model

C.A.A. inspector stops for gas at a remote salmon-drying post. His job is to make Alaskan flying safer. Below, soldiers adjust packs on dogs

The U. S. Army, busily building up our defenses in Alaska, turns to the old sourdough and learns some lessons in survival

CITIZENS of Mobile, noted for their prejudice against cows that fly, would not feel at ease in Alaska at all. Here cows not only fly high, but the fact is an everyday occurrence; as we learned this summer when we landed at the village of McGrath on the Kuskokwim. We noticed an unusual air of activity as we entered the roadhouse at McGrath. The occupant of Room Sixteen, someone explained, was fresh out of hay. Mystified, we followed an armful of hay as it disappeared down the hall, and knocked tentatively at the door of Sixteen. A gentle moo emerged. From Room Fourteen, directly adjoining, the proprietor's wife appeared and shook her head.

"I'm sorry, but that door's locked. We've had to cut a door from the outside instead. You see," she explained matter-of-factly, "we keep the new cow in there. It's warmer." We peered through the keyhole at a brown-eyed bossy, lying on a bed of straw and munching her cud contentedly. "She just flew in from Fairbanks last week," the proprietor's wife added. "It's only a couple of hundred miles." She noticed our slightly glassy look. "Oh, cows fly everywhere up here," she assured us. "Next spring she's taking the plane back to Fairbanks again, just to be bred."

Anything goes in Alaska, it seems, and it usually goes by air. Livestock, medicines, babies, dogs, grand pianos, dredge buckets, an entire grocery store from lumber to stock, Diesel engines weighing up to two tons apiece, all are freighted by plane. Last year commercial planes hauled 5,000,000 pounds of freight, flew the amazing total of ninety-five per cent of the white population of the territory. "And to think it used to take me a full month to make this run by dog sled," an old sourdough beside us remarked, as we sped from Nome to Fairbanks. "Cost a thousand dollars, and I had to pay my own lodging at night and walk most of the way besides. Now I fly it for seventy-four dollars, and get there in four hours. Travel in Alaska," he said, emitting a luxurious cloud of cigar smoke, "ain't what it used to be."

Why Alaska Is Air-Minded

In the interior, the plane is taken as casually as a taxi in New York. Prospectors scout by air for new mining country, jabbing a pencil point into a map: "How much to take me there?" They still tell the story of the cheechako who made a forced landing on a mountainside and struck, among other things, gold. Salmon canneries charter planes to circle back and forth over Bristol Bay, spotting runs of salmon and signaling the fishing fleets. Trappers fly in to the head of their trap lines in the fall—a somewhat laborious process, since they frequently have to guide the pilot by means of landmarks they remember: "Now, let's see, you head up this here canyon till you see where there's a burnt stump, then you sort of folley a little creek that cuts off to the right. . . ." A drift miner scribbles a name on the flap of an old envelope, hands the pilot a leather sack. "Here, give this five thousand dollars' worth of dust to Bob at the bank, tell him to deposit it to my account." That is all: no record, no receipt. The loneliest sourdough cabin shows the effect of Alaska's air-mindedness: empty five-gallon gasoline tins are seized by thrifty wives and ripped up for pails and dustpans, flattened to shingle the woodshed, cut out along one side and racked along a shelf for kitchen drawers. Game wardens have their own ships; mercy pilots rush emergency cases from isolated mines—there is no spot in the territory more than four hours by air from a hospital; even Ladies Known as Lou use planes to rush to the scene of the latest gold stampede. "What we could have done with these in '98," the Oregon Mare remarked to us a little wistfully.

The natives themselves take the plane for granted. Indian children do not bother even to turn their heads when you land. "All same sea gull," they shrug. Native women gather around the plane and casually scribble messages on its tail to friends in the next village. Planes are no novelty to the Eskimos, either. You set down at a remote village in the Arctic, your great white man's bird with its silver wings dropping awesomely out of the skies, and you emerge a little self-consciously and face the silent throng. "Say, mister," a young Eskimo inquires at last, "you get any better performance out of her with that new constant speed propeller?" At Nome, they told us of the Kobuk chief who chartered a special ship to fly him all the way down from the Arctic. Not that the trip was any sensation; but at Nome he was able to satisfy a great ambition. He got the thrill of riding in his first automobile.

You sense the thing as you fly from New York at night and board Pan American's new Alaska Clipper at Seattle the following morning, to drift luxuriously over the unparalleled scenery of the Inland Passage and set down that evening at Juneau, twenty-four hours after

(Continued on page 55)

An Article written by Richard L. Neuberger (later a Senator from Oregon) in *Collier's Magazine* for Dec. 23, 1944 entailed, *Go North Young Man!* concerning Alaska's wartime governor, Ernest Gruening

The Honorable Ernest Gruening, governor of the Territory of Alaska, had a message in his parka pocket which he had to deliver the next afternoon in the opening session of the Alaska Territorial Legislature at Juneau, 220 wilderness miles off to the south (from Whitehorse, Yukon).

But how to get to Juneau?

This was of Whitehorse's cold days. It was 61 below. The tiny narrow-gauge White Pass and Yukon Railroad was immobilized. The locomotives were frozen. The water towers were frozen. The roundhouse doors were frozen. The switches were frozen. Everything was frozen. Otherwise, the governor might have jolted down to the gold-rush settlement of Skagway at tidewater from where the Coast Guard would buck frigid seas to reach Juneau.

The governor trudged to the barracks of the Royal Canadian Mounted Police. Could a dog sled get through the drifts in the Chilkoot? Inspector Cronkhite regretfully shook his fur-topped head. The snow in the pass was over a Malemute's head and up to a constable's armpits.

Next, the honorable Ernest Gruening rode in a jeep at 61 below to the U.S. Army Air Force hangar on a bluff high above the frozen Yukon. Maybe it's 75 below up above. And a heavy ground fog covers the airport in Juneau like a blanket. I wouldn't advise it governor.

The Honorable Ernest Gruening fingered the speech in the pocket of his parka. "I've got to get to Juneau." he repeated. "If anyone will fly me, I'll try it."

"I'll fly you, sir," said a blond young captain. Putting on his fur jacket.

"Good boy!" said the governor.

"Are you sure it's wise, Governor?" asked Colonel Ken Bush, chief of staff of the American Army's Northwest Service Command.

"I'm going to Juneau,"said the governor.

Americans and Canadians lined the runway with prayers and crossed fingers as the Beechcraft skidded across the icy sod. And they hung grimly to the telegraph ticker until Juneau reported three hours later that the plane had slipped through the hole in the fog the size of a doily and deposited a slightly frozen Honorable Ernest Gruening on the airfield at the Territorial capital.

Alaska's governor is like that. In the five years since he came to the Far North in 1939. Ernest Grueing has tried to demonstrate personally that his country's vast Arctic outpost can be lived in and traveled in, the calendar around. In Aleutian williwaw and Yukon blizzard, he has visited every settlement in Alaska—the first governor in Alaskan history to do so—and he has journeyed by any and all possible means of conveyance in doing it.

Gruening was born in New York City in 1887. His father, Emil Gruening was a celebrated eye, ear, nose and throat specialist and Earnest followed him to Harvard Medical School and an internship at Boston City Hospital. But instead of following a medical practice he turned to journalism, getting a job with *The Boston American*. Journalism, he decided after a few weeks, was definitely his field. His next job was as an editor of the old *New York Tribune*. During the First World War he enlisted in the field artillery and in 1921 he went to *The Nation* magazine and commenced a crusade against what he called "dollar diplomacy" in Latin America. He got interested in Latin America and Canada and Alaska and started writing books advocating a "Good Neighbor" policy.

He next moved to Maine where he founded *The Portland Evening News* and became an active supporter of President Franklin D. Roosevelt. One of the president's first acts was to send Gruening to Uruguay as adviser to the United States Delegation to the Inter-American Conference. A year later he was appointed director of the newly created Division of Territories and Island Possessions, in the Department of the Interior. This took him to Alaska on numerous inspections, and he became an enthusiastic advocate of the future of Alaska.

In 1939, the president named him to be the governor of the country's largest Territorial possession. He held this position until 1953 and was elected to the U. S. Senate in 1959, serving 10 years. In 1938 the U.S. Government proposed to resettle European refugees in sparsely populated Alaska to help with infrastructure problems but there was too much opposition to this idea.

The governor/senator died in 1974.

SS YUKON
June 18, 41

Dear Pansy:

Well here we are sailing along through the water on our way to Alaska. Guess I shouldn't have said sailing it is more like chugging. Wish you could have come with me.

This boat is taking 205 men the Gov't is sending up to Kodia (sic) and the Captain told a man who eats at our table that he had to cancel a lot of tourist tickets to make room for them and that a lot of them had to go steerage. The Captain also said that he thought that this would be the last ship that would take tourists as the Gov't needs all boats and that he wouldn't be surprised if all tourists were soon ordered home on account of trouble with Japan.

We were at the beach in the spring and Jim found an agate rock that has yellow in it. He has a ring set cut and polished for you but I didn't get around to sending it before we left. Will get it to you someday.

The bell is ringing for dinner in 30 min. so will stop and get ready.

June 21st Petersburg

I didn't get this finished on the boat as we got into waters that were more scenic and stopped at the two tours. Got into Petersburg at 12:20 Thurs night. Last night Jim read a paper out of doors at 11:30 at night. This afternoon we are going out in the boat trolling.

It is a lovely sunny day and nice and cool. Wish you could have come with us. Last night drove around the island and saw a couple of deer along the road. Jim took some pictures of me and if they are good will send some.

Love, Ceva & Jim

REPORT FROM THE ALEUTIANS

In August 1942, well-known Hollywood director, John Houston was sent to Alaska to film a documentary on the American build-up and the efforts to recapture the Aleutian islands occupied by the Japanese.

The Office of War Information had established a film division and recruited some of Hollywood's best directors, such as Houston, John Ford, William Wyler, Frank Capra and Darryl Zanuck to produce films to inform the American public of the country's war effort.

Houston's first movie as director was *The Maltese Falcon* in 1941, which starred Humphrey Bogart and Lauren Bacall. He directed two more movies, *In This Our Life* and *Across the Pacific*, in 1942 before joining the army with the rank of captain.

The film crew arrived on Adak just over a month after the army had occupied the island. Houston was to film the building of the airbase and the bombing of the occupied island of Kiska. He flew on 15 bombing missions and twice narrowly escaped death. In his six months in the Aleutians he was basically given free rein to film the events as they happened with no set agenda. Shooting the film presented enormous tactical and logistic difficulties for those assigned there.

After editing the footage in New York and Hollywood the film was released in July 1943, a few months after the recapture of Attu and shortly before the evacuation of Kiska by the Japanese. Houston later commented about Report from the Aleutians "The only false note in it is one of optimism, which the country needed at the moment." *The New York Times* called it "one of the war's outstanding records of what our men are doing," and Variety called it "a successful attempt to bring to the American people a picture of the tough conditions under which their boys are fighting."

World War II Army poster promoted film directed by John Huston. Film crew worked at Astoria studio.

Report from the Aleutians was the only government documentary film made in the Alaska Theater of operations. Houston went on to make more films for the army, including *The Battle of San Pietro* in 1945, considered to be one of the best documentaries about men in combat to come out of the war. Other movies made in the North Country during the war include: *Alaska Highway* by Paramount, 1942; *Law of the Northwest* by Columbia, 1943; *Yukon Patrol* by Republic, 1942; and *Riders of the Northland by Republic*, 1942.

The crew of the B-24 that was used in the film taken at Adak in 1943. –Courtesy of Jeff Ryan

ADDITIONAL INFORMATION ON MRS. ETTA JONES

In the summer of 1941, Mr. and Mrs. C. Foster Jones took up their duties on the island of Attu. Mrs. Jones was the teacher of the community school, and Mr. Jones acted as special assistant and as a weather reporter and radio operator for the Weather Bureau. They both had long experience in Alaska. Mr. Jones had been there for nearly 40 years, 15 of which were in the Indian Service. His wife, a graduate of the Pennsylvania Hospital Nurses' training school, was qualified as a teacher, community worker and nurse. She was first employed in the Indian Service in 1928. Together they made a fine combination, for the Indian Service used married couples at the isolated stations in Alaska where the two were the only white people in the community, and where contact with the outside world was limited to the radio and one or two visits a year from the mail boat.

On Sept. 8, 1941, two weeks after their arrival on Attu, Mrs. Jones wrote to Claude Hirst, General Superintendent of the Alaska Native Service, telling him her impressions of the village and its people.

"There are 45 people in the village. They are progressive, intelligent, clean and friendly. They live and work as a community, making their living from blue fox trapping. They operate as the Native Community of Attu, pooling the season's catch of pelts, and selling them in the name of the community to a fur dealer in New York. The proceeds, after 19 dollars for each skins taken out for the trappers, is divided equally among all the members of the village, children included. Thus widows and helpless ones are taken care of. There are no indigents here."

"Their houses are models of construction, neatness and furnishings. There are nine houses, having four to seven rooms each and they are well lighted and beautifully painted, inside and out. All have excellent stoves, good linoleum on the floors, gas lamps, and all but one has running water piped into the house from a spring. The yards are neat, all refuge being carefully disposed of. The American flag, flying from the village flagpole, was one of the first sights which greeted us as we came into the harbor on the Coast Guard cutter *Atlanta*. They have a beautiful Greek Orthodox Church, electrically lighted by means of a small light plant."

"They all speak a little English, much to our astonishment, considering their extreme isolation. People from occasional boats which stop here are the only ones outside the village they see."

"The villagers have used the school for dances on various occasions but have left everything in good condition. Written on the blackboard we found the chief's orders: 'Pealse dont spate on the Flower and dont brake loking Gleese' (window). They are cooperative and helpful in all work concerning the school. All want to work without pay when there is building or lifting or special work to be done. They have an abundance of all kinds of fish and the boys are generous with their gifts of fish. At first we paid them, but the chief asked us not to pay them. The boys themselves made that request. They have plenty of fish and they wanted their gifts to be free."

"They are proud people; proud of the fact that they differ somewhat from the people of Atka and Unalaska. There has been no intermingling with the Japanese. In fact, they dislike and distrust the Japs. They accuse them of stealing their foxes, and even of killing some of their trappers years ago. But for three years they haven't seen a Jap or a Japanese boat."

In late December 1941, Mrs. Jones wrote that all was well and that no Japs have as yet made an appearance. Further east, on the island of Atka, another Indian Service couple taught the school and ran the radio station. Ralph Magee talked each day with Foster Jones by radio, exchanging weather data and other news. On June 7, 1942, they talked together at the usual time in the morning, but in the afternoon Magee was unable to make any contact with Attu. He surmised correctly that the island had been invaded, and he immediately began to plan for the evacuation of the inhabitants of Atka.

From the morning of that day until August 1945, no word was received concerning the fate of the Joneses and the 45 natives on Attu. The island was recaptured after a long and bloody campaign. The village had been destroyed, and no trace remained of the inhabitants. Many rumors were circulated, none of which had any foundation in fact. The Indian Service and the Department of the Interior made every effort to find out what had happened to the Jones's and the Aleuts, and although no information was forthcoming, hope was held out that they may have survived. In June 1944, the Board of Suggestions and Awards of the Interior Department cited the Jones's for courage and devotion to duty, giving them Awards of Excellence and especially meritorious promotions. Letters from Secretary Ickes, commending them, were sent to the Juneau office to be held for the day of their release. The remaining 45 Attu villagers were taken to Japan and endured considerable hardships.

Early in July 1945, the Swiss representative of the International Red Cross, who had finally been allowed to visit the prisoner-of-war camps, discovered Mrs. Jones in the small village of Totauka, in the Tokyo-Yokohoma area. When the Americans landed, a short time later, she was released and flown back across the Pacific.

After landing in California on September 12, she went to Seattle, where she began to straighten out a three-year accumulation of business matters, and where she received letters from the Secretary of the Interior and the Commissioner of Indian Affairs. She arrived in Chicago on Sept. 30, 1945, her 66th birthday, and was met by her sister and her niece."

At the Office of Indian Affairs, Mrs. Jones told of her long imprisonment and her release. On June 7, 1942, some 2,000 Japanese landed on the island and surrounded the village, firing at the inhabitants from every direction. One woman was hit in the leg, but there were no other causalities, and no resistance was offered. Mr. Jones put the radio station out of commission just as the Japanese landed. The invaders handled the inhabitants roughly; separated Mr. and Mrs. Jones, and Mrs. Jones did not see her husband after the second day. The Aleuts told her secretly that he was dead and that they had buried him in the churchyard. The following day a high officer, evidently an aristocrat, landed and imposed order on his command. The Japanese were forbidden to enter the village and they were obliged to return food which they had stolen from the town. The mayor was appointed liaison to handle arrangements between the military and the Aleuts, and from this time on the prisoners were well treated. After a few days, Mrs. Jones was told to pack her clothes for the voyage to Japan. She was taken directly to Yokohoma, where she was lodged temporarily in a hotel in company with 18 Australian nurses who had been captured in New Guinea.

In the Yacht Club to which they were moved and where they lived for two years there was a well-stocked library. The prisoners could read, and they passed some of the time knitting for the Japanese Red Cross. Morale was high among the nurses, and in spite of their predicament they had some hilarious times together. Because of her white hair Mrs. Jones was not allowed to do any work, and she was looked upon with special respect. The food was not satisfactory. Eventually American parcels arrived, and during the latter part of the war these were received every few months. At Christmastime, 1942, each American prisoner received a gift of 90 yen in the name of the Vatican, although there was little to buy with the money.

After two years the women were moved to a Japanese house in the village some miles from Yokohoma, where they were eventually found. There was no heat, and water had to be pumped from the well in the yard. But in the summer they had a garden where they grew tomatoes and other vegetables. They knew that the invasion was coming. They had heard of the liberation of the Philippines and they knew of the fighting on Okinawa. They often heard the bombs falling and saw the fires set by incendiaries. On July 3rd the representative of the International Red Cross came to see them and insisted to the Japanese Government that they must be allowed to send cables to their relatives at home–the first word of them to reach the world outside of Japan. The Japanese told them about the atomic bomb, and said that one bomb had killed 89,000 people, but they found it hard to believe. They went on working in the little vegetable garden and waited for the day of liberation.

Mrs. Jones could not say enough about the treatment of the released prisoners. The Army, the Navy, and the Red Cross did everything possible to help them. A planeload of oranges was flown from California for them. In Manila, where she spent a week on her homeward journey, the Red Cross had, among other morale-building facilities, a beauty parlor and a shop where ready-made dresses or material for sowing were available.

Less than half of the Aleuts returned from imprisonment in Japan. Forced to work digging clay, many died of tuberculosis and malnutrition. Those who did return were resettled on Atka, where they had friends and relatives.

Excerpted from an Office of Indian Affairs memorandum in October 1945.

After the war she lived in Margate, NJ from 1945-46, Bradenton, FL from 1956-63, Seattle, WA from 1963-65, and back to Bradenton, FL in 1965 where she died. In 1957 she took a trip to Australia and New Zealand to visit with some of the nurses who were prisoners with her in Japan. This information was supplied by Mrs. Mary Breu of Anderson, SC, the great niece of Mrs. Jones.

Wartime menu of the Canadian Pacific Railway's Café Car service featuring dinners from one dollar to one dollar and twenty five cents.

A WPA art project by artist Edward Grigware, created for the Thirteenth Naval District.

JESSE LEE HOME

The Alaska Children's Services was established as an orphanage in Unalaska in 1890 by the Methodist Church. It was known as the Jesse Lee Home and moved to Seward in 1925. The program served hundreds of Aleut orphans as a shelter as well as a loving, caring and nurturing environment and job training. Many residents went on to productive lives in Alaska including the founder of the University of Alaska and Benny Benson, designer of the Alaska flag. After the 1964 earthquake, which devastated Seward the home was moved to Anchorage.

This view of the Balto building at the Jesse Lee Home during the war shows the outside walls camouflaged by pine trees painted on the walls. –Seward Community Library Association, SCL-7-3

Boys sitting on the steps of the Balto building after the war. –Seward Community Library Association, SCL-7-50

Baranof Hotel

DINNER MENU

SATURDAY SEPTEMBER 23, 1944

COCKTAIL

V-8 Juice | Fresh Seafood | Grape Juice | Chilled Fruit

SOUP

Potage of Navy Bean | Baranof Special Clam Chowder

SALAD

Cabbage-Carrot and Celery with Russian Dressing

ENTREE

Baked Sugar Cured Ham, Madeira Wine Sauce, Rice Fritters	$1.65
Roast Stuffed Young Capon, Savory Dressing, Giblet Gravy	$1.65
Potted Swiss Steak, Bordelaise Sauce, Jardiniere Vegetables	$1.65
Grilled Fresh Halibut Steak, Lemon Butter, Cabbage Salad	$1.50
Breaded Veal Cutlet, Country Gravy, Apricot Glase	$1.50
Stuffed Ripe Half Avacado with Crab Salad, Sliced Tomato	$1.50
Dinner Omelette Filled with Diced Chicken ala King	$1.50

Baked New Potatoes | Whole Kernel Corn

DESSERTS

Delicious Homemade Baranof Pies, Fresh Daily: Vanilla Cream, Peach, Hot Mince, Hot Apple, Pumpkin, Cherry, Youngberry

Homemade Layer Cake | Vanilla Cream Pudding, Whipped Cream

Rice and Raisin Custard, Whipped Cream | Orange Sherbet

Fruit Jello, Whipped Cream | Chilled Green Gage Plums

Stewed Fresh Prunes | Peppermint Ice Cream

Choice of Chilled Fruits | Choice of Ice Cream

Coffee | Tea

DINETOIRE SPECIALS

Roast Sirloin of Steer Beef, Brown Gravy, Julienne Vegetable	$1.25
Breaded Lean Pork Chops, Country Gravy, Apple Sauce	$1.25
Ground Round Steak, Brown Gravy, Sliced Tomatoes	$1.00
Grilled Fresh Salmon Fillet, Lemon Butter, Cole Slaw	$1.00
Cold Assorted Meat Plate, Combination Fruit Salad	$1.00
Stuffed Ripe Tomato with Chicken Salad, Green Olives	$1.00
Scrambled Eggs with Diced Ham and Green Pepper	$1.00

Includes Dinner Vegetable, Potato, Hot Rolls, Coffee

"Good Food Is Good Health"

A wartime menu of The Baranof Hotel in Juneau, Alaska's newest and largest hotel at the time.

UNITED STATES

DEPARTMENT OF THE INTERIOR

OFFICE OF THE SECRETARY

DIVISION OF TERRITORIES AND ISLAND POSSESSIONS

WASHINGTON

November 10, 1942.

Subject: Censorship in Alaska.

MEMORANDUM for the Secretary.

Censorship in Alaska has been and is, to my judgment, unduly repressive, wasteful--since many people are employed in carrying out its provisions--and wholly unnecessary. Censorship falls under five heads:

1. Outgoing news and dispatches. This is controlled by the Army and Navy. During the first six or seven months after our entry into the war, the high military command felt it advisable to throw a blanket over Alaska, to obviate all mention of Alaska that even remotely suggested its relation to the war, prevented regular news men from sending out any stories, censored even the official news release of the Alaska War Council, the announcement extending the rubber drive, etc. and kept Alaskans in complete ignorance of events concerning Alaska that were being published elsewhere in the United States. I am happy to say, however, that this situation has now been largely corrected as a result of discussions with General DeWitt. While there is still room for further improvement in the handling of the news, I am convinced that the military authorities have completely altered their attitude and that we are now headed for a desirable news policy. Nothing needs to be done here for the time being.

2. Incoming news dispatches. Some news dispatches disseminated throughout the United States are censored by the Office of Censorship in Seattle. The Army and Navy now take the position that anything that has been published in the United States should be sent to Alaska. Nevertheless, the Office of Censorship has taken upon itself to delete certain matters. The President's speech was held up by the Office of Censorship for several hours, likewise a speech by Congressman Magnuson delivered in Seattle, which was sent out by the Associated Press and United Press but was held up by the Office of Censorship. There would seem to be no excuse or justification for this civilian agency moving in where neither of the military services have any desire to tread.

3. Incoming newspapers and magazines. Newspapers and magazines coming from the United States are clipped by the Office of Censorship in Seattle. There is no justification whatever for this. General DeWitt expressed to me categorically his disapproval of this performance, and his willingness to be quoted--that no justification or military necessity existed for this policy. My copies of the Washington Post, Time and News Week have been cut. This policy should be completely abandoned, and the great army of newspaper and magazine clippers dismissed for more useful work.

4. Mail. All letters to and from Alaska are subject to censorship in Seattle by the Office of Censorship and is, of course, in addition to the military censorship exercised by the Army and Navy solely for mail to and from members of the armed forces. Needless to say, this latter is universal practice for armed forces and does not concern us. The civilian mail censorship, however, is wholly unwarranted. There is no valid reason why Alaska mail should be treated any differently than California, Washington or Oregon mail. I suspect this originated as a general policy for the territories, and whatever may be the justification or lack thereof for other outlying islands, I feel definitely that this policy should not apply to Alaska. General De Witt is in agreement with this position. I could elaborate instances of the poor execution of this policy—the fact that identical letters, carbon copies, are treated differently in the same office—but I would like to rest my case on the obvious lack of need, in the waste of time in reading all these letters, and in the needless prying and snooping that takes place in consequence. Finally, the mail service, already suffering greatly through inadequate transportation facilities and shortage of Post Office personnel, is further delayed by censorship.

5. Kodachrome photos. Taking colored photographs has become a widespread hobby and thousands of people enjoy taking color pictures in Alaska. All of these pictures have to be sent either to the Eastman Kodak Co. at Rochester, New York, or at Los Angeles, California, to be developed. There is no censorship of these pictures for anyone in the United States, but pictures taken in Alaska are censored and pictures which they conceive to have some military aspects are not returned to the senders. Their judgment in this matter is wholly fantastic. Among the victims of this censorship have been Major General Simon B. Buckner, Jr., head of the Alaska Defense Command, who complained to me bitterly about this censorship. General Buckner told me of one picture of a sled which had been removed from his pictures. Presumably, the idea was that he would send this picture of a sled to an enemy who would then find out that sleds were being used in Alaska. In my own case, pictures that had no possible relation to the war were removed. The complaint is widespread in Alaska. I know the case of one man who sent four rolls, a total of 80 pictures, and got back 7. He wrote a violent letter to the Office of Censorship and got them all back which would, at least, indicate that the Office of Censorship did not have a clear understanding of its task.

It seems clear that if an enemy agent were trying to photograph strategic objectives in Alaska, the one medium he would not use would be Kodachrome which he cannot develop himself but which must be sent to Eastman to be developed and where any unusual or suspicious photographs would be detected, but that he would use ordinary black and white and develop the films himself. Both General DeWitt and General Buckner stated to me that they considered this censorship wholly unnecessary.

We have, therefore, in Alaska four forms of censorship imposed by a civilian agency which the military do not desire or require. These forms of censorship are distinctly detrimental to the morale of the people of Alaska. They greatly add, and unnecessarily, to the burden of life there. In addition to that, they must employ much personnel wholly uselessly. They are among the many irritations which would be cheerfully borne if their existence were justified, but which being rightly considered needless by their victims, serve to lessen the faith in and loyalty to our government which should instead have the fervent and enthusiastic support of the entire people.

I therefore desire, Mr. Secretary, to have the full backing of the Department in trying to eliminate these unnecessary forms of censorship. I would like first to discuss the matter with Mr. Byron Price and his staff. If relief cannot be secured there—which seems probable since the agency that voluntarily cuts down its activity and diminishes its jurisdiction is rare—it may be necessary to seek appropriate action higher up.

Ernest Gruening,
Governor.

Approved: NOV 18 1942

Secretary of the Interior.

"WILLIE WAW" is plenty tough!
GUARD AGAINST
WIND DAMAGE

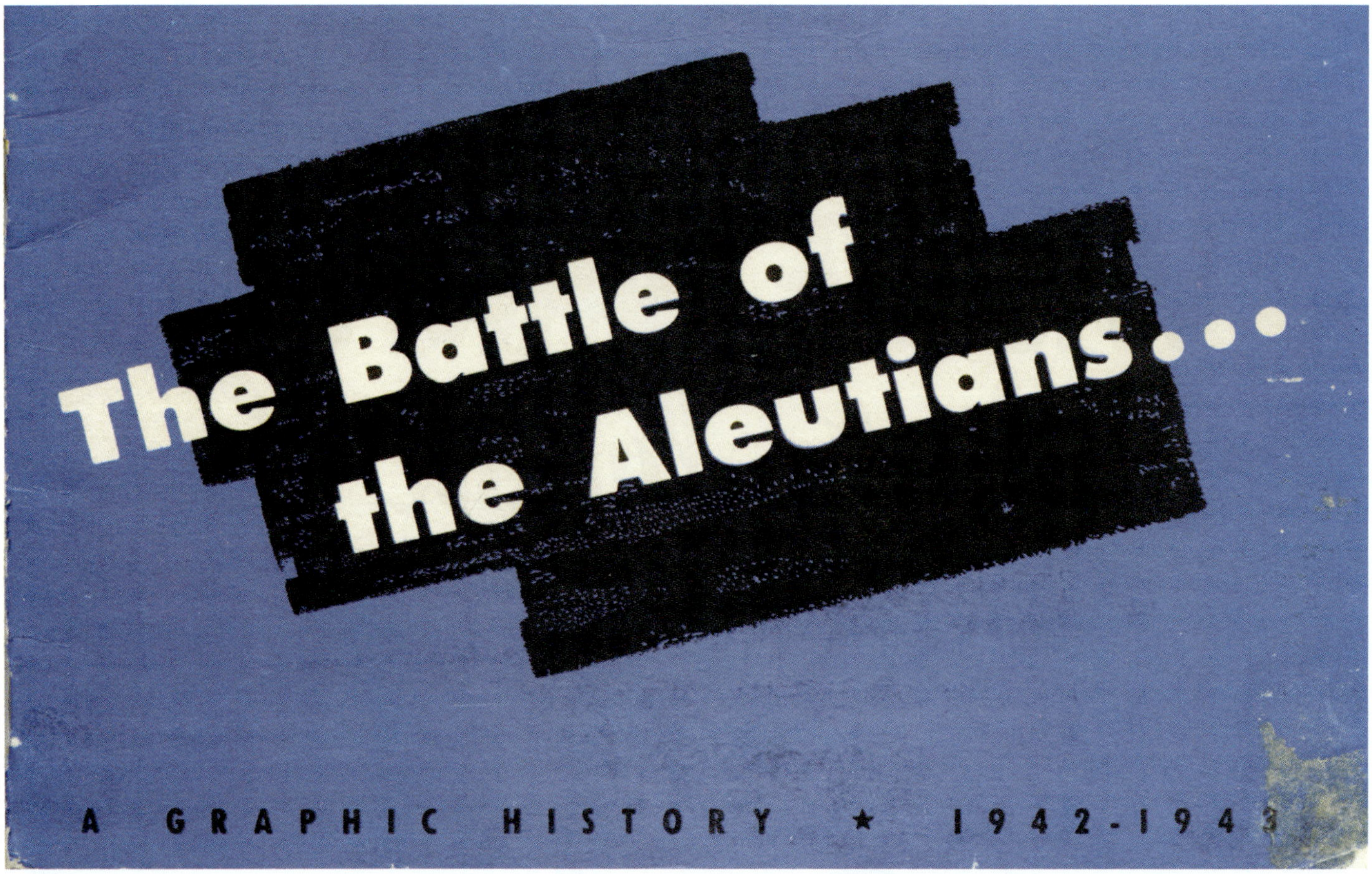

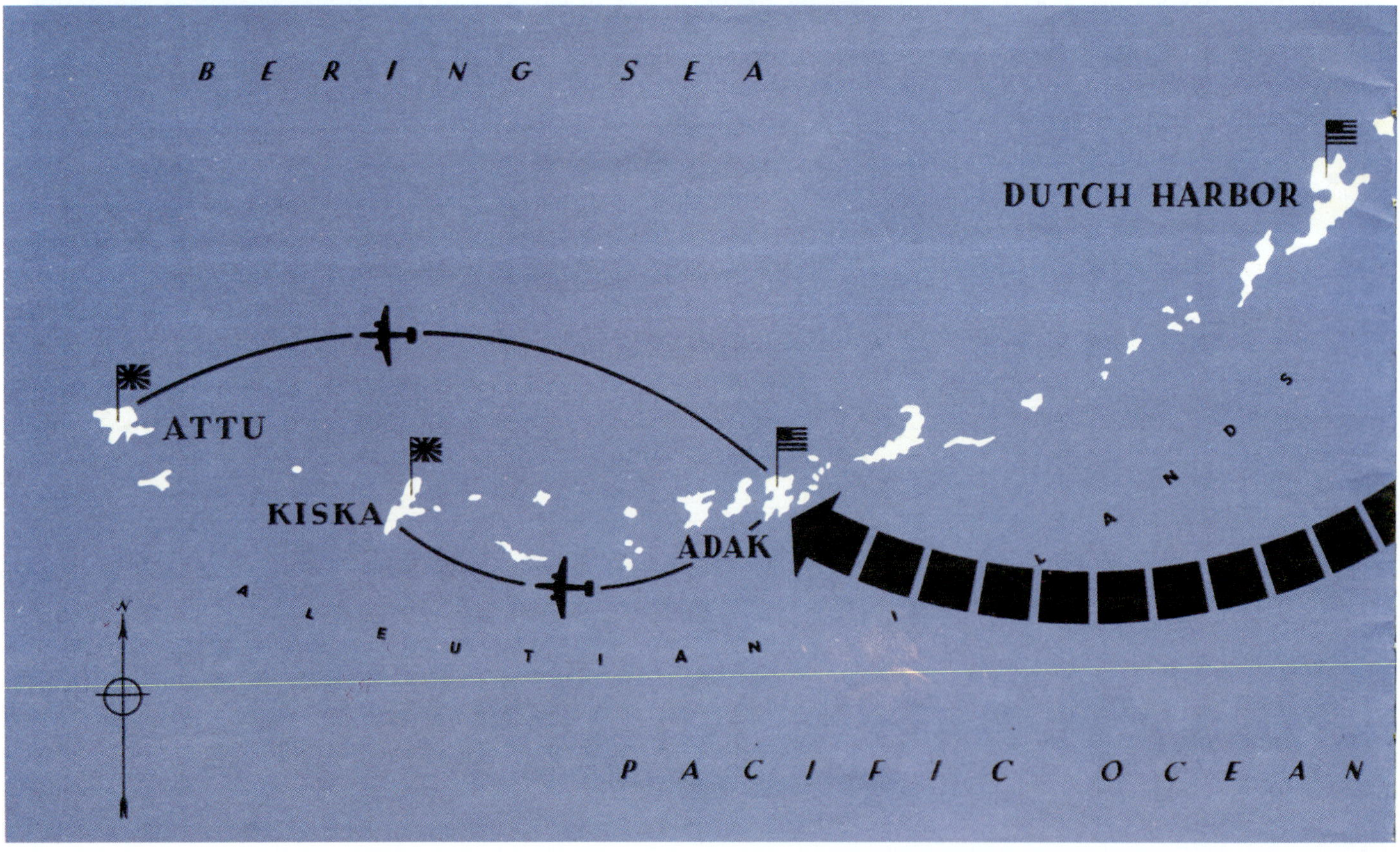

Pamphlet put out by the Intelligence Section, Field Force Headquarters, Adak, Alaska, October, 1943, two months after the Kiska invasion. This pamphlet was prepared by Dasheil Hammett and Robert Colodny.

THIS CAN'T BE ALASKA— I MUST HAVE TAKEN THE WRONG TRANSPORT!

BATTERY "D"
TWO HUNDRED SIXTY SIXTH C.A.C.
Extends
SEASONS GREETINGS from
ALASKA

THIS FEATURE IS ADAPTED FROM AN ARTICLE IN THE **READER'S DIGEST**, JUNE, 1944.

BUT THE NEXT MORNING...
AM I DREAMING—OR DO I REALLY SMELL WHAT I THINK I DO?
LET'S FIND OUT!
TROUT! ARE THEY REAL?
SURE, THEY'RE REAL. EMMY BROUGHT THEM.
THUS THE SOLDIERS MET EMMY—THE LITTLE ESKIMO GIRL WHO WAS TO BECOME SO IMPORTANT TO THEM.
AFTER THE MEAL...
IT WAS SWELL OF YOU, EMMY, BRINGING THAT FISH. IS THERE ANY WAY WE CAN PAY YOU BACK? IS THERE ANYTHING YOU WANT?
COAL!
COAL? WHAT DOES THE KID WANT WITH COAL?
BEATS ME! I THOUGHT SHE'D ASK FOR SOME KIND OF A TOY.
THEN THE SOLDIERS LEARNED THAT EMMY HAD BEEN TAKING CARE OF HER MOTHER AND TWO YOUNGER BROTHERS SINCE HER FATHER HAD DIED THE YEAR BEFORE. SHE WANTED COAL FOR HER HOME, AND SHE GOT IT!

A SHORT TIME LATER, THE SOLDIERS WERE BUILDING A PIER.
I SURE WISH WE HAD SOME BETTER MAIN SUPPORTS THAN THOSE TWO-BY-SIXES.
EMMY GOT BETTER!
I GUESS SHE MEANS WE'RE TO FOLLOW HER. COME ON!
EMMY LED THEM TO HER HOUSE.
THAT WOOD BETTER!
THAT RAMP'S BUILT OF TWELVE-BY-TWELVES. JUST WHAT WE NEED!
THE WOOD IS SWELL, EMMY, BUT WHERE DID YOU GET IT?
MAN COME IN BIG BOAT. HE HAVE WOOD. PAPA GIVE HIM FOX SKINS.
WE WILL GIVE YOU SUGAR, CANNED GOODS, AND WHATEVER ELSE YOU NEED.
THAT WAS EMMY'S WAY—GIVING OTHERS THE THINGS THEY NEEDED, AND ACCEPTING IN RETURN ARTICLES THAT WOULD HELP HER FAMILY.

IN THE WEEKS THAT FOLLOWED, EMMY WAS OF INVALUABLE AID. SHE TAUGHT THE MEN HOW TO MAKE SNOWSHOES...
...HOW TO BUILD TRAPS...
...AND HOW TO HUNT CARIBOU.
CARIBOU MAKES THE TRACKS LIKE THIS.
NOTHING WAS TOO DIFFICULT FOR EMMY TO ACHIEVE.
WE'LL NEED PLENTY OF PIPE TO SET UP THIS WATER SYSTEM.
WE'D BETTER SEE EMMY. SHE'LL HAVE SOME, OR KNOW WHERE TO GET IT.
THE SOLDIERS ALWAYS REPAID HER. BUT SOMETIMES SHE DID NOT WANT MATERIAL THINGS.
PAPA MAKE THIS MACHINE LONG AGO. YOU TEACH MY BROTHERS HOW TO RUN IT.

EMMY NEVER DROVE SHARP BARGAINS. ONE DAY...
I'LL GIVE YOU TWO HUNDRED AND FIFTY DOLLARS FOR YOUR WINDBREAKER, EMMY.
NO, IT TAKE MAMMA ALL WINTER TO MAKE FOR ME. I NOT SELL.
BUT SEVERAL WEEKS LATER...
THERE'S JENNINGS. GOOD TO SEE HIM OUT OF THE HOSPITAL.
AND LOOK! EMMY'S GIVEN HIM HER WINDBREAKER SO THAT HE CAN KEEP WARM.
ONLY ONE THING ANGERED THE GIRL—JAP FISHING-NET FLOATS THAT SOMETIMES DRIFTED IN TO SHORE.
EMMY FIX THIS SO JAPS NEVER USE AGAIN.
HER BROTHER EXPLAINED HER HATRED OF THE JAPS.
JAP FISHERMEN COME, RAID OUR NETS. EMMY SEE THEM AND SHOOT RIFLE. THEY RUN AWAY IN BOATS. NOT COME BACK!
THIS JAP RAID HAD OCCURRED JUST BEFORE PEARL HARBOR. IN SHOOTING AT THE RAIDERS, EMMY HAD FIRED THE FIRST AMERICAN SHOT AGAINST THE JAPS!
WHEN THE AIRPORT WAS FINISHED, THE SOLDIERS HAD TO MOVE ON. BUT THEY WILL NEVER FORGET EMMY, THE ESKIMO GIRL, WHOSE FRIENDLY HELP SPEEDED THEIR IMPORTANT JOB.

Alaska Life
THE TERRITORIAL MAGAZINE
NC 21711
NWA
Courtesy Northwest Airlines
JANUARY, 1944
Annual Edition
35 CENTS

This story appeared in the *Anchorage Daily Times* on July 15, 1969

WRITTEN BY HILARY HILSCHER

PIG PROBLEM ENDED IN 'CHOPS'

Usually he talks about sheep when he arrives in Alaska for his annual visit but this time, I.M.C. Anderson, grandfather of the Aleutian sheep raising industry, talked about hogs.

"Andy" Anderson is well qualified to talk about any facet of agriculture, however. With a degree in agriculture and years of experience in Oregon, Montana and Idaho, he came to Alaska in 1937 as extension agent for the Matanuska Valley. The next year he was put in charge of the experiment work at the University of Alaska, and served as livestock specialist.

Anderson moved to Anchorage in 1942 to set up the loan program for the Farmers Home Administration, which he directed until he retired in 1965.

It was this last job that led him to the subject of hogs.

"Early in the war years, President Roosevelt visited the chain and the army post on Adak Island. With the abundant grass on the islands, he felt the Army should raise livestock there to provide meat for the soldiers. At this time, any meat had to be flown in, and the weather wouldn't let that be very reliable," Anderson recalls.

Col. Lechner, then stationed on Adak, was given the job of determining the "best way to use the grass. So he came to me," said Anderson, "because I was the only husbandry specialist in the state."

On Anderson's advice, the colonel called on his commissioned officers and found 16 who had graduated in agriculture. One of the men, the son of the extension agent on Kodiak Island, had been raised on the extension station there, "They quickly put him in charge," smiled Anderson.

The committee studied the conditions on the Aleutians, and recommended that cattle be brought in.

"They sent in the order for 75 cows. An Eagle River farmer sent them 75 SOWS."

This was only the beginning. The hogs were supposed to have been bred, so the Army hadn't bothered sending for a boar. The supplying Farmer couldn't seem to convince the Army committee in his letters to include a boar as an "insurance measure," so he just sent one anyway.

"But," Anderson added, "It really didn't do any good. The boar was anti-social and ran away and hid in a ditch."

"Well, the Army did the best they could with what they got and assigned the Quartermaster Corps to hog-tending," Anderson said, "because they were in charge of garbage disposal. "Fortunately, one sergeant from the Midwest knew a lot about the animals, and "was a first-rate hogminder."

Anderson visited the island later to study the results of the President's project. The Army was eager for his knowledgeable recommendations.

"Pork Chops," he said.

Only too happy to be finished with the hog business, the Army took Anderson's advice without delay. "And with that the hog-raising industry on the Aleutians ended."

The former Alaskan, now a resident of Oregon, paused a few days in Anchorage before visiting the chain. From 1955 until he left Alaska in 1963, he served as adviser to the sheep ranchers of Unalaska and Umnak, and each year since, he visits the islands, "But I've had no pig problems to deal with since 1945," Anderson smiled.

Troops on Amchitka Island carrying stakes that augured into the tundra to string barb wire around defense positions. There were thousands of these devises lying on the ground on many islands at the end of the war and for years afterwards. –Left: courtesy of Acme Newspictures, Right: Courtesy of Blaine Cornelison

St. Paul Island Reserve Guard men in early 1941. All residents of the Pribilof Islands (St. Paul and St. George) were evacuated soon after the Japanese attack in June, 1942. –ASL-PCA-233

These photos of Amchitka during the war were taken by Norris Rockwell Griswold. He started working for the ACS in the mid 1930's in Seattle and Fairbanks before the war. His duty on the island was Radio Repairman Fixed Station 649. –Courtesy of Bill Griswold, San Diego, CA

Part of the coast line of Amchitka, which is 60 miles east of Kiska. The island is long, hilly and shaped somewhat like a gravy boat but was an ideal site for an airfield, close enough to both occupied islands for a bombing campaign.

Quonset huts and wood frame buildings were hastily put up after the occupation. Mud was a constant problem and boardwalks were needed to get around.

A theater was built for the morale of the troops stationed on the island. –Courtesy of The Williwaw

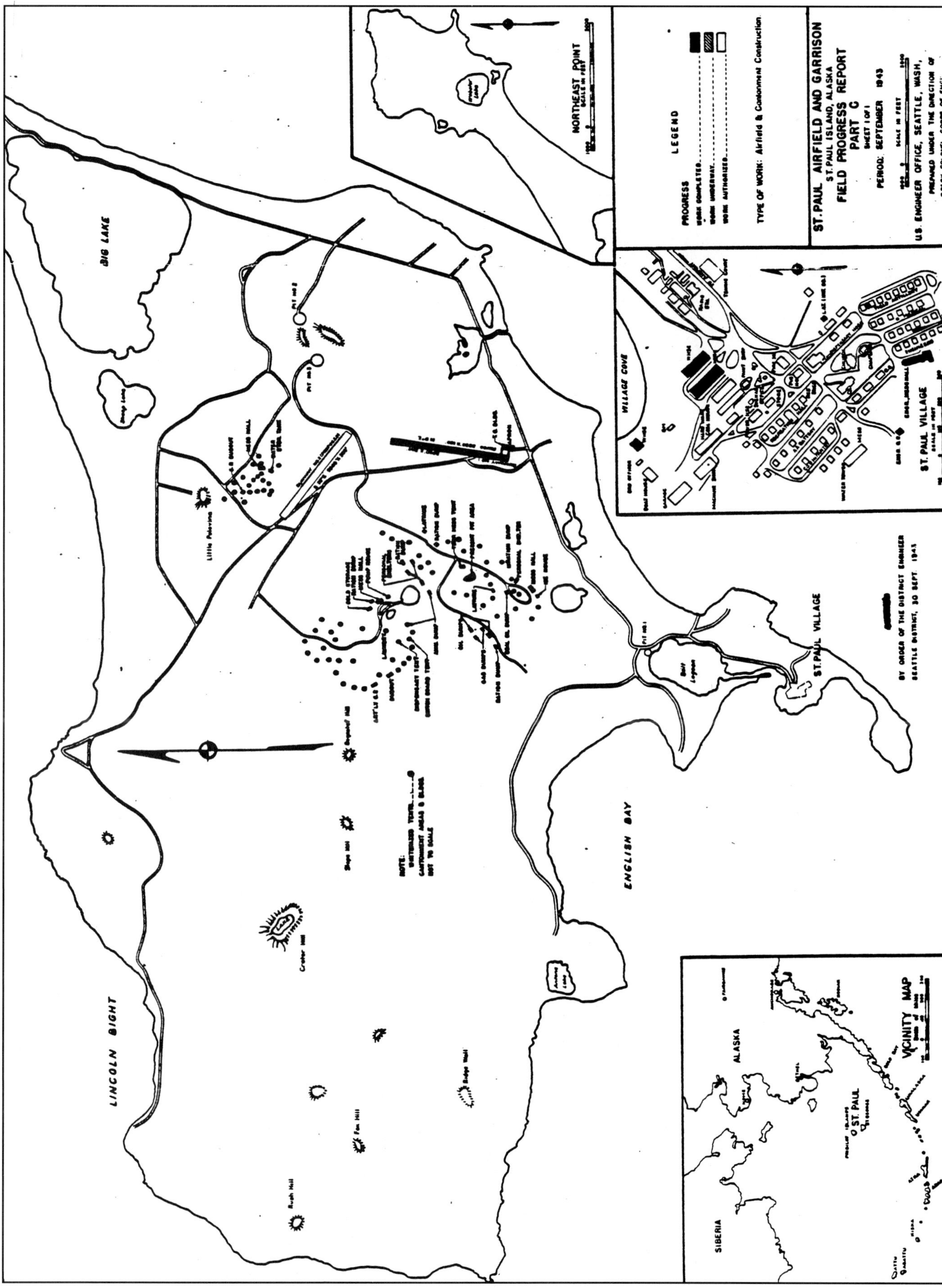
ST. PAUL AIRFIELD AND GARRISON
ST. PAUL ISLAND, ALASKA
FIELD PROGRESS REPORT
PART C
SHEET 1 OF 1
PERIOD: SEPTEMBER 1943
SCALE IN FEET
U.S. ENGINEER OFFICE, SEATTLE, WASH.,
LEGEND
PROGRESS
WORK COMPLETED
WORK UNDERWAY
WORK AUTHORIZED
TYPE OF WORK: Airfield & Cantonment Construction
NORTHEAST POINT
ST. PAUL VILLAGE
VILLAGE COVE
BIG LAKE
LINCOLN BIGHT
ENGLISH BAY
VICINITY MAP
ALASKA
SIBERIA
ST. PAUL
BY ORDER OF THE DISTRICT ENGINEER
SEATTLE DISTRICT, 30 SEPT. 1943

Line of natives with guns at Unalakleet on the Bering Sea coast.
–Courtesy ASL-P368-90

20 mm gun (camouflage off) at St. Paul Island, June 20, 1943.
–Courtesy of ASL-PCA-343, Evan Hill photograph collection

A view of Whitehorse, Yukon Territory in 1945, showing how the US Army built hundreds of buildings and Quonset huts for the construction of the ALCAN and CANOL projects.

Alaskan Vet Tells Of Tough Sledding On Aleutian Isles

Mister Lawrence Mahrkens of Squadron 4, like many of those in his squadron has seen service in the Alaskan theatre of war. With three years of duty in Uncle Sam's Army he has many interesting stories to tell of his experiences on Adak island.

"Larry" was born in a small town in Minnesota by the name of Red Wing. His athletic career in high school was hampered by a leg injury sustained while playing basketball. After graduating he worked in a clothing store for a year and then a grocery store.

These businesses held small interest for him with the result that he joined a National Guard unit formed in Red Wing. The unit left for Camp Haan, Calif., January 1941 where he was trained as a range-setter in the Anti-Aircraft.

Before leaving Camp Haan "Larry" held the rank of corporal. His new assignment was on Alcatraz island in San Francisco bay, "but not as inmate." The big day of his career came in August, 1942 when his battery joined a task force bound for Adak, a small but strategic island off the Alaskan coast.

The occupation was made with no resistance, in fact that Japs were unaware of the presence of American troops for over three weeks. The importance of this island lay chiefly in its proximity to Attu and Kiska. From there fighters could escort bombers to the objectives, for this was the only base more remote from Alaska proper than Dutch Harbor.

Larry's description of the barren rock is vivid. He lauds the Army engineers for the Herculean feat in developing an airstrip; it was 14 days from the time of the landing until the first bombers took off on their first mission to Kiska. It was necessary to drain and dam up a lake for the purpose, during which time they were hampered by foul weather and other numerous obstructions.

"Flying there is at its worst," says Mahrkens. Often a flight would leave on a mission and fail to return to their base. They just couldn't find the tiny island in the dense fog. Searchlights were set up at the end of the runways but even these could penetrate only a few feet. The use of searchlights other than as an aid to our own aircraft was limited, for the glare on the low ceiling gave away the positions to enemy raiders.

Ordered back to the United States for aircrew training, after 14 months on Adak, he eventually was sent to Amarillo, Texas where he was classified for pilot training. Where he will be sent now that the ground forces have reclaimed him is a mystery, but he has enjoyed the brief stay here in the 317th CTD, which he says is a virtual paradise.

PLATINUM, ALASKA

Platinum was and still is a strategist metal used in a variety of military equipment. The only source for it in the Western Hemisphere during the war was a site on Goodn News Bay adjacent to the mouth of the Small River and 11 miles southwest of Good News and the Kilbuck mountains. The town was named in the 1930s and the site became a boom town by 1937. A post office had been established in 1935 and incorporated as a city in 1975. A dredge, similar to the type used for placer gold mining was used to mine the metal by the Goodness Bay Mining Company. Six Alaska Territorial Guard soldiers were sent to the site to guard the dredge, during the winter of 1942-43 in case of a Japanese attack. The soldiers went to inspect the dredge and Private George "Ernie" Fiene marveled, "That is sure something to see. Just how could they assemble and run such a large piece of equipment so far away from civilization literally amazes me." In April 1943 the dredge crew returned to continue mining with the soldiers still stationed there. It was not found how long they continued to guard the facility, but after the retaking of Kiska in August 1943 the enemy threat was essentially gone.

–Courtesy of W.I. Van Der Poel

Anchorage during the war was an important trans-shipping port for supplies going by rail to interior Alaska and Fairbanks for the air and army base there and for building the ALCAN highway, which ended at Big Delta. It was founded in 1915, built around the Alaska Railroad yards.

The construction of the Fort Richardson-Elmendorf Field complex in the spring of 1940 brought in construction workers and the 4th Infantry Regiment and it became the headquarters for the Alaska Defense Command until the latter part of 1944.

President Roosevelt inspects troops in Kodiak in in a hollow formation in 1944 on his way back to Washington, DC after his three week tour of the Pacific area. AP Wirephoto

PRESIDENT FRANKLIN D. ROOSEVELT IN ALASKA

In August 1944 President Roosevelt met with military leaders in Hawaii and then went to the Aleutians to meet with his military commanders, boast morale and do a little fishing. He had lunch with the troops at Adak and caught several Dolly Varden off the side of his warship. He was to go to Dutch Harbor but the weather was not good so he sailed on to Kodiak He travelled on the heavy cruiser the *USS Baltimore* along with an escort of destroyers, keeping a wary eye for Japanese submarines. At Kodiak he ate again with the troops and reviewed them, caught one fish and then transferred to the destroyer *USS Cummings* at Auke Bay near Juneau for the final leg of the trip through the Inside Passage. The famous Fala (Roosevelt's dog) story, put out by the Republicans was that they accused the President of leaving his dog behind in Alaska and therefore having to send a warship back to retrieve the dog, costing many millions of dollars.

The dog was with the President all of the time and he later told a meeting with the Teamsters Union the following: "These Republican leaders, have not been content with attacks on me, or my wife, or my sons. No, not content with that, they now include my little dog Fala. Well of course, I don't resent attacks, and my family doesn't resent attacks, but Fala does resent them!"

Retired Air Force historian John Cloe wrote "at the time, he was suffering from severe hypertension and heart problems and needed a respite before engaging in a presidential campaign. It's fairly well known that FDR enjoyed going to sea on naval vessels and liked to fish."

Eating with the troops at a mess hall on Adak in August 1944.
–Courtesy FDR Library, NPX 48-32: 3868 (497)

As stated, the president liked to fish whenever he had the chance.

Lt. Gen. Simon Bolivar Buckner, Jr, the commander of the Alaska Defense Command from July 1940 to June 1944, was the son of Confederate General Simon Bolivar Buckner, Sr. who was a candidate for vice-president of the United States in 1896 and governor of his home state of Kentucky from 1887 to 1891. Senior was also involved in the famous Hatfield-McCoy feud in the 1880s.

The feud involved two rural families along the West Virginia-Kentucky border and the Tug Fork of the Big Sandy River from 1863 to 1891. It was caused by a land dispute during the American Civil War, and revenge killings by both sides, the Hatfields on the West Virginia side and the McCoys on the Kentucky side. Nine Hatfields were imprisoned for life and one executed. William Anderson Hatfield, known as Devil Anse was one leader and Randolph "Old Ranel" McCoy the other.

During the run-up to the Kentucky 1887 gubernatorial campaign, Perry Cline, a supporter of the McCoy clan was promised by Buckner to bring the Hatfield clan to justice if Cline could deliver the McCoy vote to him. Buckner liked to blame the West Virginia Hatfields for all the mayhem the feud caused through the years.

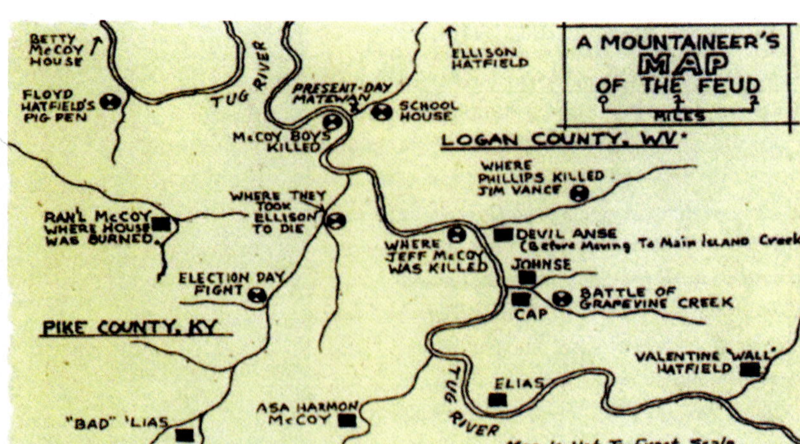

A major flood of the Yukon River hit the Galena airbase on May 29, 1945 causing major damage. Galena was a stopping point for Lend-Lease planes going to Russia. –Courtesy of Mark Milkovich via Charles Robison

GALENA

The spring breakup of the Yukon River caused major flooding on the Galena townsite and airfield. This one occurred on May 29, 1945, and caused major damage. The military airfield was built adjacent to the local airfield. The 8,000 foot runway was shared along with the flight line facilities.

It was constructed in 1942 by the Air Transport Command and used as a fueling/servicing field for Lend-Lease aircraft flying from Ladd Field to Nome and then onto Russia.

The host unit was the 1468th AAFBU, Alaskan Division, ATC. It was also used by the 11th Air Force for staging and emergency use. It was transferred to the Alaskan Air Command in 1945.

The photos are from the Mark Milkovich Collection via Charles Robison, Helena, Montana.

Cartoons from the 1944 booklet, *The Alaska Sportsman, Book of Pictures of "The Last Frontier"*

"I understand the boys at camp are going to practice camouflage today."

"He likes to be different!"

"His sweetheart is visiting him and he 'just isn't taking any chances'."

WIND BLOWN AND DRIPPING

A BOOK OF ALEUTIAN CARTOONS

By

CPL. BERNARD ANASTASIA
PFC. OLIVER PEDIGO
PFC. DON L. MILLER

Introduction

These cartoons originally were scratched into waxed paper stencils for our mimeographed daily newspaper at APO 980 in the Aleutians. This is a medium to make an artist long for the good old days when a craftsman had nice cave walls and handfuls of red and yellow ocher to work with. The hundred and fifty representative cartoons reproduced here have been dressed up a little with ink-line and wash; otherwise they haven't been tampered with.

Since our newspaper first appeared, fourteen months ago, we've run from two to four cartoons a day, depending on how much space we needed for maps, and our daily average through this period must have been at least three. That multiplies up to some twelve hundred and seventy cartoons in all. So far as I can figure out, no particular plan was followed in picking out the favored hundred and fifty for this book. Each of the three artists seems simply to have picked out the ones he happened—for one reason or another—to like. Some of my favorites are absent, but I'm too old and cagey to argue with artists unless I have to. And this lot is doubtless as truly representative as any I would select.

—Courtesy of Blaine Cornelison

Taken from an article from the CFB Esquimalt Naval & Military Museum

WRITTEN BY DEBBIE TOWELL, MUSEUM CURATOR

PACIFIC COAST MILITIA RANGERS

BRITISH COLUMBIA'S OWN HOME GUARD

They began as the Coastal Defence Guards and were finally reorganized as the Pacific Coast Militia Rangers (PCMR). The PCMR were unique to the west coast of Canada and were formed in early 1942 to protect British Columbia (BC) and calm public unease over possible enemy activities.

After the attack on Pearl Harbor and declaration of war against Japan, patrols of BC's rugged country appeared to be a necessity, one that could not be carried out by regular militia, who were deemed more suited to populated areas. Experienced men such as loggers, trappers, prospectors and ranchers were sought for this distinctive role. These men had knowledge of the local topography and terrain. Those who were close to populated centers were trained and employed in intelligence duties and local defence against minor raids at a local Ranger Training Camp. They were also instructed in tactical situations that included observation, especially coast watching against a possible Japanese invasion, anti-sabotage measures and protection of lines of communications and transportation.

All these newly formed companies of PCMR were so geographically spread out; many could not attend a training camp. Those who did attend were also trained in methods of instruction. This enabled to pass on information to their own personal upon their return. Training continued to be an issue and so it was determined that a training publication would have to be created in order to meet the needs of this widely dispersed force. "The Ranger," as it came to be known, was issued on Sept. 1, 1942 and was filled with useful information that every well-rounded Ranger should know, such as: "Know where to shoot," "Edible plants of BC," "Dig or Die'" and "What can you do with a tarp?" Age was not necessarily a consideration in the enlistment of these rugged men.

It was observed that, "young lads....in outlying areas were extremely valuable as guides to city bred men." Even those considered to be too old to join the war effort were able to contribute to the protection of BC. The PCMR's early months were met with a distinct lack of supplies in appropriate clothing and weaponry. This changed, however, after the first Japanese incendiary balloons started appearing and a standard kit issue was developed to include: steel helmets, cloth "dry-bak" shooting hat, armbands, cloth "dry-bak" cruiser coat with shoulder straps, cloth "dry- bak" trousers and battle dress drill blouse with .303 rifles issued. Although the PCMR never engaged the enemy they played a crucial role in establishing a sense of purpose in those who were unable to go overseas for whatever reason.

On Sept. 30, 1945 at Brockton Point Oval, British Columbia the PCMR were stood down. At the ceremony Major General F.F. Worthington noted that "the citizens of this country owe you a great deal of gratitude for the services you have rendered in the defence of their country." Unfortunately the personal records for the Rangers no longer exist.

A wartime view of the coastline of Tanaga, site of a fish cannery and military facilities.

For years after the war and up to the present (2018) various government agencies, using civilian contractors have worked on cleaning up the islands of wartime leftovers. –Courtesy of Steve Levi

NOTABLE PERSONALITIES WHO SERVED IN ALASKA DURING WORLD WAR TWO

There were several veterans of the Aleutian Campaign who went on to great success or were already successful as writers, movie actors or in the broadcast media. Dashiel Hammett was a well-known writer who produced the Thin Man series and was editor of the Adakan newspaper, which he started while stationed at Adak. It was first published on Jan. 19, 1944 and was printed daily with a run of between 3,000– to 6,000 copies. It was only distributed on Adak.

He was originally turned down by recruiters after the war started as he was already 48 years old and still on a disability pension from the last war. But he persisted and was inducted into the army. He spent two years on Adak and in Anchorage and wrote letters from there to his wife, children and several lady friends. They are collected in the book; *Selected Letters of Dashiel Hammett, 1921-1960*. He even bought a bar in Anchorage.

Charlton Heston was a crewman on a B-25 and after the war would become a very important actor in many epic movies. He joined the Army Air Forces after the December 7th attack, and after basic training as a radioman/gunner on a B-25 his squadron joined the 11th Air Force in Alaska in 1944. He didn't see combat this late in the war and was discharged in 1946. Marvin and Bernard Kalb stationed at Adak would go on to highly successful broadcasting careers.

Dashiel Hammett, left and Charton Heston, right.

Letter from Dashiel Hammett to his Daughter, Josephine, 2 October 1943 (from Adak)

Dear Princess—

We live here in Quonset huts—those semi-cylindrical metal things you have seen in pictures—strung out along both steep walls of a little valley, close to the walls, half dug in sometimes and spaced well apart so that if some dope wants to bomb us he can't bag too many with one shot. The huts have no openings in the sides, but a door and two square windows in either end. My hut is so well concealed under sod, tundra, and stuff, spread over chicken wire, that little light comes in even on those days when we can leave our doors and windows open. If our generator is functioning we have electric light, and can get our armed forces station (short wave) or Radio Tokyo (where all our navy is sunk every day) on our radio. And most of us have rigged up some sort of reading light over our beds.

Our beds are the regular metal Army cot. We have plenty of blankets and comforters, but of course no pillows and sheets. A Diesel-oil stove keeps the hut warm and—what's more important—dry, and our beaverboard wall lining makes a good background for pin-ups—mostly Vargas girls that look too much like Vargas girls. Long cracks between the floor and the walls let in enough fresh air to keep our canteens of water—and bottles of Coke when we have them—cool, but not enough of the outdoors to really bother us. (We're pretty comfortable when we're not wet and in the wind).

The prevailing wind—and it can do a mighty fancy piece of prevailing when it sets its mind to it—turns our valley into a funnel, and you think it's rugged going until you climb up the steep green sides to the terrain above. Then, lady, you've really bought yourself a hunk of air in motion. The only reason we don't sound like liars when we tell people how hard it blows is that we don't know. Our machine only registers up to 109 miles per hour. So we can just say it's blown harder than that.

A brook winds down our little valley, and winds is the word. Between my hut and the mess-hut—only a few hundreds yards away—we cross the brook eight times, mostly on impromptu footbridges that are as easily missed in the darkness as washed away when the brook cuts up. The brook is a lively one, busy and bustling and clear and cold, with rocky pools that sometimes have fish in them. (There's a report that a couple of pound Dolly Varden trout was seen this morning in a pool some twenty feet from my hut. I may hike that way after I finish this letter and see if I can do anything about it. I think I know where I can borrow some patchwork fishing tackle.)

I worked all night, until seven this morning, and should be sleeping now. Maybe I'll do that instead of going fishing. Or maybe I'll wash some sox and things. That's what I ought to do, so maybe I won't. Maybe I'll take a nap after all.

Kiss your mother and Mary for me—and don't bite 'em.

Much love, Papa

GORE VIDAL

Gore Vidal served as a journalist in the Aleutians and after the war would become a prolific American novelist, playwright and essayist and active in American politics. He was born in 1925 at West Point where his father was an instructor. He was raised near Washington, D.C., in the home of his grandfather, Thomas P. Gore, a populist Democrat senator from Oklahoma. Vidal learned about political life from him and when he was a teenager he adopted his first name of Gore. (His given first name was Eugene Luther).

Gore graduated from the exclusive Philips Exeter Academy and in 1943 joined the U.S. Army Reserves and was sent to the Aleutians on an Army supply ship. In 1946, while still in uniform he made his debut as a novelist with his first book, *Williwaw*, reflecting on his experiences in the Aleutians. He has written dozens of novels since then on a variety of subjects plus returning to politics and the movies.

Sam Maloof, famed woodworker was stationed at Adak where the military put his talent to use making detailed drawings of gun emplacements. His simple and practical wood furniture was prized by connoisseurs around the country. In 1949 he began his lifelong career of handcrafting furniture. He did not follow plans and his pieces were assembled without metal parts. He was the first craftsman to receive a MacArthur Foundation "Genius" grant in 1985. He died in 2009.

KERMIT ROOSEVELT (1889–1943)

The second son of President Theodore Roosevelt graduated from Harvard and in 1909 went on a year long expedition to Africa with his father.

In 1913-14 he accompanied his father again on an expedition into the Brazilian Amazon Basin which almost killed Theodore.

Kermit married in 1914 and then in 1917 he was made an honorary captain in the British Army and fought in the Middle East. He transferred to the American Army in 1918.

In between the wars he was a business man.

He again joined the British Army in 1939 and saw service in Norway and North Africa, but his health and drinking habit forced his discharge in 1941.

His cousin, President Franklin D. Roosevelt gave him a commission and he was posted to Fort Richardson near Anchorage where he worked as an intelligence officer and helped form the Alaska Territorial Guard.

Alcoholism plagued Kermit much of his adult life and he took his own life on June 4, 1943 in Anchorage. He was interned in the Fort Richardson National Cemetery with a memorial stone in 1949.

ARMY
E
NAVY
SHORT CUT TO TOKIO
KEEP 'EM ROLLING
Buy Bonds-Stamps
U.S.A.
VIA ALASKA HIGHWAY
Our Northern front is now not only protected, but is set up for attack. In this triumph of American and Canadian ability to do what couldn't be done, both men and equipment did their work well. Credit must also be given the manufacturers who delivered *on time* the trucks, tractors, shovels, bulldozers and other rugged construction equipments which stood up so well in service that was the ultimate in severity.
Kropp Forge is proud of having furnished many tough stress and shock-resisting forged parts for the many equipments used in building the Alaska Highway; also of the fact that we made our deliveries *on time* to aid the builders of these massive construction machines.
Wherever dependable forgings are needed for the war effort, the greatly increased facilities of Kropp Forge are equal to the task of delivering forged machine and equipment parts *on time*.
KROPP
SERVING INDUSTRY
18 SINCE 37
K
KROPP FORGE CO.
OVER 100 YEARS
Proudly we fly the Army and Navy "E" flag and stars, awarded and re-awarded for excellence and proficiency in the production of war materiel
KROPP FORGE COMPANY
Makers of Drop, Upset and Hammer Forgings for Ships, Guns, Planes, Tanks, Ordnance and Machine Tools.
"World's Largest Job Forging Shop"
5301 W. Roosevelt Road
Chicago, Ill.
Engineering Representatives in Principal Cities

These photos from the Yukon Archives show the tremendous difficulties of operating machinery on road building in the territory.
–Courtesy of the Yukon Archives, #30 84/73, #29 84/73, #30 84/30

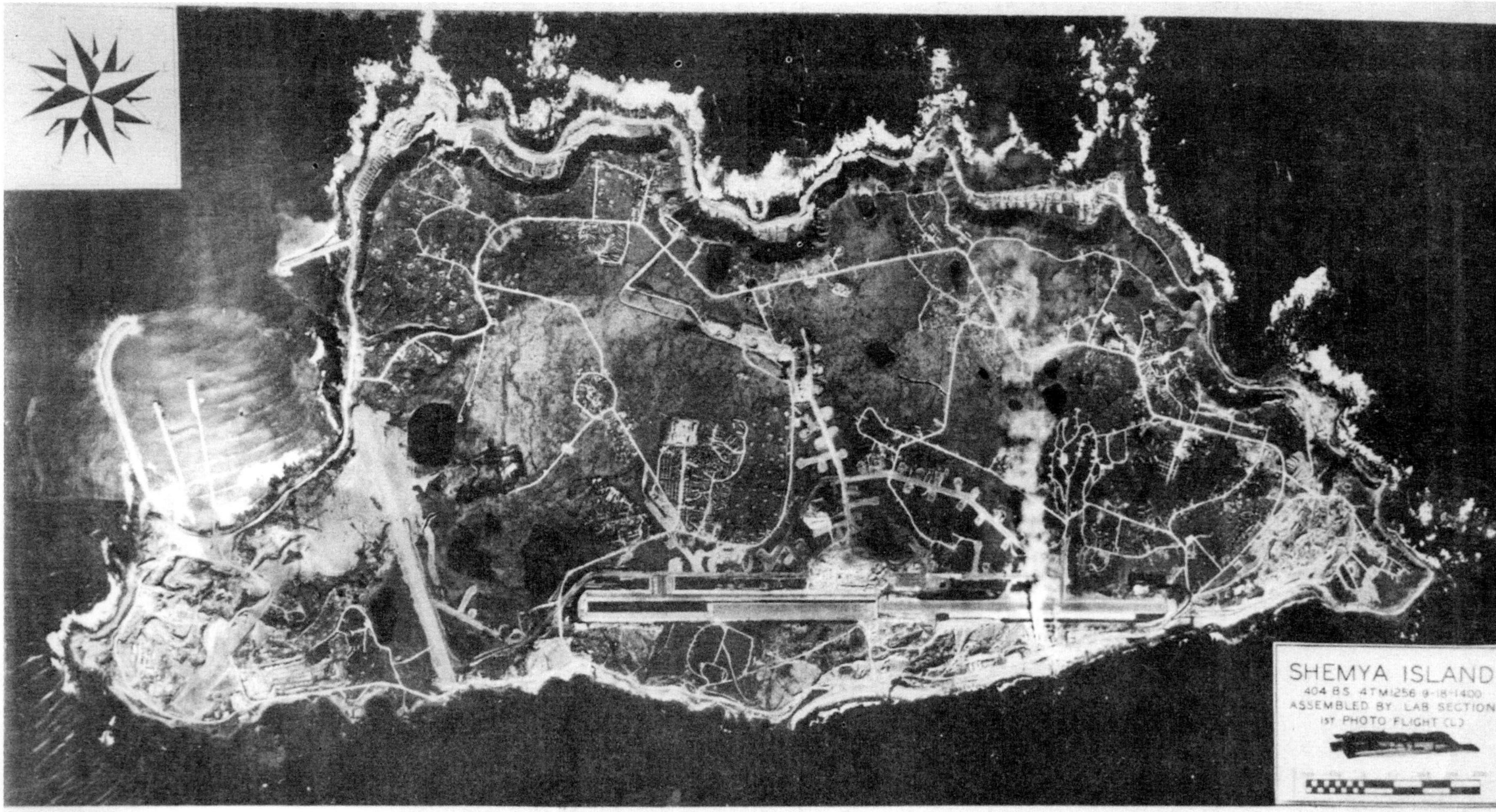

There is no date on this photo. If my memory serves me right, it must have been taken sometime in mid-1945. A clue to this date is the breakwater on the upper left, seems intact and we know the first one was blown away shortly after being completed in late 1944. The runway is completed; when I arrived in 1943 it was half this size and of steel-mat. My outfit, the 400th Air Base Squadron, was settled on the Pacific side of the Island at about a one-fourth point length of the runway from east to west. What part of the Island was your outfit located? We have the Elmendorf AFB Historian to thank for the photo. Thanks!!

E.B. (8/30/83)

Here is our favorite photo of our"home" during a most meaningful part of our lives, WWII. SHEMYA, that "secret" airbase, its location the Japs couldn't figure out and from which they were getting the hell blasted out of them!! We have Lester H. Best to thank for this photo. He was flying with the 404th Bomb Sq. as a Master Sgt., and chief photoman. Les has this to say about the photo: "Many times we endeavored to make aerial photos of Shemya. Time after time we were unsuccessful for as we would taxi for takeoff the base would be closed in. After returning from a mission we found this good weather. I luckily had a folding kodak in my pocket and made this photo." Thanks Les for the great contribution you've made to your buddies of the SHEMYA (A.P.O. 729) WWII Vets Association.

These photos were taken at Adak, the largest base during the war.

This chapel was constructed in 1943 and restored in 1989 to its wartime look by personal at the Naval Air Station.

Services held in the chapel during the war.

A vast array of quonset huts were set up around the airfield to accommodate the army troops assembling there for the Kiska invasion and the troops that were stationed there. After the war the huts were abandoned and the weather, through the years, took its toll on them.

Every base in the Aleutians, large or small had a military post office. One of the few ways to help bolster morale in this isolated theater of war was mail from home.

One of Maj. Jack Chennault's P-40 fighter planes of the 11th Fighter Squadron at Adak. Jack's father, Claire was the commander of the famous Flying Tigers, flying out of India and Burma early in the war.

CIRCULAR)
:
NUMBER 2)

HEADQUARTERS ALASKA DEFENSE COMMAND
Fort Richardson, Alaska
October 14, 1941

More than a year has passed since the Alaska Defense Command first came into being. That year has seen our numbers increase from a mere handful of men camped in snow-covered tents to a respectable force determined to meet hostile enterprises and deal with them effectively. It has seen a vast construction program, the building of air bases, the fortification of these bases and the initiation of a training program calculated to weld our units into a fighting machine.

Our year in Alaska has witnessed more than this. It has seen men from Southern States become hardened to a severe climate and enjoying the outdoors on snowshoes, ice skates and skis. It has seen men accustomed to luxurious living and highly developed artificial amusement centers laugh off minor discomforts and inconveniences and display commendable initiative in developing recreational facilities from the resources at hand. It has seen a minimum of whimpering and a maximum of straightforward American manhood among our officers and soldiers. For those who have built up this manly spirit that exists in our command, I have nothing but the highest praise, and I have every confidence that their fighting qualities can be counted on in an emergency.

With the ever increasing seriousness of our international situation, it has become necessary to reinforce Alaskan garrisons at a rate far beyond the ability of construction forces to provide the comforts and conveniences normally enjoyed by peacetime garrisons. Many of our troops are, and will be for some time to come, living under conditions which while not comparable to actual field service, are nevertheless less comfortable than can be expected under normal conditions. This is taken as a matter of course by every good soldier and in no way dampens the spirit of a man of fortitude and patriotism. At times, perhaps, it may cause a little temporary grumbling on the part of individuals who have been softened by luxury and have not yet come to a full realization of the fact that a nation and institutions built by manhood and fortitude can continue to exist only so long as it is defended by men of like fiber.

Ample evidence exists that the enemies of our country are, at the present moment, conducting an insidious campaign of propaganda calculated to undermine morale by attempting to make our soldiers feel sorry for themselves, become disgruntled and complained of mistreatment. Our papers, our magazines and some of our associates are full of subtle propaganda of this nature. If we are not on guard against it, we are likely to play into the hands of our enemies.

I feel confident that a word of warning will suffice in this matter. We are here on a serious mission but, after all, we can have plenty of fun if we look for it and don't wait for it to look for us. Let your letters home be cheerful, harden yourselves against minor discomforts, and let your enemies learn not only that you can "take it" but that you are prepared to hand out to them a good deal more than they can take.

/s/ S. B. BUCKNER, Jr.
Major General, U.S. Army.,
Commanding

/jws
DISTRIBUTION: "A" and "B"

— CHAPTER TWO —

RECREATION AND THE USO

Famous heavyweight boxer, Joe Louis appeared in the Aleutians to visit the troops and referee boxing matches.

USO

A number of private agencies had provided comfort and social services to American troops in France toward the close of World War One. Representatives of these organizations were called together in October 1940 in New York City for a first of a series of meetings hosted by Frank Weil of the National Jewish Welfare Board to discuss what could be done for the recent buildup of American forces.

Meanwhile, the Federal Government had also become concerned with maintaining morale among the troops and with offsetting the negative input the mobilization was having on local communities. Although some wanted the morale effort to be under government control, President Roosevelt believed that what was most needed was a way with civilian life, a life that nearly all of them had recently left behind so abruptly.

Six of the organizations that had met in New York City- the Young Women's Christian Association (YWCA), the Young Men's Christian Association (YMCA), the National Catholic Community Service, The National Jewish Welfare Board, the Traveler's Aid Association and the Salvation Army, pooled their resources to form the United Service Organization for National Defense, later shortened to the United Service Organization (USO).

In January 1941 Roosevelt summoned the USO leaders to Washington, DC to set the ground rules for the organization. It was to handle the on-leave recreation of the men in the armed forces. Funds were raised and USO centers were established in various locations in the United States.

On February 4, 1941 the USO was incorporated in New York State with its financial chairman, Thomas Dewey, who helped raise over $16 million. In October the USO created "Camp Shows, Inc." for the purpose of coordinating entertainment for the troops both at home and abroad.

The first Hollywood star to tour front-line bases was Joe E. Brown, who performed before Alaska troops in 1942. Bob Hope would become synonymous with USO tour shows during the war and his first tour was to mainland Alaska and the Aleutian Islands in 1942. He dubbed his tour the "Great White Way."

Along with his sidekick, Jerry Colonna and Frances Langford and musician Tony Romano, he performed at Anchorage, Annette Island, Cold Bay, Cordova, Naknak, Nome, Unimak and Whitehorse, Yukon. Other entertainers would perform in the territory along with movie stars such as Olivia de Havilland who made a trip to visit hospitals in Alaska in 1944 and Ingrid Bergnman, although a Swedish citizen made bond tours around the country, reading poetry, telling stories and making speeches. As she related in her autobiography:

" I thought I should entertain the soldiers somehow or other, but of course that was much more difficult because I was an actress not a cabaret star or entertainer. I volunteered and got signed up by the USO and they said, "Would you go to Alaska because no one ever wants to go there? They all want to go to the South Pacific."Well, I thought, the South Pacific would be full of insects and snakes, and I didn't like either of those things, so I said sure, I'll go to Alaska."

She went with three other girls and Neil Hamilton, who preformed magic. They preformed an O. Henry story and sang and danced. As she related: " We danced with the soldiers, and we ate with them and visited the hospitals, and then I caught a cold because the huts were so hot I was going out of my mind. I used to open the door and go out into the snow saying, "I'll die with this heat." Ad I almost did because I got pneumonia. I was in the hospital on New Year's Eve with the boys, but not in the way I intended. We flew in five little planes, just the pilot and one person behind; five tiny people and there were no roads. All snow. You'd say, "What's that down there?...." and there it was....just one little collection of huts and about two hundred boys sitting with nothing to do. They hadn't seen anyone for months. They hadn't even got a war to fight, not a bullet went off in Alaska (forgetting Attu and Kiska in 1943), and when they saw these five little planes coming in, they were so happy.

She became friends with Lieutenant General Simon Bolivar Buckner, the Army's Commanding Officer and they kept up a correspondence into 1945, until he was killed on Okinawa. He was always "Buck" to her.

These photos of Hollywood actress, Olivia de Havilland were provided by Jane Tucker of Hayesville, North Carolina. Ms. Tucker was with the American Red Cross in the Aleutians and was directed to serve as Miss de Havilland's escort during her 1944 trip to the islands. She was asked by the US Army to visit hospitals throughout the US and Alaska. In a 2003 interview with the author, Miss de Havilland stated that she was not a singer or dancer, but being a well-known actress, the army felt her presence in hospitals would be a great morale booster for the sick and wounded.

THE OLDEST PAPER IN THE ALEUTIANS

LAST OUTPOST

Most 948 O Units were 2 wks

Vol. II, Issue 33 APO 948, Seattle, Washington March 12, 1944

BOXING TOURNEY STARTS WEDNESDAY

Bouts opening the post's second annual boxing tourney will get underway Wednesday, March 15, at 7:00 PM. Entry lists for both the novice and open class tourneys closed March 10.

At stake in the series of Open bouts which begin Wednesday night will be seven local championships, with every class represented except the bantamweight.

Bouts in the Novice class will get underway about one month after the beginning of the Open competition. There will be seven classes in this group, also, with National Boxing Association weights prevailing in both groups.

FOR FULL DETAILS, SEE PAGES 10 and 11.

SGT. STEIN WINS BOND

Is reading other peoples' mail a private vice of yours? Whether or not, you must have the common trouble at APO 948, difficulty in writing letters. In either case, you'll be interested in reading the letters printed on page 6, which are the prize-winning entries in last week's LOP letter-writing contest.

Winners, in one-two-three order, are: S/Sgt Alvin C. Stein, Base; PFC Arthur E. Mosher, Posters; T/5 Morton L. Leavy, Livewires.

"SHOULD THE GOVERNMENT SUBSIDIZE COLLEGE EDUCATION AFTER THE WAR?" This is the essay contest subject for the coming week. There's a $25 war bond at stake, so keep your entry to the usual 300 words or less, and have it in the hands of the LOP by Wednesday morning at 9:00

TAX INFORMATION - PAGE 3

DOUGHGIRLS ARRIVE; PREMIERE SLATED IN ABOUT TWO WEEKS

another week

The Doughgirls, Unit Number 173 of USO Camp Shows, arrived here Tuesday and immediately began preparations for the presentation of Joseph Fields' smash Broadway hit after which the unit is named.

The Doughgirls, (Priscilla Newton, Jane Harven, Virginia Dyer and Jean McKenzie) have chosen the entire male cast of the show from among soldiers of the Post, who will play opposite the girls. The entire cast is given on page 9, except for one nurse who will be selected later.

The opening date has not been set, but will probably be within two weeks. The local premiere will be held at the Uptown Theatre, and will continue to play there twice daily until all units have seen it.

In a way the Doughgirls can be referred to as a stock company, only minus its male cast. The original production is still going strong in New York City and has caught the eye of critics.

(Continued on page nine)

AIR MAIL RATES INCREASED

All men are urged to note the change in air mail postage rates to and from this post.

Beginning 26 March 1944, air mail postage rates between the US and APO's in care of Postmaster at Seattle and Minneapolis will be increased to 8 cents per ounce or fraction thereof.

Be sure to repeat this information the next time you write anyone home.

Pvt. LOOGAN by WES.
WHEN THE USO SHOW HITS TOWN
THE WOLVES WILL GATHER AROUND!
THE GIRLS WILL SING, DANCE AND SHAKE
WITH EVERY 'G.I.' ON THE MAKE.
LET'S GET GOING! IF WE'RE FIRST IN LINE, WE CAN COP THE FRONT ROW I DON'T WANNA MISS DIS USO SHOW!
YA SED IT SPORT! I WANNA DANCE DE "BUMPS-A-DAISY" WID DEM GOILS
I WANNA BE DE GUY WHO GETS PICKED OUT OF THE AWDLE-ENCE --- GORSH! A KISS FROM LUCILLE, AND THEN I CAN MISS DA BOAT
WOW! WHAT A MOB OF 'G.I.'s'-- LUCILLE, YOU BETTER PICK OUT YOUR "SHY AND MODEST", NOW.
RIGHT! THERE'S ONE RIGHT THERE! THOSE OTHER CHARACTERS ARE TOO SHARP FOR ME TO HANDLE !
C'MON BIG BOY-- COME AND SING WITH ME...
WHO ? ME ?
HOPE HE DOESN'T PASS OUT ON ME--
YOU MADE ME LOVE YOU
WELL, HERE GOES LESSON NO. 1
THIS ONE IS EASY
AH!! CHEERIE - MY LOVE ARF - ARF - ARF - ARF ARF - ARF - ARF, ETC.
YE GODS! "REVERSE ENGLISH" -AND HOW!
HM-M-M-M-M
LESSON NO. 2 HOW TO LOVE
SO--DATS WHERE HE LEARNED HIS STUFF! FROM A BOOK !
THAT'S NO LIBRARY BOOK
WONDER, IF THE ARMED FORCES INSTITUTE CARRIES THAT?

WEEKLY BULLDOZER

23 August 1943

Published at APO 724

Vol 2 No. 43

WOMEN! IN PERSON TONIGHT USO SHOW!

Women in a USO Show! Here! We hope Eddie Burnette, Magician and manager of the troupe won't mind if we just sit here and knock ourselves out over the idea. This is not to his discredit because we know it took a magician - and a good one - to get a show with female embellishments into this Service Command.

Look at 'em all. There's Lucille Burnette, she works with Eddie in a novelty magic act which has amazed and amused serviceman audiences all over the states. Eddie does both magic and dancing simultaneously. She helps him.

Marcella Blanton, tap and acrobatic dancer, novelty roller skater, has been playing in the variety circuits of America for the past 14 years, brings with her a wealth of experience and a very entertaining and unusual act, and the man next to us, who says he's seen the show, says she's pretty, too.

Helen McClure, singer, is well known for her singing over WCCO and KSTP in Minneapolis. In 1933 and '34 she was chosen Television Girl at the World's Fair in Chicago. She has worked in Movies for all the major studios and in Musical Comedy.

Lucille Lane - this one is described in the publicity sheet as "beautiful" (!) - sings old fashioned songs with comical and romantic lyrics, and is equally good as a singer of hit-parade stuff. She has just completed 10 months as featured singer at Gounar's Gay Nineties in San Francisco.

Besides these 4 beautiful (and most welcome) women, there's Stanley Erickson, from Chicago, with comedy and novelty songs in Swedish dialect, accompanying himself on the accordion. He's a member of the Polar Bears, a Chicago Club that only goes swimming when they have to break the ice to get to the pool. When he signed up with USO he asked to go to a cold climate. He should have been here last winter.

The show will follow the movie at the Post Theater, Monday, Tuesday and Wednesday at 8:30. The movie starts at 6:30. Come early and get a seat. WOMEN!

USO show at warehouse #10 at Dutch Harbor, May 3, 1943. Photo by H. Marion Thornton. –Courtesy of ASL-P338-0915

Actress and singer Frances Langford on right in print dress, was on a USO tour in April 1943 in Dutch Harbor. She was a regular member of Bob Hope's touring group and became a favorite of troops around the world. Her film career began in 1935 after singing on radio shows. Her song "I'm In the Mood for Love" became her theme song. She first appeared on Hope's tour in May 1941 and was soon dubbed the "Sweetheart of the Fighting Fronts." She appeared in 28 films and several TV shows. Her USO tours continued through the Korean and Vietnam conflicts. She died in 2005 at age 92. –Courtesty of ASL, P338-0908

World-famous violinist, Yehudi Menuhin, in sweater, visited and performed at Dutch Harbor in April 1944. Menuhin was a child prodigy on the violin. In April 1945 he performed for liberated inmates of the Bergen-Belsen Concentration camp in Germany. In 1947 he was the first Jewish musician to return to Germany to perform. –Courtesty of ASL, P338-1759

A USO tour in full costume even visited the small island of Agattu south of Attu.

In the fall of 1943 National League president, Ford Frick, sent a group of major league ballplayers to the Aleutians. This was the first attempt by the major league organization to entertain troops during the war. The group, which included Frankie Frisch, manager of the Pittsburgh Pirates, second from left; Danny Litwhiler, outfielder for the St. Louis Cardinals, third from left; and Stan Musial outfielder for the St. Louis Cardinals, fourth from left; Also in the group were Dixie Walker, outfielder for the Brooklyn Dodgers and New York Yankees pitcher, Hank Borowy. The USO tour lasted about three weeks and the players showed the latest World Series film, answered questions and signed autographs. This photo was taken by H. Marion Thornton at Dutch Harbor on Dec. 26, 1943. –Courtesy of ASL, P338-1770

THE RIPCORD THEATRE

6:00
8:15
10:15

Adak Alaska

FEB. 20 Sunday PERILS OF NYOKA Chapter # 14
THE LODGER **** Merle Oberon -- Laird Cregar -- George Sanders

FEB. 21 Monday
ROOKIES IN BURMA **** Alan -- Carney -- Wally Brown

FEB. 22 and 23 Tuesday and Wednesday
ALI BABA AND THE FORTY THIEVES **** Maria Montez -- Jon Hall & Andy Devine

FEB. 24 Thursday
SPRINGTIME IN THE ROCKIES **** Betty Grable -- Harry James and Orch.

FEB. 25 and 26 Friday and Saturday
THE MIRACLE OF MORGAN'S CREEK **** Betty Hutton -- Eddie Bracken

FEB. 27 Sunday PERILS OF NYOKA FINAL CHAPTER #15
CAREER GIRL **** Francis Langford -- Edward Norris

FEB. 28 Monday
CASANOVA IN BURLESQUE **** Joe E. Brown -- June Havoc

FEB. 29 Tuesday MAR. 1 Wednesday
THE FIGHTING SEABEES **** John Wayne -- Susan Hayward -- Dennis O'Keefe

MAR. 2 Thursday
LIFEBOAT **** Tallulah Bankhead -- Henry Hull -- William Bendix

MAR. 3 and 4 Friday and Saturday
MADAME CURIE **** Greer Garson -- Walter Pidgeon

During 1938-39 the US Government built the Mount McKinley Hotel to promote tourism using the Alaska Railroad to get to Mount McKinley National Park. It was built near the southwest base of Mount Healy, at the start of the park road. The hotel was operated by the railroad but during the war the entire railroad was taken over by the US Army Transportation Corps and the hotel became the US Army Recreation Camp. Recreation activities included skiing and the main ski run was located on the south slope of Mount Healy, north of the park road. During the winter of 1943-44, the Army rigged up a ski tow and warming hut at Mile 6 of the park road. It was used December through April. Several other sites were also used.

SKIING IN WARTIME ALASKA

When one thinks of Alaska it is usually of snow and cold weather. Troops from the Arkansas National Guard were sent to Dutch Harbor to protect the military facilities built or under construction. Most had never seen snow or experienced the harsh weather that was typical of the area. Especially in the Aleutians, the weather affected everyone and the aircraft and heavy equipment. But snow in interior Alaska did provide recreation opportunities for troops on rest and recreation leaves.

The Anchorage Ski Club and the US Army built the City Ski Bowl including a ski jump, on the bluff northwest of Gambell and 3rd, overlooking Ship Creek, to provide skiing for civilians and troops. The two Alaska Railroad hotels, The Mount McKinley and The Curry, along the route also provided winter activities. There are even Japanese photos showing their troops on skis on the occupied islands.

Nurses stationed at Dutch Harbor on skis with an army tracked vehicle called a "weasel" pulling them.
—Courtesy of the Museum of the Aleutians

These Alaska National Guard troops on the Valdez Glacier are practicing on skies for possible combat, January 1943.

From 1941-45, a garrison of the Alaska Army National Guard was established in Valdez. The 297th Infantry Battalion consisted of 265 men organized into three companies. Their mission was to protect the Port of Valdez and the Richardson Highway. Their duties, however, also included unloading freight ships carrying materials for military construction in Alaska's interior and building their own facilities there. The garrison's housing site was located on a glacial moraine approximately one and one half miles west of the original Valdez town site

The facilities included housing for 15 officers and 250 enlisted men, a 25-bed hospital, motor repair shop, and 20,000 square feet of storage space. Later, a dry cleaning plant and a small laundry building were built. The 297th infantry worked on construction "between boats." Preparation of the ground and foundation work was done in April 1943 when two feet of snow was still present and was finished before the end of October.

The unit also conducted ski patrols on the Valdez Glacier. One such patrol in February 1943 ended in tragedy with 20 members of the unit requiring hospitalization; one member of the patrol–a Corporal Birdwell was lost in a crevasse.

The photo to the left shows a skier, probably his first time on skis at the Mt McKinley Hotel in 1942. This photo made the pages of Life *magazine. The bottom photo states, Soldiers on Ski Patrol somewhere in Alaska, 1942.* –Courtesy of AP Wirephotos

Even the Japanese on Attu found time to enjoy the snow on skis.

Soldiers of the 7th Division and Navy Seabees cooking lunch on the beach at Attu during battle. The ski would be Japanese as there were no ski troops involved in the battle.
—Courtesy of Alaska Air Command

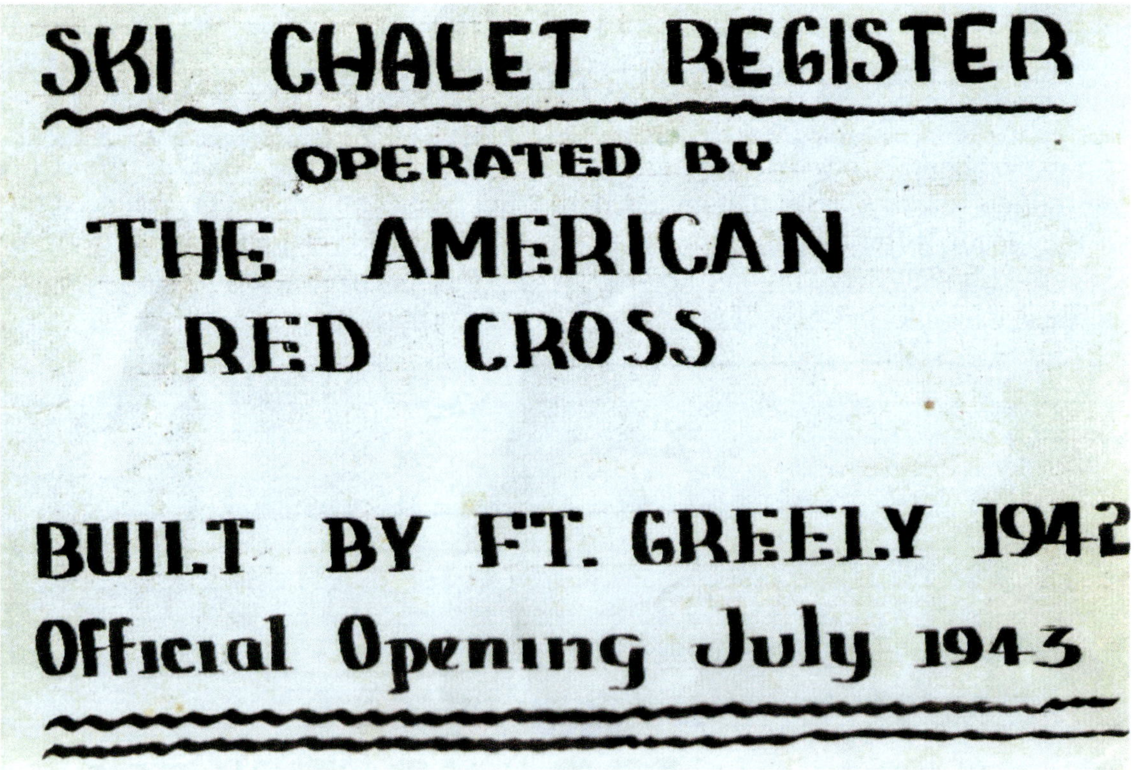

SKI CHALET REGISTER

OPERATED BY

THE AMERICAN RED CROSS

BUILT BY FT. GREELY 1942

Official Opening July 1943

Kodiak Island had a major naval facility and the Fort Greely Army base during the war. A ski chalet was built by army engineers and dedicated during the Winter Carnival in February 1943. It was managed by the Red Cross. A Ski Patrol was formed and ski instruction was provided on Old Womens Mountain. In the final test of a student's ability on skis, he was taken by truck to a place about a half days journey away and had to ski back to headquarters. Notice the number of different jobs on the charts and where they were from. –Kodiak Historical Society

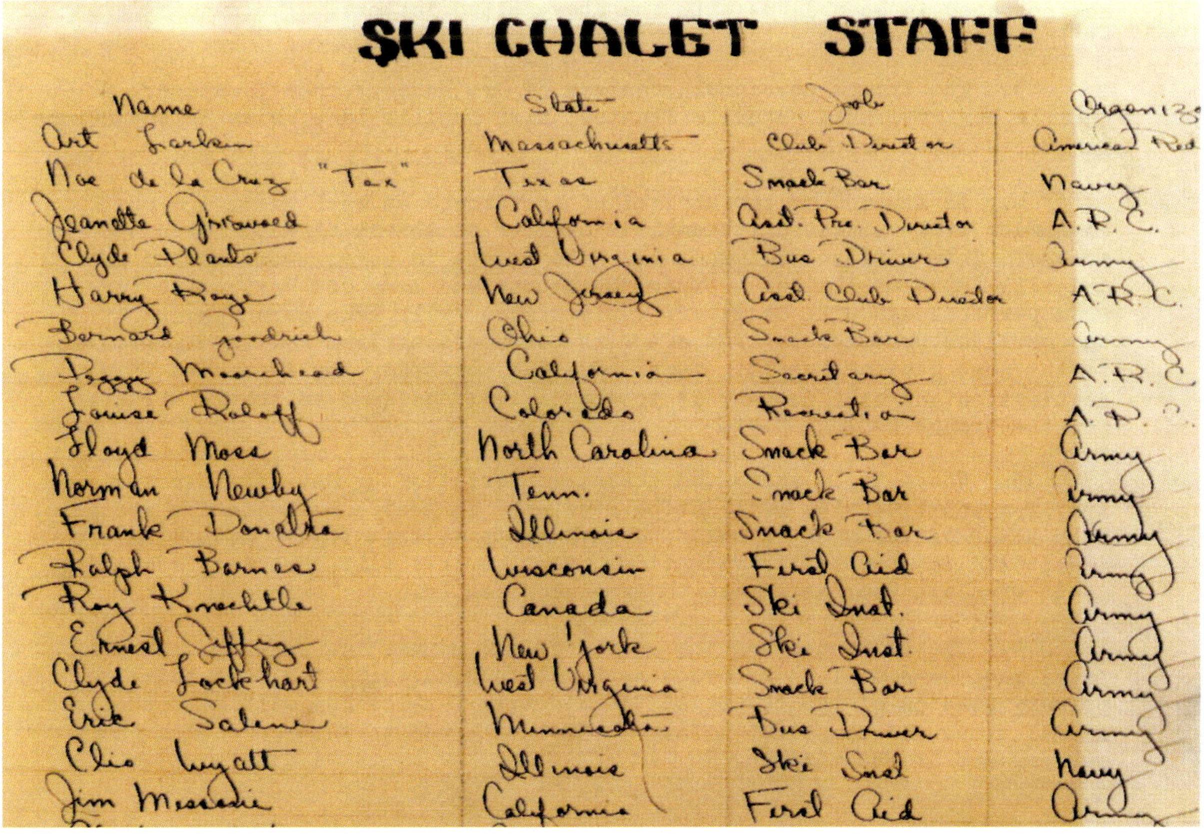

SKI CHALET STAFF

Name	State	Job	Organiz.
Art Larken	Massachusetts	Club Director	American Red
Noe de la Cruz "Tex"	Texas	Snack Bar	Navy
Jeanette Girouard	California	Asst. Pro. Director	A.R.C.
Clyde Plants	West Virginia	Bus Driver	Army
Harry Roye	New Jersey	Asst. Club Director	A.R.C.
Bernard Goodrich	Ohio	Snack Bar	Army
Peggy Moorhead	California	Secretary	A.R.C.
Louise Roloff	Colorado	Recreation	A.R.C.
Floyd Moss	North Carolina	Snack Bar	Army
Norman Newby	Tenn.	Snack Bar	Army
Frank Donaldson	Illinois	Snack Bar	Army
Ralph Barnes	Wisconsin	First Aid	Army
Roy Knechtle	Canada	Ski Inst.	Army
Ernest Jeffrey	New York	Ski Inst.	Army
Clyde Lockhart	West Virginia	Snack Bar	Army
Eric Salene	Minnesota	Bus Driver	Army
Clio Wyatt	Illinois	Ski Inst	Navy
Jim Messadie	California	First Aid	Army

USO CAMP SHOWS TROUPE #100

This was an experimental troupe-the first group of USO entertainers to go to Alaska that included women. If they made it through all right, more would be sent. Although they couldn't keep to their prescribed schedule, because of poor road conditions and bad weather, the trip was very successful and other units followed them to the North Country. Lucille Lane Fetterly, one of the performers from Renton, WA provided these official orders.

Headquarters Alaskan Department
OFFICE OF THE COMMANDING GENERAL
APO 942, c/o Postmaster, Seattle, Washington

28 November 1943

SUBJECT: USO-Camp Shows Troupe #100.

TO : Post Commanders All Posts Concerned, Alaskan Department.

1. References:

a. Letter, this headquarters, dated 16 April 1943, subject: "Handling of USO-Camp Shows, Troupes, and Other Entertainers."

b. Letter, this headquarters, dated 25 August 1943, subject: "Local Scheduling of USO-Camp Shows Troupes."

2. USO-Camp Shows Troupe #100 will report to your station for the purpose of entertainment of troops as indicated on the attached schedule. It will proceed to the next station on the itinerary promptly in accordance with this schedule. Scheduling and handling of the troupe will be accomplished in accordance with the above cited letters. The running time of the show is approximately seventy (70) minutes.

3. The troupe personnel consists of Mr. Eddie Burnett, manager, & Lucille Burnett, Miss Marcella Blanton, Miss Lucille Lane, Miss Helen McClure and Mr. Stanley Erickson.

4. In advance of the arrival of the troupe at each post, the post commander will appoint a responsible officer as travel director with the troupe. This officer will accompany the troupe to engagements at the post, and will serve as liaison between the troupe and Army and Navy units for whom performances will be given. This officer will make arrangements at the earliest practicable time after the troupe's arrival for transportation to the next post on the itinerary. He will accompany the troupe to this destination and will deliver it to the officer assigned as travel director for the troupe at that post.

5. Where it is indicated that transportation by Navy Air, Army Air or Army Transport Service will not be available in accordance with the schedule, this headquarters will be notified in advance so that timely action may be instituted to correct the situation. Such reports will include a statement as to when transportation can be arranged locally.

6. These troupes are the guests of the Commanding General, Alaskan Department, and will be accorded appropriate handling. The fact that the primary mission of the troupe is to entertain Service Men will be emphasized at all times and no social affairs will be allowed to interfere with the performance of the mission.

USO-Camp Shows Troupe #100-continued.

When entertainment or social affairs are held, the entire troupe may be invited to participate, but private social engagements with individual members of the troupes will be discouraged. In such cases, invitations to the troupe as a unit will be extended to the troupe manager by the officer travel director.

By command of Lieutenant General BUCKNER:

FRANK L. WHITTAKER
Brigadier General, U. S. Army
Deputy Commander

NORRIS B. CLOUGH
1st Lt., A. G. D.
Asst. Adjutant General

2 Incls:
#1 Itinerary
#2 Publicity

DISTRIBUTION
"AAA"

Ft. Richardson	3	Yakutat	3
Ft. Greely	3	Juneau	3
Ft. Mears	3	Excursion Inlet	3
Ft. Glenn	3	Annette	3
Ft. Randall	3	Ketchikan	3
Ft. Morrow	3	Prince Rupert	3
Ft. Ray	3	Comalsec	3
Adak	3	13th Naval Dist	3
Atka	3	Base Echelon	3
Naknek	3	Adv CP	3
Whittier	3	PRO	3
Valdez	3	Trans O	3
Cordova	3	SSO	10

- 2 -

ITINERARY FOR USO-CAMP SHOWS TROUPE #100

POST	FROM	TO
Ft. Richardson	4 Dec 43	15 Dec 43
Ft. Greely	16 Dec 43	28 Dec 43
Ft. Mears	29 Dec 43	11 Jan 44
Adak	12 Jan 44	26 Jan 44
Atka	27 Jan 44	29 Jan 44
Ft. Glenn	30 Jan 44	9 Feb 44
Ft. Randall	10 Feb 44	20 Feb 44
Ft. Morrow	21 Feb 44	
Naknek	22 Feb 44	
Ft. Richardson	(travel)	
Whittier	25 Feb 44	26 Feb 44
Valdez	27 Feb 44	
Cordova	28 Feb 44	
Yakutat	29 Feb 44	1 Mar 44
Juneau (& Ex. Inlet)	2 Mar 44	3 Mar 44
Ft. Ray	4 Mar 44	8 Mar 44
Annette	9 Mar 44	12 Mar 44
Ketchikan (incl. Coast Guard)	13 Mar 44	16 Mar 44
Prince Rupert	17 Mar 44	24 Mar 44
Seattle	---------	

Our itinerary was shot to blazes due to weather. It took us nearly two months to go up the Alcan highway. We were stuck at Atka for over a week due to storms. We were stuck at Lake Bennett over a week due to slides and washout of trestle - Boy - is that a story!!!

Incl. #1

TROUPE #100 TOURS THE ALEUTIANS

USO-CSI Troupe #100, comprised by four women and two men, will entertain troops at ____________________ on ____________________.

* * *

Troupe #100, having completed a three months' run throughout the Alaskan mainland, is making it's way with a successful one hour show through the outposts in the Aleutians. One of the reasons for the success of #100 has been its peculiar policy of shunning publicity, which gives this troupe a rare and pleasing individuality. Their mainland stand has proven popular in each instance. This troupe promises to be among the most successful USO aggregations ever sent up here. Following is what little information Manager Eddie Burnett released concerning the individual members of #100:

BURNETT, EDDIE - From Chicago. Manager, emcee. Dances with manipulations.

BURNETT, LUCILLE - From Chicago. An accomplished magician.

ERICKSON, STANLEY - From Chicago. Accordianist and singer of songs in Swedish dialect. Erickson is also a member of the Chicago Polar Bear Club, all of whose members go for long swims in Lake Michigan about the time of year when it shows signs of freezing. Erickson says he took this trip in order to take a few dips in the Bering Sea. "I hear the water is nice and cold in the Bering Sea," he said.

BLANTON, MARCELLA - From Los Angeles. From a show family, and a trouper since she was four years old, or about 17 years. Miss Blanton has a roller skate specialty which she will not do up here. "I heard they only ice skate in Alaska, so I didn't bring my rollers." But Marcella's acrobatic dance routine is popular in its own right.

LANE, LUCILLE - From Seattle. Miss Lane is a personality singer, who believes in audience participation as a surefire thing in soldier shows. Lucille left after a successful stand as a singing comedienne at San Francisco's "Gay 90's" to join Troupe 100.

McCLURE, HELEN - From Los Angeles. Sings popular ballads like "Let's Get Lost". Has done extensive work in Hollywood where they make motion pictures, and has had her voice dubbed in for numerous of the "big name" actresses who looked as though they were singing, when actually it was Helen McClure whose voice everybody heard.

- but even if #100 were not the talented group it is, they would nevertheless have proven commendable for their refusal to promote their own publicity. Posts on the mainland liked that.

A USO boxing match at Fort Richardson in Anchorage with comedian Joe E. Brown as Master of Ceremonies. –AM AMRC b90-4-11

— CHAPTER THREE —

THE ALCAN AND CANOL CONSTRUCTION PROJECTS

Drivers ready to pick up their trucks for the drive north over the still rough ALCAN Highway.
—Courtesy of APWire photo

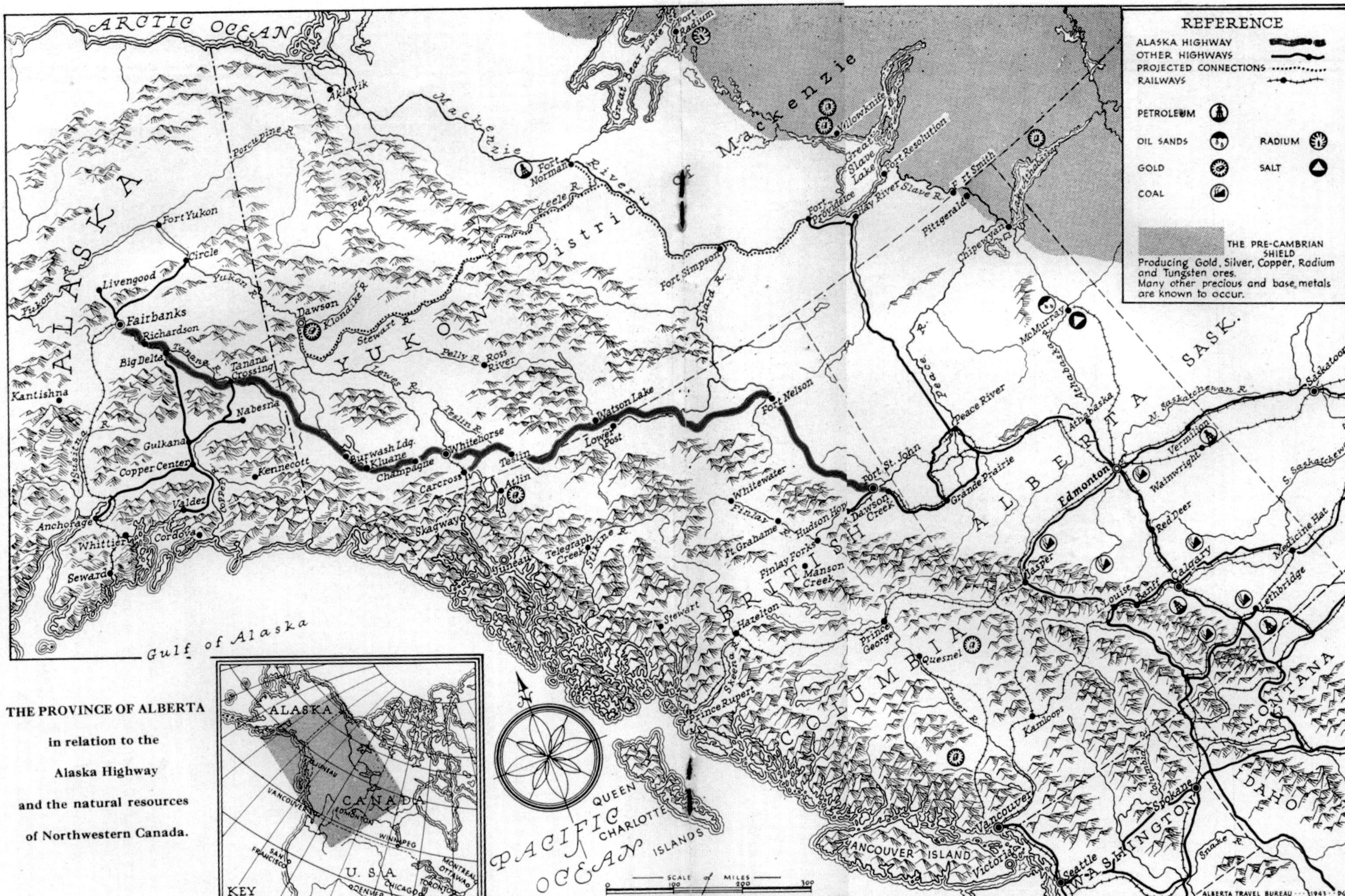

THE PROVINCE OF ALBERTA

in relation to the

Alaska Highway

and the natural resources

of Northwestern Canada.

INFORMATION REGARDING CANADA'S GREAT NORTH-WEST WILL BE SUPPLIED FREE BY WRITING TO ANY OF THE FOLLOWING

District Superintendent,
Dept. Colonization & Agriculture,
Canadian National Railways,
10418 101st Street,
EDMONTON, Alta.

District Superintendent,
Dept. Immigration & Colonization,
Canadian Pacific Railway Company,
C. P. R. Building,
EDMONTON, Alta.

Alberta Travel Bureau,
Dept. of Trade and Industry
Legislative Building,
EDMONTON, Alta.

British Columbia Government Travel Bureau,
Dept. of Trade and Industry,
Parliament Buildings,
VICTORIA, B. C.

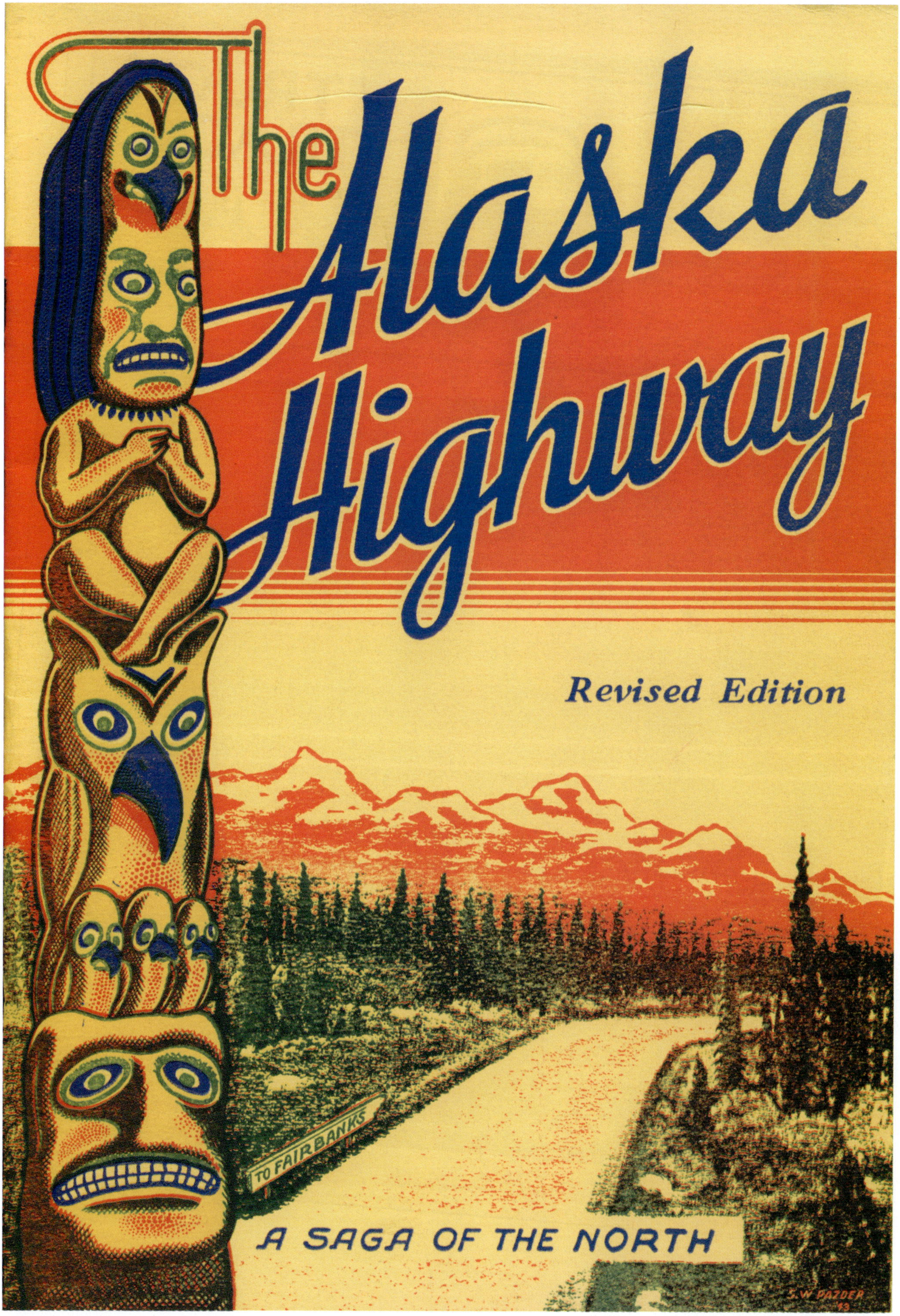
The Alaska Highway
Revised Edition
TO FAIRBANKS
A SAGA OF THE NORTH

The Alaska Highway

"TRUCK TRACKS"

16 February, 1944

Vol. 2, No. 8

Special Souvenir Edition

Collier's
DECEMBER 23, 1944
TEN CENTS
©THE CROWELL-COLLIER PUBLISHING COMPANY—PUBLISHERS OF COLLIER'S—THE AMERICAN MAGAZINE—WOMAN'S HOME COMPANION
El Paso 3000 MILES
QMC USA
THE SECRET of the RED ARMY
By HARRISON E. SALISBU

Dedication of the Peace River Bridge 38 miles from Dawson Creek, British Columbia on Aug. 27, 1943. The bridge was officially opened with the cutting of the ribbon with the representatives of the United States and Canada. It was the largest bridge construction project on the highway and took 18 months to complete, crossing 2,000 feet of navigable water and high enough for river-craft to proceed under it.

Gen. James A O'Connor, commanding general of the northwest service command, and Fiorello H. LaGuardia, Mayor of New York City and a member of the joint United States and Canadian Commission that selected the site for the highway, stand at a point named in the latter's honor.

UNIQUE CHAPEL SERVES ROAD

An article from *Truck Tracks*, Feburary 16, 1944

A vehicle, unique on the Alaska Highway is driven hundreds of miles each month by Chaplain William J. Brown, one of two spiritual advisers assigned to the highway project.

The vehicle is a Dodge pick-up 4x4 with a replica of an Army chapel built on the back. This little chapel is the composite work and voluntary effort of soldiers in five or six different stations within the Central and Northern Divisions, each group adding details as the project progressed.

It all began when the Chaplin requested some form of permanent protection for his equipment during the winter months. A small detachment of men at Haines Camp had ideas of their own. Elaborating on the Chaplin's suggestions, they built a small house and added windows on all sides, with doors opening from the center at the rear. Cathedral Bluffs decided that paint was essential. Big Delta painted crosses on each side. After several weeks travel, an Ordnance Company suggested a second coat of paint with stenciled crosses.

Someone at McCrae began calling it "The Chapel" and soon that name became general. One day a couple of soldiers at Cathedral Bluffs said a chapel needed a steeple. The Chaplin laughed and agreed. He went to chow and upon returning to the garage found the steeple built and in place. Canyon Creek painted the steeple and cleaned the entire vehicle.

Now after several months of winter driving in all kinds of weather and road conditions, "The Chapel" had become known on the Alaska Highway from Fairbanks to Watson Lake. The Chaplin drives "The Chapel" approximately two thousand miles a month.

Many soldiers and officers have expressed their appreciation of the visible and tangible evidence of the work of the Chaplin. This undoubtedly has deeper emphasis because no station on the Highway has anything remotely resembling a chapel. Services have been held in mess halls, day-rooms, barracks and out-doors.

BUILDERS OF THE ALASKA HIGHWAY
Arctic Ocean
ASIA
Bering Strait
PT. BARROW
NOME
ALASKA
Yukon R.
FAIRBANKS
RICHARDSON HIGHWAY
TOK CUTOFF
CANADA
ALCAN HIGHWAY
WHITEHORSE
VALDEZ
HAINES CUTOFF
HAINES
SKAGWAY
JUNEAU
DAWSON CREEK
EDMONTON
FOR YEARS PEOPLE SAID IT WAS IMPOSSIBLE TO BUILD A 1,671-MILE ROAD THROUGH THE BARREN WILDERNESS OF CANADA AND ALASKA. BUT TEN-WHEELED TRUCKS ARE NOW ROLLING ALONG THE HIGHWAY THAT LINKS OUR INLAND AIRPORTS, BRINGING WAR SUPPLIES TO OUR MEN...AND THE ENGINEERS' MOTTO IS: KEEP 'EM ROLLIN'!
WITH TEMPERATURES RANGING FROM NINETY ABOVE TO SEVENTY BELOW ZERO, NATURE SOMETIMES SEEMED TO BE ON THE SIDE OF THE AXIS, BUT 16,000 AMERICANS AND CANADIANS DOGGEDLY BATTLED THE ELEMENTS!
EVEN GREAT TWENTY-THREE-TON BULLDOZERS FOUNDERED!
I'M MIRED! THIS MUSKEG SLIPS LIKE CUSTARD AND STICKS LIKE GUM!
SPECIAL GARMENTS HAD TO BE WORN IN SUMMER TO PREVENT BITES OF ALMOST INVISIBLE INSECTS.
THE DUST OF THE GLACIAL SILT WAS SOMETIMES SO THICK THAT TRUCKS HAD TO BURN THEIR HEADLIGHTS ALL DAY AND MEN HAD TO WEAR DUST RESPIRATORS IN ORDER TO BREATHE!
A SIGN HUNG IN EDMONTON HALL, WHERE 6,000 CANADIANS WERE HIRED. IT WARNED THEM AGAINST THE DANGERS AND HARDSHIPS THE MEN WOULD HAVE TO FACE.
THIS IS NO PICNIC

THE COLD WAS SO PROLONGED THAT EVEN STEEL LOST ITS ELASTICITY.
THE TREADS SPLIT DURING THE NIGHT!
LUCKY THERE'LL BE NEW SUPPLIES TOMORROW!
WHEN THE WORK WAS BEGUN, THE MEN COULD DRAG EQUIPMENT ACROSS THE ICE, BUT AS WARM WEATHER APPROACHED...
WHAT'S THE IDEA OF THE SAWDUST, JOE?
THE THAW HAS STARTED! THEY'RE USING SAWDUST TO SLOW THE MELTING OF THE ICE! WE WANT TO GET MORE EQUIPMENT ACROSS WHILE IT'S STILL SOLID!
THE K. P.'S HAD PROBLEMS, TOO!
HEY, CHARLIE! SOMETHING'S BURNING!
SURE-THE PANCAKES! AND YET THE BATTER'S FROZEN ON TOP FROM STANDING OUTSIDE
THEIR MEAT HAD TO BE PROTECTED FROM DOGS AND WOLVES.
WE'VE OUTSMARTED YOU, BUTCH! YOU STOLE OUR MEAT ONCE TOO OFTEN!
CLOTHES CAME BACK FROM THE LAUNDRY IN SOLID CHUNKS!
WHY DON'T YOU USE AN ICEPICK?
THE STOVE WILL MELT IT FASTER!
HARDWORKING AMERICANS AND CANADIANS FINALLY FINISHED THE ROAD IN NOVEMBER, 1942, BUT THEY STILL HAVE THE JOB OF KEEPING IT OPEN AGAINST THE BLIZZARDS THAT SWEEP DOWN FROM BERING STRAIT THIS IS NO JOB FOR SISSIES-THE MEN HAVE TO BE TOUGH!
Season's Greetings!

DURING THE SPRING THAW AND AUTUMN FREEZE, THE AIR WAS HEAVY WITH FOG FOR WEEKS!
ARE WE LOST?
NO! WE'RE FOLLOWING THE RUTS THAT THE OTHER TRUCKS MADE!
PILOTS BRINGING MATERIALS BY AIR SOMETIMES FLEW OVER THE ST. ELIAS MOUNTAINS, WHERE HEADWINDS OFTEN BLOW AT EIGHTY-FIVE MILES PER HOUR!
IN THE WINTER, PLANES ON THE GROUND HAD TO HAVE THEIR MOTORS COVERED WITH TARPAULINS FOR PROTECTION.
THE ENGINES WILL NEVER START! IT'S TOO COLD!
THIS HOT MACHINE AIR WILL WARM 'EM UP!
SOLDIERS WERE PUT ON DUTY TO GUARD A TEMPORARY BRIDGE ACROSS THE WHITE RIVER.
ICE IS PILING UP, BILL!
WE'D BETTER BLAST IT AWAY AGAIN! THIS SPAN IS PLENTY IMPORTANT!
EVEN TRUCK DRIVERS HAD TO BE DAREDEVILS!
TAKE IT EASY, BOY!
DON'T WORRY! I'VE SKIDDED A DOZEN TIMES AND I'M STILL HERE!
STORMS AND FREEZING WEATHER WERE NOT THE ONLY DANGERS THESE MEN HAD TO FACE. OFTEN THIS HAPPENED...
LOOK, PETE! A GRIZZLY!
I'LL GET MY GUN, QUICK!

Camp life along the highway construction route went on in all kinds of weather conditions. –Courtesy of ASL PCA-193

A White Pass & Yukon Route train at the Whitehorse roundabout with steamboats in the background. Both means of transportation were vital for construction projects. –Courtesy of YA 98/73,Albert & David Bloomstrand Colletction

These photos are from Luke Johnson of Monroe Township, NJ, whose grandfather Richard F. Johnson from Jersey City, NJ (1911–1989) was a member of the 35th Engineers Regiment who worked on 350 miles of the ALCAN from Ft. Nelson, BC to 50 miles east of Watson lake, Yukon. He had joined the Army in June 1941 and his unit worked from March to the fall of 1942 on the road. Then to the spring of 1943 the regiment built a winter road from Fort Nelson, BC to Fort Simpson, NWT and then on the road from the ALCAN Highway to Norman Wells, NWT on the Mckenzie River. In 1944 he was stationed at Noumea, New Caledonia, then New Guinea and finally in the Philippines until he was sent home in August 1945.

The men who worked on the initial building of the road had to endure the harshest of conditions in the Canadian wilderness—rain, mud, snow, ice, bugs, isolation and loneliness.

Mail call was very important for the troops who were working in isolated and harsh conditions. R. F. Johnson is holding his drinking cup.

It was not all work for the troops on the road construction.

The initial road was built in a hurry and was know as the "Crooked Road" because of its meandering around swamps, bogs, and other obstacles.

Heavy equipment was essential to building the road.

The initial road was more a rough trail, but it still provided a vital means ot getting supplies into central British Columbia, Yukon and finally to Alaska.

B. F. Johnson posed in his uniform in front of a typical tent that was home for many months in all kinds of weather.

The idea was to cut a rough road from Dawson Creek, BC to interior Alaska through the muskeg to provide a vital supply line to interior Canada and Alaska. Later the US Public Roads Administration would come in with private contractors to upgrade it for year-round use.

A postwar brochure of the White Pass & Yukon Route bus trip on the Alaska Highway.

Roll North Over The

ALASKA HIGHWAY

in Luxurious New B.Y.N. Busses

Swift, Regular "Pony Cruiser" Service to the Heart of America's Last Frontier Operated by the White Pass & Yukon Route

New B. Y. N. "Pony Cruiser" bus, seating 20 passengers.

When Your Bus Reaches Whitehorse There Are Inviting Side-trips to Take

1. For a complete change of pace, sail down the Yukon River, aboard a B. Y. N. steamer, to the Klondike and Dawson City. The round trip takes about a week and is a perfect contrast to your bus ride, giving you a chance to re-live the colorful gold-rush days of '98.

2. For an indescribably glamorous experience, take the train to Carcross for the overnight steamer trip to Ben-My-Chree, the former home of a romantic couple who found supreme happiness in this wilderness of glacier-mantled mountains mirrored in glassy blue lakes.

3. For a thrill-packed day, ride the White Pass & Yukon Railroad all the way down to Skagway, a 110 mile trip during which the perilous first leg of the "Trail of '98" can be plainly traced through your parlour-car window. (*Those wishing to return home via the Inside Passage may make southbound steamer connections at Skagway for Seattle or Vancouver.*)

On to Alaska

The bus trip over the rest of the Alaska Highway, from Whitehorse to Fairbanks, takes two days and includes an overnight stop at the White Pass & Yukon lodge at Dry Creek. From Fairbanks, among other things, you can fly to Nome; visit Circle Hot Springs; go by rail to McKinley National Park and Anchorage; or continue by bus over the Richardson Highway to Anchorage.

Airplane connections may also be made at Whitehorse for practically any point in Alaska.

The Best Time to Go

B. Y. N. busses operate throughout the year, but those traveling solely for pleasure will probably find the period from late May through September most enjoyable. Temperatures at this time range between 60 and 80 degrees.

Your travel agent will gladly help you plan your trip. Or write to:

F. G. DOWNEY	J. G. BLANCHARD
General Agent	General Passenger Agent
W. P. & Y. Route	W. P. & Y. Route
17 Commerce Building	P. O. Box 1846
Vancouver, B. C.	Seattle 11, Wash.

FORM P-73 LITHOGRAPHED IN U.S.A.

America's Newest Travel Sensation . . . Exploring the Alaska Highway

Nisutlin Bay Bridge, crossing a corner of Teslin Lake.

DO YOU picture the Alaska Highway as a pair of ruts slashing a ragged path through a vast, solitary wilderness of forbidding mountains and treacherous tundra? Do you imagine traveling over it would involve hardship and even danger? *Nonsense!* It's a broad, graveled, all-weather road, and you can cover its entire 1522.8 miles from Dawson Creek, British Columbia to Fairbanks, Alaska, cradled in an individual, reclining "Pony Cruiser" bus seat, without a worry in the world.

Regular, year-'round bus schedules are maintained by the British Yukon Navigation Company under the supervision of the White Pass & Yukon Route, which is an old hand at providing dependable, first-class transportation in the "North Countree."

Three modern lodges, located at suitable intervals between the larger towns, were built by the White Pass & Yukon in 1946 to assure you of a hot shower and a good bed in an immaculately clean room at the end of each day. The meals served in these lodges, as well as in the road houses where stops are made along the way for lunches and snacks, are inexpensive and hearty, and you are likely to find your appetite would do credit to a sourdough just out of the bush.

The great Peace River suspension bridge, 2130 feet long.

Although all travel costs are extremely moderate, B.Y.N. bus passengers can count on being completely comfortable and well-fed throughout their journey.

Your driver is more than the skillful pilot of your bus—he is your host as well, doubling your enjoyment of the trip by answering such questions as: "Where do those mysterious side roads go?" or "What kind of fish are caught in the lakes and streams?" or "What were all these abandoned buildings used for?" But *please* don't expect him to identify each towering, snow-capped peak! There are so many of them that only a very few have names.

Your driver is never in too much of a hurry to stop at especially spectacular scenic spots so you can take jiggle-free photographs, or to pause at a lonely ranch house to pick up a package or deliver a message. Big game is often seen along the Highway and whenever he spots a moose or a bear, a caribou or a wolf, your driver will call out—but remember, if you sight one first *you're* supposed to shout the news!

You'll Wish the Days Had More Hours

Friendships develop quickly on the busses, and you'll be tempted to put off going to bed because you're having so much fun. Nevertheless, it's best to say an early "Goodnight!" lest you doze off next day and miss some of the wildest, most wonderful scenery on earth. You ought not to sleep through a single mile of this land of opportunity for the energetic pioneer, of incomparable vacation experiences for those who love soaring mountains, sparkling lakes, and great forests.

Rancheria road house, one of the stops where you pile out for food.

Right: One wing of the Ft. Nelson Hotel.

Front cover, top: The Highway from the air, courtesy National Film Board. Bottom: Peaks circling Muncho Lake.

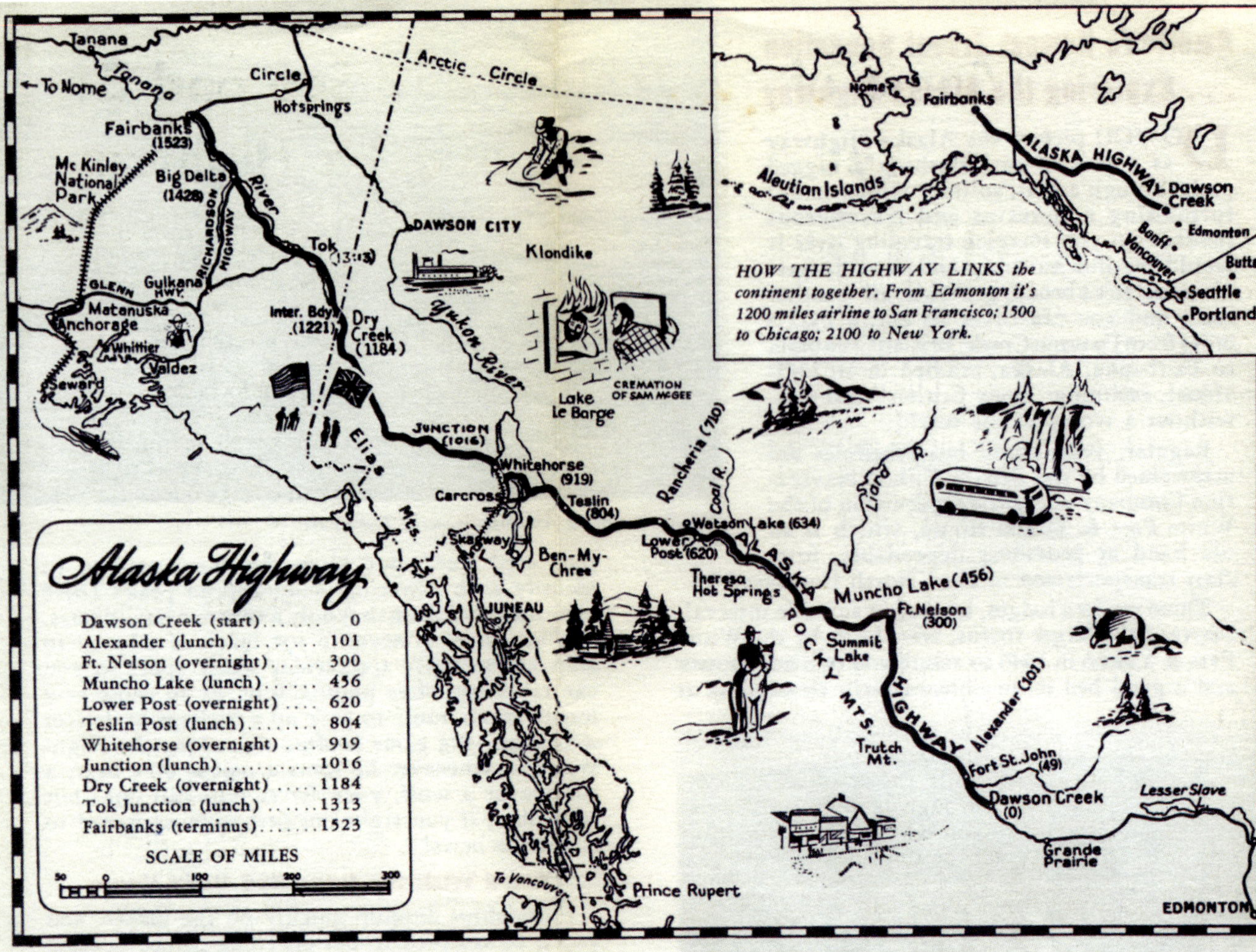

"Allen's Lookout" above the Liard River. In a few years, perhaps, this promontory may afford a view of a thriving new river community.

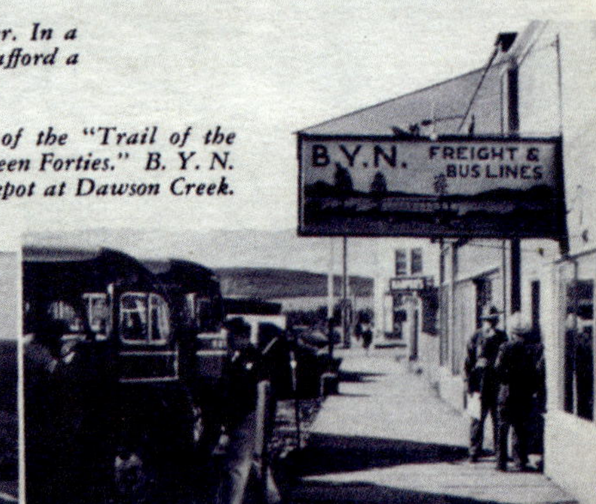

Start of the "Trail of the Nineteen Forties." B. Y. N. bus depot at Dawson Creek.

Teslin River Bridge at Mile 800. ("Teslin" means "long water.")

Lodge at Lower Post, one of the W. P. & Y. inns that provide you with big meals and soft beds.

At this spot construction gangs from the south first met those working down from the north

Milepost at Dawson Creek.

Some of the Things You'll See and Do as You Travel the Alaska Highway

THE Alaska Highway is all neatly marked off with numbered signposts, and it's lucky it is or you'd never know where you were. Unlike the Lincoln Highway, which ran through many towns even back in the days when it was the only road spanning the continent, the Alaska Highway cuts through a country that is just opening up, where settlements are yet to be, and where established landmarks are few and far between. Here are a few of your journey's highspots:

At Mile 35 you cross over the most impressive of the Highway's 133 bridges—a 2130 foot suspension job spanning a river known as the Peace because it separated a couple of hostile Indian tribes.

At Mile 181 is the summit of Trutch Mountain, âltitude 4134 feet. This is the second highest point on the Highway. The engineers were working against time when they built the road, so they went *around* rather than through or over obstructions. (This is the real reason why the road twists and turns so erratically, although some folks insist it was laid out by following a friendly moose who responded to a plea of, "Where do we go from here?")

At Mile 392 is Summit Lake, a green jewel set in a ring of snow-streaked mountains. Here is the

highest point on the road—4256 feet—and the next hundred miles lead through one of the most scenically enchanting stretches of the Highway. You're in a world of mountains, threading your way through a series of valleys, passes, and gorges. Sometimes you are hemmed in between brilliantly colored rock walls which seem to block the way ahead. Sometimes you ride the crest of a great plateau and must strain your eyes to see the far horizon. Now you are in a shadowy spruce forest, and then you are out in the sunlight where rushing streams and tumbling waterfalls struggle to carry away last winter's melting snow and ice before the long summer days are gone. And just when you begin to think you must have sampled all the kinds of scenery there are in the world, you come to mountain-girt Muncho Lake, which is so primordial in its sheer rugged grandeur that you would not be surprised to see dinosaurs grazing along the banks.

Between Dawson Creek and Whitehorse, overnight stops are made at Fort Nelson (Mile 300) and Lower Post (Mile 620) where comfortable accommodations in White Pass & Yukon lodges await you. (Those handsome fellows you'll see in dark brown uniforms aren't soldiers. They are British Columbia Police, and if you can engage one in conversation you may hear some fine tales.)

There are all sorts of things which will impress you as the miles roll past. For instance, you will notice how clear are the waters of the streams flowing down from the north, how heavy with silt those from the west. You'll be surprised at how the rivers narrow down to dig their way through rocky chasms, then widen out until they look like lakes; at how they suddenly stop flowing towards the Arctic Ocean and head for the Bering Sea. And you'll be amused by little things, such as the Indians' log huts with grass growing on the roofs.

Excitement mounts as you approach Whitehorse. You pass Teslin Lodge and Marsh Lake Lodge, two of the finest hunting, fishing, and tourist resorts in the Northwest. You bridge the Lewes River, which is really the upper Yukon, and cross the tracks of the White Pass & Yukon Railroad that runs south to Skagway. Way up there on that high plateau is the huge Whitehorse Airport. Those deserted buildings to the north once housed the personnel of the Canol project. And finally comes Milepost 919, and you are in Whitehorse, Canadian gateway to Alaska.

There are so many ways to proceed from Whitehorse! Busses, airplanes, steamers, and trains are all there to take you wherever you want to go. Just turn the page for a few suggestions.

ALASKA HIGHWAY MOVIE

The story line goes as follows: In February 1942 a road construction gang working in Northern California is summoned to a meeting. The boss of the gang has been commissioned as a major in the US Army Corps of Engineers and signs up the entire crew with his two sons gaining direct entry as Technical Sergeants to build the Alcan Highway. One of the brothers wishes to enlist in the US Marine Corps to fight the Japanese rather than build another road. He changes his mind when he meets the daughter of one of the heads of the project with the two brothers fighting over her as they build the highway. Their feud is forgotten when the Japanese invade the Aleutian Islands.

December 15th, 1943.

To All Employees,
Miller Construction Company, Inc.

Gentlemen:

In behalf of the Miller Construction Company, Inc., its officers and directors, it is my pleasure to extend to you and to yours their sincere wishes for a Merry Christmas and a Happy New Year.

Your Company is justly proud of the work which you have accomplished during the year 1943, in building the Alcan Telephone Line. The project is now completed and in service and you can look with a deep sense of satisfaction to having had a hand in a job well done and in the knowledge that you have contributed in no small way to the success of our Country's defence.

It is now our task to complete the telephone line from Johnson's Crossing to Norman Wells at the earliest possible moment. Our Government has entrusted this job to us for it has confidence in our ability to get the job done. Let us assure our Government that its confidence has not been misplaced by exerting our every effort toward the early completion of this new job. Such an accomplishment will help to make the coming year 1944 a happy one for all of us for it will aid in bringing about the early defeat of the axis powers.

Yours sincerely,
MILLER CONSTRUCTION COMPANY, Inc.,

P. F. Size

P. F. SIZE,
Treasurer.

CONTRACT No.
W-412-eng-58

BECHTEL-PRICE-CALLAHAN

INTER-OFFICE MEMORANDUM

To

Copies to

Date October 14, 1943

From

Dept.

At

Subject HOUSE RULES

Anderson, Louise
Bacon, Marjorie
Bauer, Bettie Lou
Boring, Mary
Brawner, Mamie
Buch holz, Mathilda
Connoy, Donna
Cyr, Violet
Dahl, Mary A.
Devine, Delores
Flack, Mary
Frommyer, Effie
Gadney, Virginia
Keeney, Mary
Lanam, Darlene
Lane, Lula Belle
Le Page, Mae E.
Murray, Anne
Ofstie, Rosalie
Pharis, Nelle
Powell, Hattie
Redmon, Alice
Reynolds, Jean
Roberts, Lucy
Shively, Georgia
Shoemaker, Elizabeth
Thomas, Ann C.
Ure, Doris J.
Valliere, Edwina
Volz, Leona
Walters, Wilma
Watson, Una

There have been complaints of noise and visitors after hours in the Girls' Barracks practically every night and, in view of the house rules as set up by Bechtel-Price-Callahan, we must ask you to refrain from excess noise and violation of hours.

It has been brought to the attention of the Johnson's Crossing office and the Whitehorse office that in some girls' rooms there have been male visitors as late as 2:00, 3:00, and 4:00 in the morning and, inasmuch as this is a direct violation of the house rules, it is only fair to warn each and every girl that any violation of the 11:00 week day and 12:00 Saturday Night rule will subject those concerned to immediate dismissal.

If, at any time, any male is visiting the girls' barracks in an inebriated condition, creating a disturbance, and reluctant to leave, please notify the Camp Management and immediate steps will be taken to handle the situation.

We are endeavoring to leave everyone their full rights and privileges, with minor stipulations, but unless this situation is straightened out immediately, the management will be forced to install a house matron to prohibit visitors entirely.

Thanks for your cooperation.

BECHTEL-PRICE-CALLAHAN

T O   A L L   E M P L O Y E E S:

At the start of the telephone line between Edmonton and Fairbanks it was felt that the line could be completed in six months' period by our Company and its Sub-Contractor, the Oman-Smith Company. However, due to the many developments beyond anyone's control it was found that more time would be required and as a result the work has extended beyond the time limit of six months as originally contemplated.

In addition to the original line we have since been asked to build a line from Johnson's Crossing a distance of approximately 350 miles along the Norman Wells Pipeline, therefore requiring still additional time, material and manpower. Many of our employees signed Contracts for six months' period of employment and as a result are now terminating, feeling that they have fulfilled their original obligation, which is true, and wish to go home at this time. We are appealing to all of you to reconsider the matter of termination and stay with this job, which is one of the most important jobs in connection with the war program in this area. By so doing you will assist in eliminating the great inconvenience which will be caused in attempting to replace you with new personnel, to say nothing of the additional cost involved in such a program, all of which, of course, will have to be paid for by you and I as citizens through the medium of taxation.

As our plans are now formulated, we should complete all of the Project on or about the first of December and we are appealing to you to reconsider any plans you may have to terminate and stay with the job until it is completed. We will assure you as Contractors and fellow workers on this Project that everything possible will be done to make the job as satisfactory as at all possible to you during this extended period.

Very truly yours,
MILLER CONSTRUCTION COMPANY, Inc.,
CONSTRUCTOR

J. F. Miller

J. F. MILLER, Vice-President.

JWR/D

A road had to be built from the ALCAN Highway 620 miles northeast through the mostly uncharted Mackenzie Mountains to reach the shore of the second largest river system in North America, the Mackenzie and the oil fields at Norman Wells and build a pipeline beside the road. The mere task of reaching Norman Wells by water, with the massive amount of equipment needed for construction fell to the U.S. Army Force 2600. Leaving Waterways in northern Alberta, construction equipment moved by boats and barges by the Athabasca River, to Lake Athabasca to a 310 mile trip on the Slave River, including a grueling 16-mile portage at old Fort Fitzgerald. Then to Great Slave Lake to the Mackenzie River for the last 550 mile float to the oil fields, a 1,171-mile route.

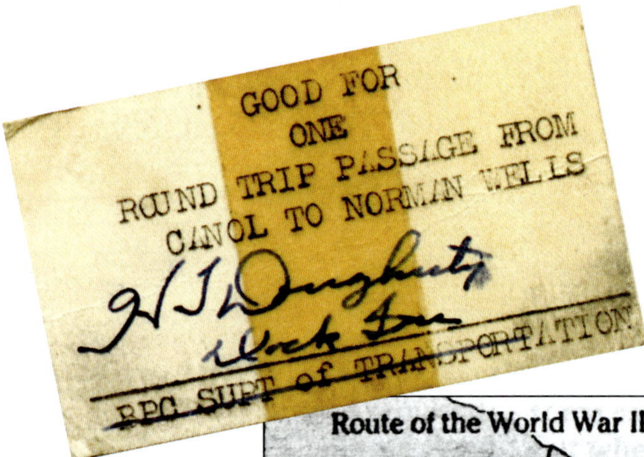

Route of the World War II Canol Pipeline and winter haul roads for the project.

A sawmill was set up to provide lumber for various uses along the CANOL road.
–Courtesy of YA, C.M. Lorence Collection 85 84/73

Camp 204 of the Dowell Construction Company along the road. –Courtesy of YA, C.M. Lorence Collection 70 84/73

EMBANKMENT SECTION

Fig. 1

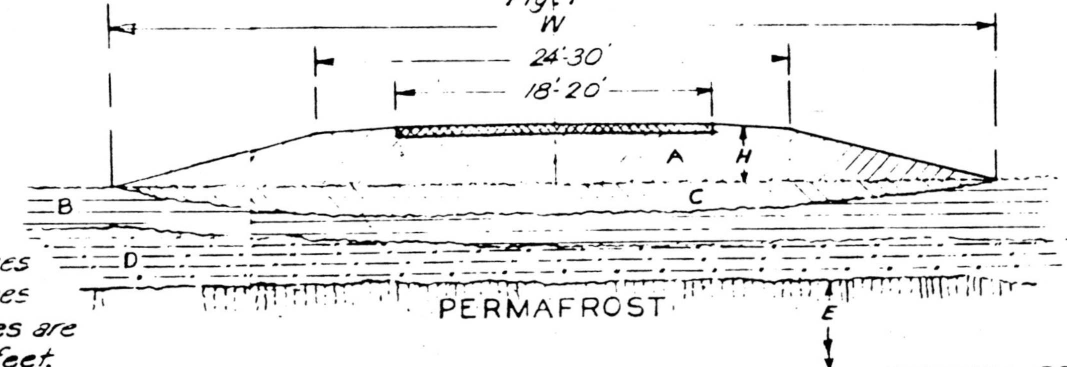

Note: When 'H' is 3 feet and fill slopes are 4:1 'W' will be about 50 feet.

Note: When 'H' averages 3 feet, slopes to ditches are 4:1 and back slopes are 2:1 'W' will be about 80 feet.

CUT SECTION

Fig. 2

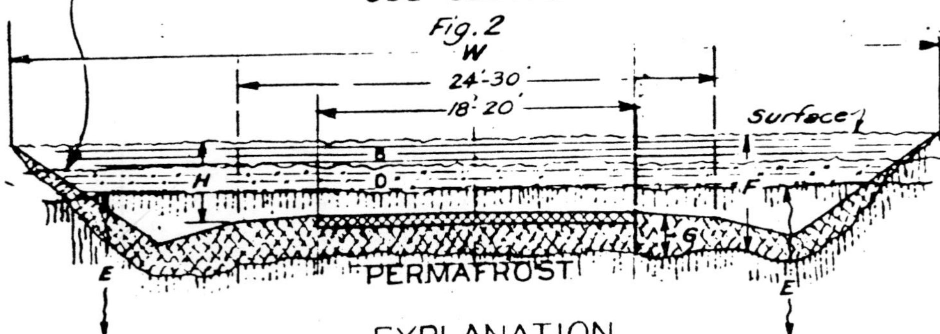

SIDEHILL SECTION

Figure 3

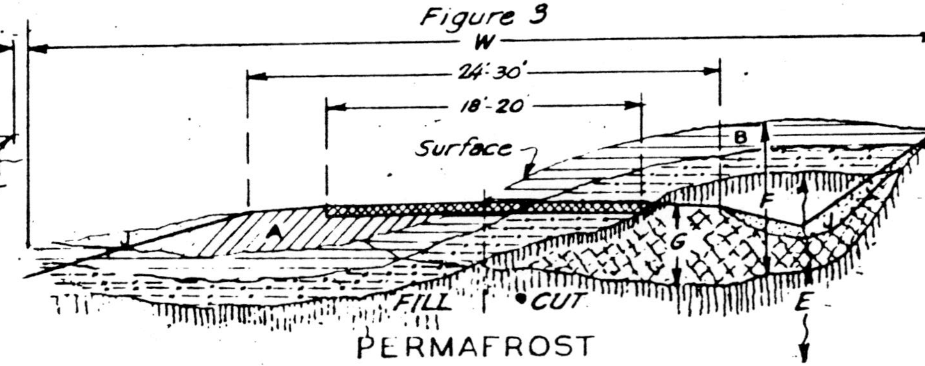

EXPLANATION

A-Embankment materials.

B-Moss and vegetal cover-Natural insulation materials. Thickness is variable, estimated to be 4 inches to 4 feet or more depending upon locality.

C-Area occupied by embankment materials because of compaction of moss and vegetal cover by the construction equipment and weight of embankment. The amount of compaction is estimated to be 30 to 70 percent of the original thickness if no stripping is done.

D-Materials in the seasonal freezing and thawing zone. Thickness of this zone is variable from zero feet to an unknown depth. The study will likely be a means to ascertain expected thickness according to surface appearance of the terrain.

E-Permafrost = permanently frozen ground.

F-Excavation below surface.

G-Backfill in cut, could be all inorganic embankment materials or same type of materials over some organic materials placed on top of the permafrost to act as a heat insulator.

J-Organic matter (moss and vegetal materials) could be placed on any of the type of sections tested. This would simply be one variation of the many combinations which should be tested.

W Width of test sections.

TYPES OF CROSS SECTIONS OVER PERMAFROST AERAS

The government put out several booklets on the virtues of the importance of building the pipeline to connect the oil deposits from the Norman Wells area, Northwest Territories on the Mackenzie River to Whitehorse, Yukon, where a refinery was built. At this time fuel for aircraft and vehicles had to be brought up the Inside Passage of Alaska or across the open seas to mainland Alaska, a treacherous route with possible Japanese submarines. A possible solution was to develop the existing oil fields in Canada and transport the crude oil by pipeline. As it turned out, by the time the project was completed in 1943 the Japanese threat to Alaska was gone and only a few barrels of oil was refined. The project tied up thousands of troops and equipment that could have been used elsewhere in the war effort. In the fall of 1943, Harry S. Truman led a congressional investigation of the project, which had cost close to $100 million, but the Army went ahead and finished it in 1944.

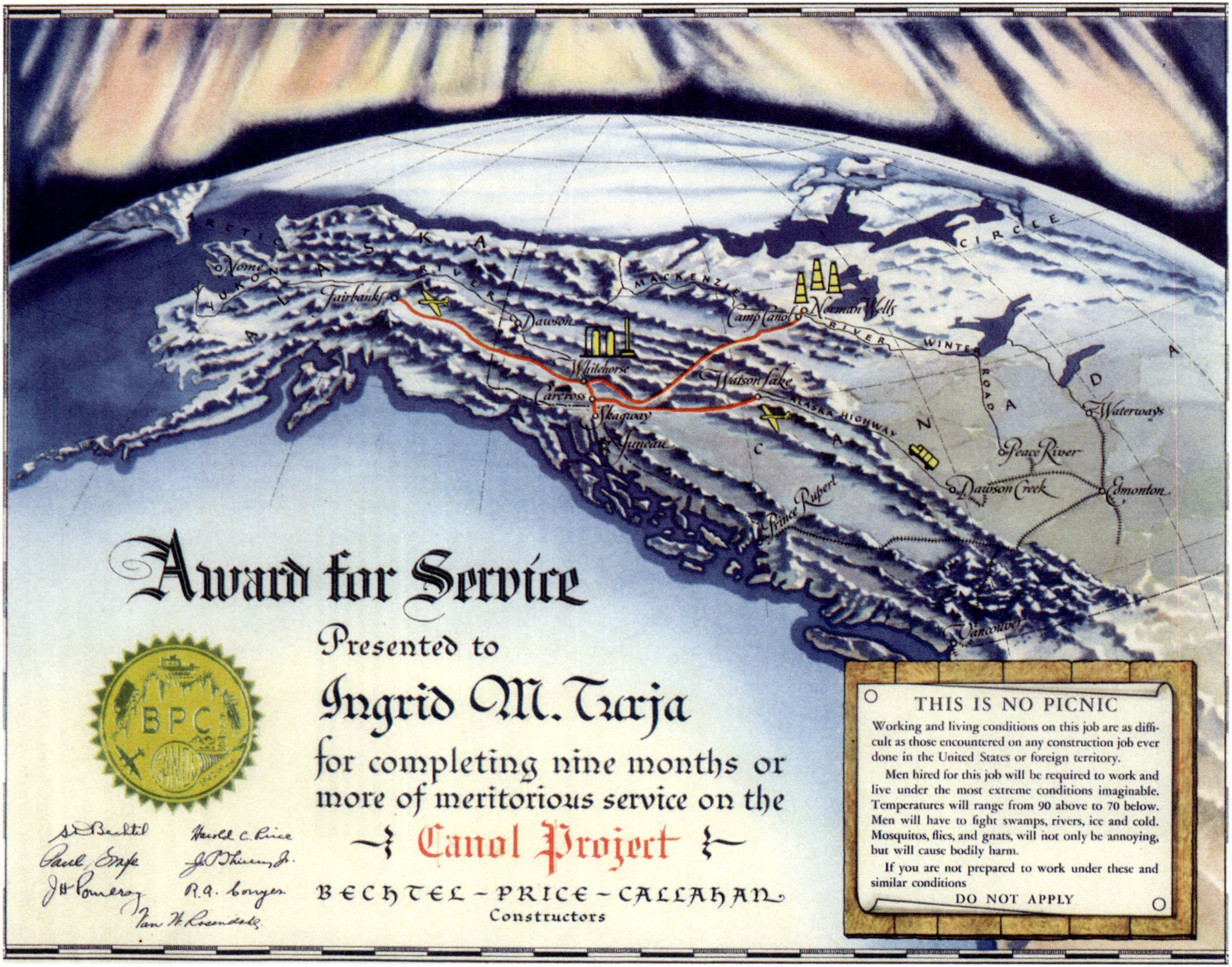
Award for Service
Presented to
Ingrid M. Tarja
for completing nine months or
more of meritorious service on the
Canol Project
BECHTEL - PRICE - CALLAHAN
Constructors
BPC
THIS IS NO PICNIC
Working and living conditions on this job are as difficult as those encountered on any construction job ever done in the United States or foreign territory.
Men hired for this job will be required to work and live under the most extreme conditions imaginable. Temperatures will range from 90 above to 70 below. Men will have to fight swamps, rivers, ice and cold. Mosquitos, flies, and gnats, will not only be annoying, but will cause bodily harm.
If you are not prepared to work under these and similar conditions
DO NOT APPLY
ARCTIC CIRCLE
ALASKA
CANADA
YUKON RIVER
MACKENZIE RIVER
WINTER ROAD
ALASKA HIGHWAY
Nome
Fairbanks
Dawson
Whitehorse
Carcross
Skagway
Juneau
Camp Canol
Norman Wells
Watson Lake
Waterways
Peace River
Dawson Creek
Edmonton
Prince Rupert
Vancouver

— CHAPTER FOUR —

CIVILIAN CONTRACTORS

Edited and published by Civilian builders of the Companies and the Alaskan Department at A.P.O.980. The Bering Breeze is dedicated to members of the U.S.Armed Forces with whom we work and live. (No. 21 ... August 11, 1944)

O N E   W E E K   N E A R E R   T O   V I C T O R Y !

TELL YOUR FRIENDS NOT TO QUIT

In a large group of men such as we are, there are bound to be some who have good reasons for quitting the job. When the U. S. Army hired our companies to help them build this base, they did so because the Army needed help, needed help badly, needed it fast. The Army and the contractors figured that some men would quit. BUT TOO MANY OF US ARE QUITTING!

There must be reasons. Is it because the pay is too low? because the hours are too long? because the job is too tough? Isn't the housing satisfactory? Aren't there adequate toilets and showers? Perhaps the foremen work the men too hard?

REASONS FOR QUITTING

We investigated, asked the Personnel Departments, asked the reasons men gave for quitting? Here they are, reasons taken from the records of men who no longer are here - quitters: "I do not like this climate." - "I have decided to quit and go back to the States." - "I feel that I am needed at home." - "No snuff-poor meals." - "I have business at home." - "My wife wants me to return." - "This weather does not agree with me." - "This climate is not good for my health." - "I want to go home to have my tooth fixed." - "I haven't been feeling well." - "My presence has been requested at home." - "I don't feel well and I don't like the job."

There were other reasons for quitting, a few were legitimate and worthy. Most of them are as poor as those quoted above. Don't quit. Ask your friends not to quit. There's a job to be done.

We won't compare our job and our pay and our circumstances with that of the soldiers. You do that, Let's just take a look at ourselves.

ONE YEAR AGREEMENT

We signed our name to a contract, an agreement which stated in black and white that we were to come to the Aleutian Islands and work for one year at good pay. When we signed that contract we pledged that we'd come and that we'd work and that we'd STAY for one full year. We signed our names to that. Isn't that enough?

If you should quit tomorrow you'd hinder the prosecution of the war. You'd postpone Victory. You'd (con't. next col.) place the responsibility on the shoulders of those of us who stay. Maybe, because of you, another soldier would die. You wouldn't willingly do that. And yet that is what the ones who quit have done!

Ask your friends not to quit. Tell them to "tough it out" - see it through to a finish - get the job done! Let's work and sweat and swear and BUILD this base for the Army ... and for our own satisfaction. What's a little year in the life of a man? You CAN take it! Don't quit. -WA

ARABIAN OIL JOB

There are reports current that the Arabian oil development will require a large force of men.

The fact is that Mr. Ickes' plans for governmental development of the Alaska and Arabian oil fields were vetoed in Congress, and the proposed program for Alaska and Arabia has been abandoned.

ATTENTION ALL CIVILIANS

The following item was received from Mr. J. E. Cooper, Area Director, War Manpower Commission:

"Many cases have arisen where men have terminated their contracts with the expectation of getting jobs in foreign countries. These men will be disappointed. Those who are leaving before their contracts are completed and who are not given releases will definitly find themselves behind the 'eightball' so far as foreign contract work is concerned. This information is furnished for the protection of those men who are considering breaking their contracts with the hope of getting work on other jobs."

SOFTBALL NEWS - PAGE 3

EMPLOYMENT WITH WAR DEPARTMENT IN ALASKA

1. Jobs offered here are in the Alaska Area and are directly under the War Department and under the jurisdiction of the Alaskan Department. Wages are paid twice a month by Government check. However, due to clerical and transportation difficulties the first check may be delayed as much as six weeks. The work is air base and cantonment construction.

2. (a) Before being employed by the Alaskan Department a man must be in draft classification 1A(H), 1B, 1C, 3, or 4, and able to obtain a permit from his draft board to leave the United States for a period of at least six months.

(b) Applicant must have Certificate of Availability.

(c) Applicant must be between 18 and 55 years of age.

(d) Applicant must be able to prove American Citizenship, and must take the documentary proof with him to Alaska.

(e) All applicants must be in sound physical condition. The loss of any member, one eye, or seriously impaired hearing disqualifies. Diabetes, Heart Trouble, Nephritis, Asthma, Bronchitis, Rheumatism, Chronic Catarrh, Arthritis, history of Tuberculosis, any communicable disease, and Hernia of any size or type, will disqualify. Slight physical defects where function is not seriously impaired, will be accepted. It must be borne in mind that any physical defect affected by rigorous climatic conditions would, in all probability, cause serious loss of time. Physical conditions requiring intermittent or continuous medical attention would become aggravated as many of the projects are isolated to the extent that medical attention, and/or hospitalization are not readily available.

(f) Applicants are not allowed to take dependents into the Alaska Area for the duration of the war.

3. Men hired will be required to sign a contract calling for one year's service from date of contract, and will be expected to fulfill this contract, unless reasons of health, or serious difficulties at home might interfere. Failure to complete contract for personal reasons will result in Discharge with Prejudice, which will make an employee ineligible for further Government Service.

4. Wages paid in Alaska range from $1.015 per hour for common labor to $1.50 for Carpenters and up to $2.00 for other skilled trades. It is anticipated that ten (10) hours per day and six (6) days per week will be the established work week. However, this schedule is not guaranteed, and is subject to change by authorized representatives of the United States Government. Time and one half is paid for any time over eight hours in one day or over forty hours in one week. Wages will commence, and contract will go into effect on the date of departure from point of hire, and will terminate at conclusion of service at place of duty and any leave accrued to employee's credit. The employee is guaranteed a monthly minimum wage of 170 times his basic hourly rate of pay, commencing upon departure from point of hire and continuing through the life of this contract.

Rev. 16 Nov. 1943

5. Employees may send money to their dependents, either by wire, mail, or through a Power of Attorney directing the Government to pay a portion of their wages directly to any designated person. If a Power of Attorney is desired, arrangements may be made through the finance office of the project on which they are employed.

6. Transportation will be paid from the point of hire to the Alaska Area, and return to the point of hire on the completion of the contract. Men will be required to buy their own meals on the train from point of hire to Seattle. This expenditure will be reimbursed at the rate of $5.00 per day upon employee's application for per diem at destination in Alaska. The cost will average $1.00 per meal. Meals are furnished on board boat between Seattle and Alaska. Upon reaching Seattle, men will report to the Alaskan Department Office, and be assigned to quarters in a Government camp where they will receive their meals and room until such time as transportation can be arranged to the Alaska Area. This period of waiting in Seattle may vary from five days to five weeks, depending upon the availability of boats. It is expected, however, that transportation will be available within very few days after arrival in Seattle.

7. If the Employee is delayed for a period of more than three (3) days while en route to place of employment, he will accept any available and suitable temporary employment in the position offered him by the Employer or the Employer's authorized representative, at the wage rate designated in his contract. In the event the employee refuses to accept such employment while in pay status, his guaranteed wages will be suspended during the period for which such temporary employment is available and not accepted.

8. Men employed as Carpenters, Mechanics, or other skilled trades will be required to have and take with them their complete set of hand tools.

9. While in Alaska men are required to pay their own room and board, which varies at different projects from $45.00 to $66.00 per month. At some of the projects employees will eat and sleep in the same class of accommodations as used by soldiers. At other projects room and board is furnished by Government supervised commissaries. The food is good, plentiful and varied. Bunk houses are warm and comfortable. In some cases men will be quartered two men to a room, and in some cases in open bunk houses.

10. As far as this office is concerned, when a man signs a contract as a laborer, he will be a laborer for the duration of that contract. However, if he has the ability or skill to qualify for a better job and can convince his foreman or superintendent that he is qualified for a better job, there is nothing to prevent that foreman or superintendent from reclassifying him. It is entirely up to the employee, his skill and ability to sell himself to his superiors. It must be thoroughly understood that if he does not bring about a reclassification himself, he will be a laborer for the duration of his contract.

Rev. 16 Nov. 1943 -2-

GENERAL INSTRUCTIONS & INFORMATION

"WELCOME TO YOUR NEW JOB"

We have attempted to set forth in this instruction letter, pertinent facts which we believe will give you a general picture of your new home and advise you of certain rules and regulations in force on this Army Base.

After you have been cleared by the Personnel Department, you will be given a yellow "assignment slip". Present this slip to your foreman when you report to work.

As soon as cleared by Personnel, go to the "Camp Office", (located at rear of Mess Hall - entrance is from street in rear of Mess Hall). Here, you will be assigned to your quarters. UNDER NO CONDITIONS are you to move out of your regular assigned hut without first obtaining permission from Mr. William Noyes of the Camp Office. Should it be necessary to locate you at any time, we must know where you live as well as work. THIS IS IMPORTANT - PLEASE COMPLY.

MEAL HOURS: For day men, the following meal hours are applicable:

Breakfast 5:45 to 8:00 A.M.
Lunch 11:45 to 1:30 P.M.
Dinner 6:00 to 7:30 P.M.

Swing-shift men consult the Mess Hall Steward, Mr. Pat Wallace for their hours.

The food served in the Mess Hall is rationed to us by the Army. We are serving the same rations that the soldiers in the Army here are served. The rationing is figured on a point basis of so many ounces per man per day. You are requested to be on time for your meals as no meals will be served after the above stated hours--the doors will open promptly on announced time and close promptly. Do not try to get meals between the regular posted hours. At no time will food be allowed to be taken from the Mess Hall. All equipment used in the Mess Hall is the property of the U. S. Government, therefore, you are warned not to take any of this equipment to your huts for personal use. Any Mess Hall equipment found in your huts will be confiscated and you will be personally held responsible.

TIME CHECKING: It is most important that you check in and out before and after each shift at the Check Shack (6th and "B" Street).

TRAVEL TIME CHECKS will be ready for you within three to four days after your arrival in camp. Inquire at the Time Shack for hours of payment.

PAY DAYS: Regular Pay-day is Friday of each week. Night shift men will be paid at the TIME SHACK between 3:30 and 5:00 P.M. Fridays only. Day shift men will be paid Fridays between 7:30 and 9:00 P.M. at the Time Shack. Mr. L. D. Kretzmeier is your paymaster and Chief Timekeeper.

CHECK CASHING: Guy F. Atkinson Company payroll checks will be cashed at the General Business Office behind the Time Shack daily, (except Tuesday), between 3:00 and 5:00 P.M. and 7:30 and 9:00 P.M. Only Company checks will be cashed, no personal checks nor any checks bearing a double endorsement--only pay checks ISSUED TO YOU. You must identify yourself when cashing checks by presenting your badge. Mr. Donald Paxton is in charge of this office.

SENDING MONEY OUT: No currency can be mailed out through the mails. You are instructed to purchase Money Orders. Due to the shortage of currency on the island, it is necessary to ask you to help keep what money we have here in circulation.

DISPENSARY PROCEDURE: The Army maintains and operates a dispensary at 9th and E Streets for your use. It is in operation 24 hours a day for emergency or illness. Should you have occasion to phone for an ambulance in case of accident, call Hockey 16.

SHOTS: Those of you who have not had all your shots, may report Tuesdays and Thursdays at 3:30 and 7:30 P.M.

SICK CALL: If you should wish to consult the Doctor personally, his hours are daily 8:00 A.M. and 7:30 P.M. For minor cuts, colds, etc., you may call at the dispensary at any hour. If you wish to leave your job to make a call to the hospital, be sure and get a signed slip from your foreman and present same to hospital.

BLOOD TYPING: All civilian personnel of this base MUST have their blood typed. This is a precaution and for your benefit. It is very necessary to know every man's blood type so that should the occasion arise that a blood transfusion is necessary, they would have a record of your particular blood type. All Atkinson employees are to report for typing the first Monday after arrival at 3:30 or 7:30 P.M.

-2-

ARMY PASS: You were given a Pass, signed by the Depot Engineer. <u>DO NOT LOSE THIS PASS.</u> <u>HAVE IT IN YOUR POSSESSION AT ALL TIMES.</u> At times, you will be stopped and questioned by the M.P's who will want to see your pass, your Company Badge and, if you are driving a truck, your Driver's License. Do NOT go out AT ANY TIME WITHOUT THESE NECESSARY PAPERS.

GUNS: No Civilian is allowed to have a gun in his possession on this base - ARMY ORDERS. All those possessing a gun will make immediate arrangements to ship it to the States at once. Take your gun, ready for mailing, to the M.P.'s, 10th and C Streets, who will inspect and seal package for mailing out. If these regulations are not carried out immediately, your gun will be confiscated.

CAMERAS: You will be allowed to have a camera in your possession providing you observe the regulations as to its use. If you have a camera, make immediate application at the Personnel Office for a Permit to have a Camera. The permit will carry all rules and regulations regarding the taking of pictures, development and mailing of pictures. If you use your camera without first securing a permit, your camera will be confiscated.

RADIOGRAMS: The A.C.S. Radio Station is located some seven miles from this camp. Unless you have a "REAL NECESSITY", do NOT wire. Air Mail to the States has been averaging four to five days to West Coast Cities.

DRAFT BOARD: Advise your Draft Board of your new address as soon as possible. Even though the Company has procured a release from your Board, the Law states that each Registrant must notify his Board, in writing, of any changes of address or family status. This is your obligation to your Board.

POST OFFICE: The Post Office is open from 11:00 A.M. to 8:00 P.M. daily EXCEPT SUNDAY. Here, you may purchase stamps, envelopes, Money Orders, Registry and War Bonds. This Post Office is operated and staffed by the U. S. Army.

ADDRESS: Address all your mail as shown below on this sample envelope:

Your name Guy F. Atkinson Co. Depot Engineer APO #980, c/o Postmaster Seattle, Wash.	Postage Stamp
	******************, ******************, ****************, ***************.

-3-

To facilitate and speed censoring, do NOT seal your envelopes - leave them open, (unless and ONLY UNLESS it contains money). EACH LETTER HAS TO BE CENSORED BY THE ARMY CENSOR HERE ON THIS BASE. Use discretion in writing letters. Remember this is a secret base and of vital importance. It and its building is of a secret nature. You will be advised further on Censorship at the Articles of War meeting, (see below).

ARTICLES OF WAR: Each and Every Civilian MUST hear, (and at such hearing, register his name, badge number and name of employer), the "ARTICLES OF WAR". These Articles will be read in the Mess Hall by the U. S. Army personnel. You will be notified when to appear. This is COMPULSORY for all men on this base. At these readings, you will also hear a course of instructions in use of gas masks; different gasses and bombs will be explained as well as First Aid measures to counteract injury done by gas and bombs.

SAFETY: Larry Carlson is here as Safety man and is anxious to see to it that we have as few accidents on this job as is humanly possible. He is here as a representative of the insurance company carring your protection. His office is located in the office building facing "C" Street between 4th and 5th Streets.

CARPENTERS: B. C. (Curley) Canoles, Building Superintendent, is in charge of all building. His office is located in office building facing "C" Street between 4th and 5th Streets. All Carpenters, on arrival, will report to him for assignment to duty.

ELECTRICIANS: Everett L. Govan is Electrical Superintendent. His office is located in office building facing "A" Street between 4th and 5th Streets. All Electrical employees will report to him for assignment to duty.

WATER & SEWERS: George Chica is Water & Sewer Superintendent. All PLUMBERS, STEAMFITTERS, PIPEFITTERS, SHEET METAL WORKERS and SEWERMEN will report to him on arrival for assignment to work.

COMPLAINTS - BEEFS - SUGGESTIONS: Mr. E. B. Skeels is the Job Manager for the Guy F. Atkinson Co. His is a tough job and it keeps him busy doing that job - that is why he has assistants, men delegated to do certain phases of the work. He will be only too glad to listen to you any time <u>but</u> he would like you to consult the following fellows if you have a complaint or beef who will, in turn, compile these complaints and present them to him for corrective suggestions:

If it pertains to the Mess Hall, Quarters or Camp in General, contact Mr. C. O. (Ted) Hardison in the Camp Office.

If it is about your Time or Checks, etc., consult Mr. Larry Kretzmeier, your Paymaster.

Matters concerning working conditions around the job in general, transfers and the like, consult Mr. J. J. (Whitey) Standish, the General Superintendent, with offices at 5th and C Streets.

Matters of personal nature, personnel problems, Notary, Draft information, anything relating to your contract, rate of pay, etc., will be taken up with the Personnel Office whose staff is here to help you.

Mr. Chester Smith is your Commissary man and is here to help you get the things you want and need. He is in the Camp Office.

We are all here for one reason - "to help speed the winning of this war" and it takes men to win wars whether on the line of battle or in the rear, building bases. You came here to build a base - the sooner it's built, the sooner we can turn it over to our Armed Forces to use as a stepping stone toward Japan. Hard work and, above all, cooperation, will do the trick. The folks back home are counting on you to do your part.

Thanks fellows!

GUY F. ATKINSON COMPANY

Matt Shields

Matt Shields,
Personnel Manager.

MS:RG.

<u>THIS LETTER CAN NOT BE MAILED FROM THIS BASE</u>!

Company crew.

STORY OF MATTHEW HENRY GORDON OF MISSOULA, MONTANA

Two things that would drastically change my life—December 7 and an early winter. With the declaration of war the market for experienced construction workers became unlimited. About mid-December it began to snow. We didn't have a roof over the gym where I was working; hence there was no way to keep the snow out. This meant closing down the job. I couldn't afford to be without work for long. Immediately after New Year's a company named Siems Drake was hiring men to go to Alaska. For those hiring on, wages would begin upon boarding the ship in Seattle. My parents were visiting me, and I told them I was going. Dad decided to go along with me. We drove to Seattle in his car. He failed the physical exam and returned home. When leaving he asked me if I had money for the ten days I had to wait until the ship sailed. I knew how short of money he was so I said I had plenty. Counting up after he left, I had ten dollars to keep me for ten days. January is cold in Seattle, too. I paid ten days rent on a cheap room, and somehow fed myself with the little money that remained.

I sailed from Seattle aboard the *SS Columbia* late in January 1942. I had just turned twenty-five, was skilled at a trade and employed at a high paying job. During my first couple of days aboard, while the ship traveled the Inside Passage which was calm as a river, I made up for the meals that I had missed in Seattle. But as soon as we exited into the Gulf of Alaska we encountered stormy seas which left most of us too seasick to eat. We got some relief from stops at Ketchikan and Kodiak Island. The ship then continued on to Dutch Harbor where I was assigned to a work crew.

The crew that I joined was composed of craftsmen to be able to build specialized buildings that did not lend themselves to mass production methods. When my brother Jack arrived two months later I was able to get him placed in my crew. Recreation was not a concern as we worked ten hours a day and seven days a week; in emergencies we would take a night unloading a lumber ship. This did not stop the confirmed gamblers who always managed to start a crap game or to play a few hands of blackjack.

My chief concern was to get some money home. It took a long time to get my first pay, and when I did some of it was already spent. I had arrived without the proper clothing for working outside in the Aleutian winter. My colleagues who had been there awhile had money to burn, and loaned me what I needed. We were paid in cash, and the unwritten law was that friendly loans be paid while still in the pay line. I was finally able to wire $500 home; it arrived there two days before my son, Kenneth , who was born April 23, 1942.

Had it not been for the tragic fate of so many young soldiers at Fort Mears, the Japanese attack on June 3rd and 4th may have looked upon by some as a break in an otherwise monotonous routine. Our crew was sleeping on the second floor of a newly completed barracks. Daylight is nearly continuous at Dutch Harbor in June; I had awakened half an hour early, got out of bed, and stood looking west at Fort Mears out the fire escape door. The weather was perfect as the sun reflected off a flight of planes approaching the fort. Watching, it didn't cross my mind that they were hostile. Even when shiny objects began to fall from the planes it seemed incredible that they could be bombs. My effort to rouse the crew was greeted with derision until the din of explosions got their attention. A jeep carrying three soldiers careened to a halt at the foot of the fire escape; they got out and began setting up a machine gun. It was time, too, for just then a Zero flew within thirty feet bouncing tracer bullets as big as oranges off the street. My companions needed no more prodding; we fled, half dressed, to the hillside behind our barracks. The military thought the raid, which lasted about thirty minutes, was the prelude to an invasion.

The army began to set up field guns behind the first hills that lined the harbor. We formed groups that carried ammunition and other supplies up to the gun positions. That evening we all dug slit trenches in the vicinity of our barracks.

The next morning mess halls opened. After breakfast our crew was taken by truck to Dutch Harbor, a distance of not more than a couple of miles, where we again helped the army lug equipment around. Suddenly the air raid siren, so silent the morning before, began to wail. We were close to the seashore were rocks as big as Mack trucks were jumbled all over the place. One enormous boulder at the ocean's edge was undercut like a mushroom. Most of crew stood beneath the overhang of this rock, or ones like it nearby, and waited. In a short while we heard a buzzing like a huge swarm of bees that signaled the approaching planes. Soon a flight of perhaps thirty dive bombers were attacking all over the place. Our forces were shooting back with little perceivable damage to the enemy, but they sure made the water just beyond our rock boil. What goes up must come down. The surface of the ocean looked as if it was rained upon. Ours was a ringside seat to a display of planes bombing buildings and oil tanks. All ships, except for one which was being used as a warehouse, had left the harbor earlier. The warehouse ship was bombed.

When the raid was over we helped the military put out fires. We found that a huge store of ammunition was piled and covered with tarps not far from our shelter. Some of the tarps were afire, but we put the fires out without incident. Had one of these fires exploded one shell we may have been blown higher than the dive bombers. The military still felt that we might be invaded. After a few days they found that the Japanese had been defeated at Midway, and our attack had only been a diversion.

STORY FROM JACK GORDON'S NOTES OF MISSOULA, MONTANA

A friend, Sherman Morehead and I, took the Empire Builder (Great Northern Railroad) to Seattle and the ship *Alaska* up the inland passage to Kodiak and then on to Dutch Harbor. Sherman was homesick and took the ship right back to Seattle. I probably would have gone with him if Matt (brother) hadn't have been there. It was the first part of April and the weather was windy and rainy most of the time. After a month of building forms for concrete ammunition bunkers at Dutch Harbor, I got a transfer to the crew Matt was on. They were working across the channel on Unalaska Island building barracks. The weather kept getting better, and things were going along smooth, until the morning of June 3, 1942, when we were rudely awakened by the Japanese flying back and forth over the barracks, strafing and bombing. Needless to say we made a hurried exit from our beds, and scratched gravel getting off to the side of the activities. They had complete control of the sky, as the only planes we had were a couple of PBY's. It all happened so fast that we really didn't have time to get too scared. That afternoon and night we unloaded a ship at Dutch Harbor, so it could sail, and get away from the action. On June 4th the Japanese came back again, and the anti-aircraft artillery worked on them some, so their bombs didn't do as much damage as was done the day before. We found out later, that the Battle of Midway was in progress, and that the attack on Dutch Harbor was only a diversionary tactic.

Matt left soon after the raid to go back to the states on the ship *Columbia*. They had some excitement, when they ran aground in the Inland Passage and had to be transferred to another ship. I stayed on until the latter part of August, when I quit and got passage on a Navy transport. That was the first time I'd ever heard of having beans for breakfast. We stayed on the open ocean all the way to the Straits of Juan de Fucca. It was partly foggy, and the ocean was like glass all of the way to Seattle. I caught the next train for Cut Bank (MT), and was home for the Labor Day Weekend.

DESIGN FOR *ALASKA MAGAZINE* ARTICLE, AUGUST 1944

The Seattle District, U S Army Corps of Engineers, has, as a part of its many construction projects, the furnishing of special services for the Alaska military program, including the design of housing and service installations, and the procurement and preparation for shipment of construction materials and equipment for approximately seventy-five percent of all authorized military construction work for all armed forces in Alaska.

All types of construction are involved requiring various designs. Already built or now being worked on are runways and airfields, docks, breakwaters, hangars, storage systems, marine repair yards, railroad modifications, tunnels, roads, housing, barracks, administration buildings, warehouses, hospitals, chapels, water, sewage, heating and electric utilities.

These features in all their ramifications and in spite of the many limitations, including difficult terrain at many project locations, often required specialized designing. Many contractors were utilized in various construction projects and their experience together with that of experienced civilian helpers proved of great aid to the program. But on the whole, only with the help of troops and related army battalions was the consummation of the construction possible.

Due to the location of many projects, it was necessary to build harbor facilities designed for the locations in order to obtain construction supplies and equipment at the projects. Un-sheltered waters were surveyed and island facilities developed in such a way that a complete unity of operations was possible for armed forces in the North.

In general in regard to design for Alaska projects, from the inception of a directive for the construction of an authorized project, there is a line of positive action in which the engineer prepares the necessary designs, directs procurement of materials thereon and continues with the follow-up of shipment to assure delivery of such material to the project where the field engineers take over and complete construction.

Perhaps the part of the designer to this program is relatively small, though it has been proven to be of considerable importance. It is the designer who must determine the suitability of available plans or prepare new plans which must meet the requirements of a directive. This has not at all times been an easy task, for many directives are for non-orthodox construction for which there is no precedence.

The designer has been faced with the fact that the production of many materials have been curtailed or eliminated and many materials have been placed on a critical list so they could only be used in a limited way. Factors to be considered by the designer also have had to include the matter of cost, shipping tonnage, so even for simpler temporary structures design had to deviate from standard practice.

It has been necessary to resort to light structures and prefabricated units and hangars, housing facilities, warehouses, and various cantonment structures which have been designed to meet the specialized requirements for a rugged combat area. Heavy construction necessarily was required many times in order to meet a particular need such as docks, marine ways, shops or trans -shipment facilities. The related utilities, together with their ever-present problems of hydraulics, distribution, development of power and related problems constituted a large part of design work. Many particular conditions in topography or soil were present in this land of the north which required ingenuity as to design and use of construction materials.

Continual vigilance was necessary to keep shipping requirements to a minimum. Lack of engineering data from the field which was often in previously undeveloped or uninhabited regions often reduced design to mealy schematic plantings or drawings, with field men to master field conditions with materials and designs supplied.

Photos from the collection of Morris "Whitey" Langberg of Seattle, WA who was a civilian operating engineer working for Atkinson and Macco construction companies at Adak, Amchitka and Shemya from 1940-45.

— CHAPTER FIVE—

DUTCH HARBOR

A US Army truck destroyed during the Japanese raid of June 3-4, 1942.
—Courtesy of AP Wire photo

Weather

Continued rather warm today.

Highest, 87; Lowest, 70

The State

'For Columbia and South Carolina'

Spot Cotton, 18.75

18,662—FOUNDED FEBRUARY 18, 1891 COLUMBIA, S. C., THURSDAY, JUNE 4, 1942 DAILY, 5c; SUNDAY, 10c

Japanese Bomb Alaska Twice

Libyan Battle Now Struggle For Position

Score Still Stand-Off Between Tanks

Cairo, June 3—(AP)—The nine-day battle of Libya became to-night a savage struggle for position and supply on the blazing, twirling sands of the desert, with the score still a destructive stand-off between the tanks of British Eighth army and German African corps.

Two Axis forces, boring toward each other from gaps already created in the mined and semi-fortified Ain El Gazala—Bir Hacheim line, ripped out a nine-mile wide hole in the center, to open up a better connection with German forces which had withdrawn to the west.

Court Denies Rehearing In Santee Cooper Case

In an order filed yesterday, the supreme court of South Carolina denied the petition of the South Carolina Public Service (Santee-Cooper) authority for a rehearing of the case in which the court granted a permanent injunction restraining the authority from purchasing privately owned

All Out of Sheep By Thomas

America Declares War on Axis Satellites

Bulgaria, Rumania and Hungary Added to List of United States Foes

Washington, June 3—(AP)—In rapid fire order, the house passed without a dissenting vote and sent to the senate today three resolutions declaring war on Bulgaria, Hungary and Rumania.

The action carried out a recommendation made yesterday by President Roosevelt in a special mesage to congress.

Three separate roll-calls were taken as members went on record for the sixth time since last December 7 for a declaration of war. Named as enemies in the earlier resolutions were Japan, Germany and Italy.

In sharp contrast to the somber atmosphere that prevailed in

Second Raid Made 6 Hours After First

Few Casualties, Little Damage Inflicted at Dutch Harbor by Four Bombers and 15 Fighters

Washington, June 3—(AP)—Two Japanese air raids were launched at Dutch Harbor, United States naval base in Alaska, within six hours today, setting off intensified precautions against any unexpected Japanese thrust along the vast Pacific frontier.

Four bombers with an escort of about 15 fighter planes carried out the first attack at 6 a. m. (local time), setting warehouses ablaze and causing a few casualties.

While details of the results from this assault were still incomplete, the navy department here received at 9 p. m. (Eastern War time) tonight a brief report on the second raid. There were no details at all of the second attack beyond the bare fact that it had occurred.

The latest naval communique said merely:

"1. A brief report just received in the navy department states that for the second time today enemy planes have attacked Dutch Harbor.

"2. The second attack was made about 12 noon, local time (6 p. m., Eastern War time), six hours after the initial attack.

"3. No further details are available at this time."

ANTHONY J. DIMOND
DELEGATE FROM ALASKA

Congress of the United States
House of Representatives
Washington, D. C.

July 22, 1942

W. M. Floyd
108 Maple St.
St. Johns, Michigan

Dear Mr. Floyd:

Your welcome letter of July 19th came in this morning.

It would be valuable to me to have a first-hand account of what happened recently at Dutch Harbor and in that vicinity, but it is asking too much to put you to the expense of making a tripe from St. Johns, Michigan to Washington in order to tell me what occurred. I am wondering if you could not write a statement telling what you saw and heard and know and send that written statement to me. I shall gladly pay whatever expense you are put to for the typing.

Of course it would be much better if we could sit down and talk it over personally, but I realize the expense of a journey from St. Johns to Washington would be considerable.

My own efforts at this time are being directed to having the Army and Navy send in enough force to drive the Japs out of the Aleutians and keep them out.

With kind regards, I am

Sincerely yours,

A J Dimond

Anthony J. Dimond
Delegate

DR. EARL GILL of Bentonville, Arkansas Remembers Dutch Harbor

I left Monticello Arkansas with Battery "B" of the 206th Coast Artillery "AA" on Jan.6, 1941. Our troop train joined other batteries as we moved south into Louisiana and then west to Fort Bliss, Texas. The regiment trained there and around Alamogordo, New Mexico, where we had enough open space to fire our 3" anti-aircraft guns at towed targets. The guns were somewhat obsolete, but the best we had at the time.

Around the first of August 1941, the regiment went to Los Angeles and then to Camp Murray in Washington State. We shipped out of Seattle and arrived at Dutch Harbor about Sept. 1, 1941. We had always been told that it was a "toss of a coin" between commanding officers that sent the 206th to the Aleutians and the 200th C.A. "AA" from New Mexico to the Philippines. The men of the 206th really complained at first when they found out they were being sent to the cold, rainy, windy and snowy Aleutians instead of the Philippines. When the story of the Bataan Death March came out we all felt good about being sent to the Aleutians in spite of having to fight williwaws, rain, snow etc.

Battery "B's" 3" guns were located on Hill 100 at the end of Main Street at Fort Mears. Upon arrival at Dutch Harbor we lived in the barracks at the fort. The first couple of months we spent a lot of time unloading the ships as they brought supplies into the harbor. We were also establishing the gun positions on Hill 100.

After getting the four guns with the accompanying equipment-the director and range finder hooked up by cable to the guns-in position, we started making "dugouts" to sleep in while manning the guns. We spent most of the winter of 1941-42 living in the "dugouts" part of the time and the barracks part of the time.

The Japanese attacked us on June 3, 1942 in the morning and on June 4th in the afternoon. Unfortunately our 3" guns were not very effective on the high-flying bombers. I do remember a Japanese Zero fighter strafing the area, just below or at the same level as our positions on Hill 100, close enough for us to see the pilots sitting in the cockpits. Just why they were not strafing our positions on the hill has always been a mystery. One man from our battery was killed near Fort Mears.

Soon after the bombing raids our battery was moved to Hog Island across the bay. After getting established on the island we stayed there until departing in the early spring of 1944. I recall while we were on the island an airfield was built off the side of Mount Ballyhoo. A navy fighter plane landed one day on the runway but was unable to stop and ran off the end of the runway, nosing over into the bay. The pilot did manage to get out of the plane before it sank. I also experienced an earthquake while on the island. Huge boulders rolled off Mount Ballyhoo and the island shook quite noticeably for a few seconds. This was my first earthquake experience.

JOHN J. BIELAK of Jupiter, Florida Remembers His Experiences at Dutch Harbor

I served two and one half years at Unalaska and Dutch Harbor. I was carried on the roster of Battery F, 210th CA AA, Battery F 503rd CA, and Battery B 594th AAA, all that time I was posted to the Post fire department at Fort Mears, as they need firefighters, as some were lost during the air raid. I was a replacement but in time I became the assistant fire chief.

I was on the ship Fillmore and our own guns fired on us as we were coming in to port on June 1, 1942. Luckily we weren't hit as we were really loaded with ammunition. The fire station was the visitor's welcome center for Marines, Sailors, Seabees, Russians and Aleuts, so we got to know everything that was going on to the west along the chain. I really heard some real stories as the firemen could work as clerks at the Northern Commercial Company store and wait on all the different customers. The photos were censored with no military facilities allowed to be shown.

THE NORTHWESTERN

The battered *SS Northwestern* was a hard-luck ship from her launching at the Philadelphia ship yard in 1883. Built as a luxury liner, the *Arazaba* as she was then called sank a tow boat in sliding down the ways to begin her jinxed career.

The *Arazaba's* first run was between New York and Havana as the flagship of the tourist fleet, followed by a taste of military service in the Spanish-American War, transporting troops from New Orleans and Mobile to battlefields in Cuba and Puerto Rico. Returning to her original run she continued to sail to Havana until 1907 when she was bought by the Black Ball Steamship Company of Seattle, renamed the *Northwestern* and routed to Alaskan ports. When the line changed its name to the Alaska Steamship Company shortly afterwards, the vessel had already confirmed her reputation as an unlucky craft by running aground 16 times in North Pacific waters.

During the lean thirties the *Northwestern* was tied up, out of commission in Lake Washington in Seattle. But in 1940 Siems-Drake Puget Sound, contractors for the Alaskan military bases, bought the old liner and reconditioned it to bring civilian workers and the first US Marines to Dutch Harbor. Arriving there in August 1940 the ill-fated ship was moored at Unalaska until a fierce winter williwaw drove her on the beach. She was then towed to a dredged position by the Naval Operating Base dock and became a barracks for civilian workers.

Hit twice by Japanese bombs in the June 4th raid, the old vessel's usefulness was not entirely destroyed by the ensuing fire. Her boilers were flooded and thus saved and she supplied steam and heat for many months after the raid.

The S.S. Northwestern *showing her fore part badly buckled by the Japanese attack* –Courtesy of AP Wire photo

Here is a closeup from a newsreel film sequence of the damage done by a Japanese bomb to the S.S. Northwestern *in raids on this US Naval base in Alaska on June 3–4, 1942. A few shacks in the dock section were also hit and burned.* –Courtesy of AP Wire photo

THE BOMBING OF DUTCH HARBOR BY ZENJI ABE

Former Imperial Lieutenant Commander of the Carrier Junyo

The *Junyo* and *Ruyjo* of the 4th carrier division together with the heavy cruisers *Maya* and *Takao* and assorted escorts left for the Aleutians on May 26, 1942. Up to that date, the Navy had fought victoriously at Pearl Harbor, Malaya and the Indian Ocean to deal the US fleet a devastating blow. Vice Admiral Hosogaya's Northern Strike Force was going to make a diversionary attack on the Aleutians and also trying to land army troops on the islands of Attu, Adak and Kiska. Our 4th Carrier Division was to attack Dutch Harbor and guard the fleet against enemy air attacks.

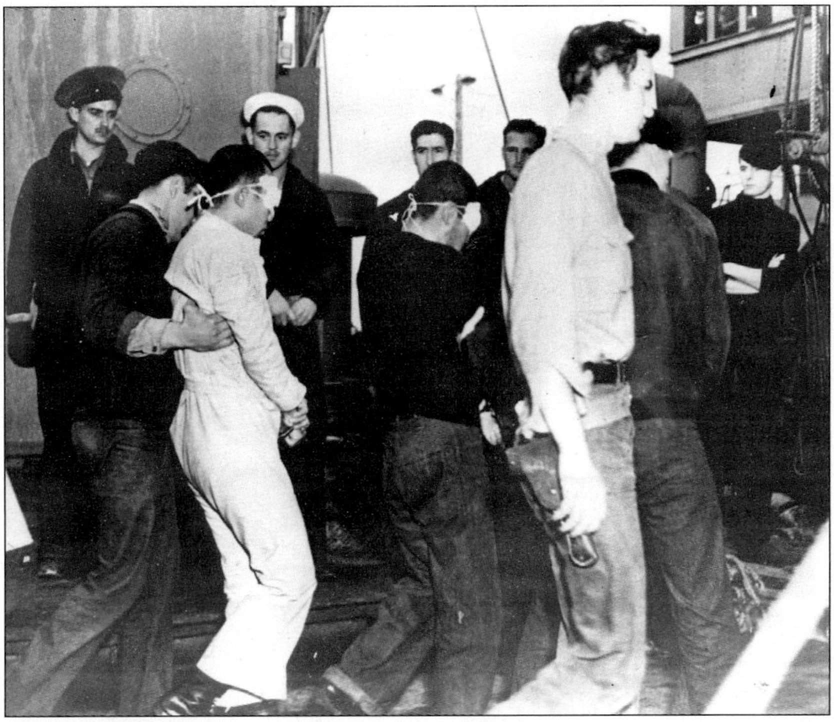

Several of the 28 Japanese prisoners from the battle of Attu, shown in this Acme wirephoto, were brought to Dutch Harbor where a large POW camp was constructed in the valley assuming that there would possibly be many enemy prisoners. The battle was an early indication that the enemy were going to fight to the death. Five Japanese sailors were captured after their submarine was sunk off of Atka after it torpedoed the seaplane tender the Casco. –Courtesy of AP Wire photo

At that time I was a squadron leader on the new carrier *Junyo*. I was transferred there in May 1942 from the carrier *Akagi*. The *Junyo* was part of the 4th Carrier Division which was part of the second Striking Force under Rear Admiral Kakuji Kakuta. I had taken part in the attack on Pearl harbor and in other battles but it is hard for me to believe that the dark waves ahead of us belonged to the same ocean as the tropical waters in which we had fought until now.

When I was transferred to the *Junyo* shortly after my return from the Indian Ocean a new bombing squadron was established with 18 bombers and 36 crewmen. We went to train at the Saeki airbase in Kyusha but were pressed for time. Over half of the men had just graduated from high school and needed to practice not only landings and takeoffs, but also bombing. As in the Navy song "getsu Ka Sui Moku Kin Kin" (this means Monday, Tuesday, Wednesday, Thursday and Friday) an indication that there were few days off for the Navy. We drilled day and night without rest to improve the airmens' performance.

The *Junyo* was the first fleet carrier converted from a passenger liner so our crewmen had difficulties at first to get used to it but in time they learned how to deal with the ship. I myself went to the staff officers to tell them that we needed more time. Until now it was unheard of, if in the Navy, to send a new carrier and aircrews into battle with only one month of training, but my superiors told me to literally leave the men who couldn't preform properly behind. I was very surprised that we would be sent into battle under such circumstances. Rear Admiral Kakuta told me that the schedule could not be changed and that a decisive battle lay ahead of us. The Admiral was originally a gunnery expert but well respected in the Navy as an intelligent model Navy officer. He was later promoted to Vice Admiral and died in August 1944, committing seppuku (ritual suicide).

The
ALEUTIAN
DUTCH HARBOR
ALASKA
VOL. I
JULY 8, 1943
NO. 2

Northwestern Was Jinx Ship

The battered S. S. Northwestern, long a landmark of last June's Jap raid, was a hard-luck ship from her first launching at a Philadelphia yard in 1883.

Built as a luxury liner, the Arazaba, as she was then called, sank a tow boat in sliding down the ways to begin her jinxed career.

The Arazaba's first run was between New York and Havana as the flagship of the tourist fleet, followed by a taste of military service in the Spanish American War, transporting troops from New Orleans and Mobile to battlefields in Cuba and Puerto Rico.

Aground 16 Times

Returning to her original run, the Arazaba continued to ply to Havana until 1907 when she was bought by the Black Ball Steamship Company of Seattle, renamed the Northwestern and routed to Alaskan ports. When the line changed its name to the Alaska Steamship Company shortly afterwards, the sharp prowed vessel had already confirmed her reputation as an unlucky craft by running aground sixteen times in North Pacific waters.

During the lean thirties the Northwestern was tied up, out of commission, in Lake Washington at Seattle. But in 1940 Siems-Drake Puget Sound, contractors for the Alaskan air bases, bought the old liner and reconditioned it to bring civilian workers and the first Marines to Dutch Harbor.

Hit Twice In Raid

Arriving here in August, 1940, the ill-fated ship was moored at Unalaska until a fierce winter williwaw drove her on the beach. The Northwestern was then towed to a dredged position by the NOB dock and became a barracks for civilian workers.

Hit twice by Jap bombs in the raid of last June 4, the old vessel's usefulness was not entirely destroyed by the ensuing fire. Her boilers were flooded and thus saved and she supplied steam and heat for many months after the enemy onslaught.

JUNE, 1942

This year-old picture shows the Northwestern smoldering after being hit by two Jap bombs in the June 3-4 raids.

Raid Vets Broadcast

Exactly one year after the first Jap Zero zoomed in over Unalaska to begin the memorable June 3 and 4 raids, Army and Navy veterans of those days spoke proudly and defiantly of the progress of this base in an anniversary broadcast over WXLC.

E. J. Irvine, Cox. of NAS, and Cpl. Dell Gore of Antiaircraft, both told of their feelings as enemy planes dived on then weakly armed Amaknak.

Musical highlight of the commemorative program was the singing by Sgt. Bob Coner of the Arkansawyers of his ballad, "The Bombing of Dutch Harbor."

C&B School's Out

Better chow will be on the menu for Army men at six Alaskan stations, if 58 new graduates of the Western Alaska Sub-School for Bakers and Cooks have learned their lessons well.

Four 1st Lieutenants and seventeen 2nd Lieutenants comprise the first class of 21 officers to complete a new one month course in mess hall management.

Eight Mess Sergeants finished a one month course, while 29 Mess Cooks received certificates for completing two months of study.

Finest Service Studios Opened

"The finest radio studios in the armed forces," is the description given WXLC's new quarters by officers from the Radio Section, Army Special Service who recently inspected the Radio-Morale Center in Fort Mears.

In addition to two soundproof studios, one able to accomodate a 25-piece band, there are control and transmitter rooms, an office, a sound lock, storage space, and a work room. These facilities topside in the new building behind the Army hospital are supplemented by a stage and 200 seat auditorium below.

Housed in the same building are offices of the Subsector and Seabee Morale departments, the College of the Aleutians, and THE ALEUTIAN, as well as a 3,000-volume library, a coffee shop, and dressing rooms.

The Black Jack Seabees commanded by Lieut. Comdr. F. M. Thomson, CEC, built the Center, replacing Quonset hut accomodations for the station and magazine. Lt. (jg) R. L. Jones was in charge of construction.

A gala housewarming program, broadcast from the packed auditorium, informally opened the new studios. Jo D. Hamilton, ARC, and H. G. Theis, Y3c, were in charge.

Infantry NCOs Open Club

"Fourth and only" is a claim the new Non-Commissioned Officers Club of the Littlejohn Infantry can make stick. Three other NCO clubs have been started at Fort Mears, but all folded because of transfers or lack of a club room.

Billeting won't bother the newest organization. A deluxe clubroom, complete with a combination radio-phonograph and a slug of games, opened recently.

President of the NCO club is 1st Sgt. Norman D. Jones of Lawrence, Kan. Other newly-elected officers are: 1st Sgt. Herron I. B. Warren of Dexter, Mo., vice president; Cpl. Arthur H. Frohman of Chicago, secretary; S/Sgt. George G. Dunlap of Hollywood, treasurer.

The ALEUTIAN
DUTCH HARBOR
ALASKA

Published by and for all service men in the Dutch Harbor area

Editor: Lieut. William H. Price, USNR
Associate: Major J. V. Brereton, AUS
Assistants: L. S. Rosen, CSp, USNR
H. F. Mertens, PhoM1c, USNR
M. W. Openshaw, PhoM1c, USNR
D. E. Nease, PhoM1c, USNR
Pfc. A. L. Cabiati, AUS
Pvt. W. B. Murray, AUS
Offices: Navy Administration Building and Radio-Morale Center
Telephones: Navy 476-M, Tillie 90-M

BETWEEN ROUNDS

This North Pacific war is something like a prize fight. We're in the corner now after round one, waiting for another chance to sail into that yellow rat across the ring. We got in some good wallops in the opener but we took a couple of jolts ourselves.

Now we're ready to start punching again. Make no mistake about it, we'll have to battle plenty to get that KO. If we've got the guts, the condition and the punch, we'll be able to do it. But the best thing of all to remember when we hear the bell is this—championship fights aren't won in first round flurries.

SPRUCE UP, MAC!

You've heard that saying from the tropics that the jungle has begun to get a man when he stops shaving regularly. It's pretty true up here too that when a guy begins to look like a Poland China hog, his military snap and personal drive are gone to pot.

All those memos from the braid about cleanliness aren't aimed at turning us into lavender scented lilymen. They're based on the sound view that an unshaven galoot with stinking duds and hair like a weed patch is likely to be a pretty sad sack of a fighting man.

When you skip washing your clothes and yourself, is it a necessary concession to your living conditions or just a piece of slipshod laziness? That uniform you wear is something to be proud of, brother. Wear it that way.

ROUND ONE!

The MAIL SACK

Q. M. SHOW

Dear Sir:

I think the Q.M. Show was a good example of one kind of morale, people going along making their own fun, taking time out to entertain other people....

When you and you saw the show, did you stop to think of the preparation that went into it, or the handicaps involved because our Detachment work comes first?....Well, friend, show me a squad, platoon, company or division, corps or army that has stuff like that and I'll show you a country that can't be beaten today, tomorrow, or ever.

1st. Sgt. Hollis Nosker

BOOTS

Dear Sir:

Every $25 bond that you or your people at home buy pays for six pairs of shoes or three pairs of boots. That bond is wasted if you and a couple of your buddies neglectfully leave your boots on a hot stove.....

Restoration of your shoes when worn too long before sending them in for repair also wastes money and material and shipping space. Now that the shoe shop has plenty of material let's get our shoes and boots in for repair as soon as they show wear and tear....

S/Sgt. Thomas E. Monzo

RIDES?

Dear Sir:

I have to walk a lot of miles each day. How about suggesting to truck drivers that we on foot would be grateful for a lift once in a while?

Tom Meany, S1c

Watch the next issue, Tom.

PAINT REMOVAL

Dear Sir:

I was reading in the paper from home that some shiny pants back there is asking the skirts to quit using rouge and powder for the duration and some babe says let's leave it up to the soldiers and then asks "How do you like us, painted or plain?"

I don't know about the rest of you guys, but right now I can't figure out a more interesting way to spend Sunday than scraping a couple of layers of paint off of Rita Hayworth.

Dogface Dave of Battery D

Page 12 THE ALEUTIAN July 8, 1943

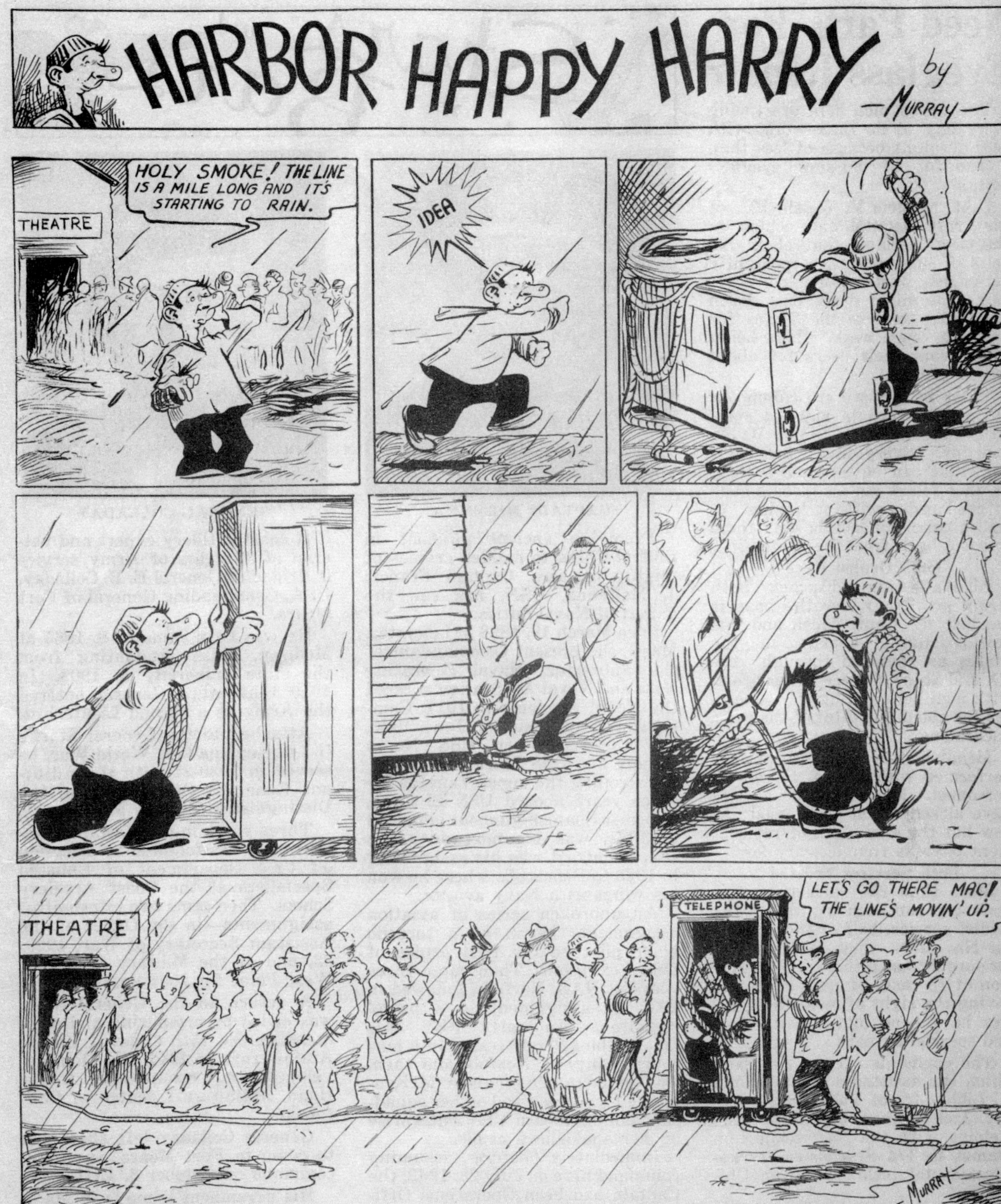

WILLIAM H. WORRELL

William H. Worrell unlisted in the Arkansas National Guard in 1940 and went on active duty on Jan. 6, 1941. He was assigned to the Medical Detachment 1882 Service Command Unit and joined the 206th Coast Artillery Regiment. He was a trained Medical Technician attached to the Arkansas National Guard and was part of a field unit trained to handle field emergencies and also an ambulance driver in combat zones.

The unit transferred to Ft. Lewis and then headed to Dutch Harbor in February, 1942. He was there during the attack and stayed until February, 1944.

He was honorably discharged at Camp Chaffee, Arkansas on July 5, 1945.

–Story and photos courtesy of Dan and Joyce Worrell

— CHAPTER SIX—

TRANSPORTATION SYSTEMS

Part of the 300 officers and men and equipment loading on the* USS St. Mihiel *in Seattle on June 21, 1940, to be stationed in Alaska. —Courtesy of US Army

During the war, tracks of The White Pass & Yukon Route, which was taken over by the US Army Transportation Corps, ran down Broadway, Skagway's main street, to the docks to pick up supplies to haul to Whitehorse, Yukon Territory for construction of the ALCAN and CANOL projects. –Courtesy of US Army

The railroad had to deal with massive snowfalls on their route north. Here a combination freight and passenger train crosses the steel cantilever bridge across Dead Horse Gulch, made famous during the 1898 Klondike Gold Rush. –Courtesy of US Army

MUSIC BY- SGT FELTYSCH
SOLDIERING AT SKAGWAY
WORDS BY-LT MORRIS
WE are sol-dier-ing at the port of old Skag-way, on a gra--vel bar at the le--vel of the sea, Hemmed
We are sol-dier-ing at the port of old Skag-way, in a spot knee deep with mud we made our camp, For
In by moun--tain walls be--decked by wat--ter falls in a can-yon where the wind blows rather fr
Weeks we lived that way for it rained most every day with out no floors and a can-dle for a lamp
We'd like to go fish---ing but we can't spare the time, and hunt---ing in those rug--ed mount-ains
'Till we built a little city and we built it out of tin , and built a house with lots of plumbing
high Or pan the creeks for gold as did the men of old, But it ain't done and heres the rea--son why the
too The docks we had to rob to get men for the job, But heres the reason we couldn't spare the crew th
Colo-nel said its ton-nage that I crave, off the boats and and mov-ing up the hill this
Colo-nel said its ton-nage that I crave, but to move the stuff a sol-dier must be fit we
Ain't no game we play we can't win the war that way and to Hell to them that' saying that we wil
Can't un-load the barges if the men are hospital charges and to Hell to them that's saying that we can
Load the car and move it Get the stuff to those that use it, for they are going to use it right a--
Get the men out of the cold The winter's bit-ter I am told, And hear them sing when they are warm and
way And the Transporta-tion Corps will keep send-ing more, Sol-dier-ing with Ahr-ens at Skag-way.
dry For the Transporta-tion Corps asks for noth-ing more, Sol-dier-ing with Ahr-ens at Skag-way.

The US Army Transport, St. Mihiel, *and the* S.S. Yukon *at dock in Seward.*

Supplying defense forces in Alaska was an operation that included ocean, rail, truck and river arteries. The 878th Port Company at Nenana ran a barge transport of critical fuel down the Tanana and Yukon rivers to Galena, the site of an air transport command airfield in 1944. –Courtesy of ASL-PCA-8

The steamer Klondike at Eagle, Alaska pushing a barge loaded with military equipment and supplies. –Courtesy of the National Archives of Canada, C4033

A menu from the Princess Louise.

The
ALASKA
RAILROAD
★
United States
Department
of Interior
Serving the Nation's Most
Strategic War Area in a
World at War.
HELPING TO SPEED
THE DAY OF VICTORY
★
DEDICATED TO THE BUILDING
OF A GREATER ALASKA
★
For further information, write:
O. F. OHLSON, General Manager
ANCHORAGE, ALASKA

ENGINE 557 RESTORATION COMPANY

For over 100 years, The Alaska Railroad's story lead developments in the Railbelt from the founding of Seward and Anchorage to connections with Fairbanks and the interior rivers. Missing since the late 1950's has been the sight and sound of a steam locomotive and the lonesome echo of its whistle. The non-profit Engine 557 restoration Company has been performing a multi-year restoration of ARR steam locomotive #557, the last Alaska Railroad steam locomotive to operate.

Engine 557 represents the 2120 s-160 locomotives built for the U.S. Army Transportation Corps and sent off to support the allied war effort around the world. Only 18 of these locomotives were retained in North America and 12 of those came to Alaska. Built in 1944 and brought North to help with the increased wartime traffic, 557 was retained for special trains long after all the other steam equipment was retired. After many special charters and then pulling trains through flood waters at Nenana in 1962, she was finally sold for scrap in 1967. Purchased by Monte Holmes, he saved 557 from the torch at his House of Poverty Museum in Moses Lake, Washington.

557 at Anchorage, September 5, 1959.
–Courtesy of Ken Reuben alaskarails.org collection, via Patrick Durand

The last revenue run of 557 was to the "first" Alaska State Fair, September 5, 1959.

557 along Turnagain Arm about 1948.
–Courtesy of the Ostrom Collection, alaskarails.org collection

557 along Turnagain Arm about 1948
–Ostrom collection, courtesy of alaskarails.org

557 arrived in Whittier on the S.S. Crowley *November 2, 1944 along with two other S-160 locomotives. The photo was by John Parys then on active duty in Whittier, Alaska. His son Ken Parys shared his dad's extensive collection, now part of the alaskarails.org collection.* –Courtesy of Patrick Durand

Upon Monte's passing, friends Jim and Vic Jansen, who own Lynden Inc. a major Alaska transportation service, bought 557 and donated it to the Alaska Railroad on provision it be restored and operated for special trains. 557 moved on a flat car from Moses Lake to the Lynden terminal in Seattle. Lynden then provided barge transport to Whittier where 557 was treated to a special movement on the Alaska Railroad to Anchorage.

The Alaska Railroad transferred the locomotive to the Engine 557 Restoration Company upon delivery to an empty warehouse in Wasilla, Alaska. Volunteers immediately began the job of up-fitting the building to perform the restoration. Monthly status reports reflect steady progress with hopes of doing steam tests in 2020.

557 restoration is a total overhaul, including a new firebox, tubes, flues, rebuilt suspension and driving boxes, shoes, wedges and everything that connects them.

Funding is all from private individuals and foundations. Rasmuson Foundation began the effort with a $350,000 matching grant in 2012 and progress has continued as funding developed. Donations toward completion are always welcome. For status reports and the latest information you can go to: w.w.w.557.alaskarails.org

–Copy provided by Patrick Durand

an Alaska Interlude
THE ALASKA STEAMSHIP COMPAN

SIBERIA
BERING SEA
KOTZEBUE
DEERING
TELLER
KEEWALIK
NOME
ARCTIC CIRCLE
ST. MICHAEL
FORT YUKON
YUKON RIVER
TANANA
CIRCLE
TANANA RIVER
STEESE HIGHWAY
FAIRBANKS
MT. McKINLEY NATIONAL PARK
NENANA
ALASKA
DAWSON
CURRY
BAXSON
PALMER MATANUSKA VALLEY
ANCHORAGE
VALDEZ
UPPER TONSINA
KENNECOTT
COLUMBIA GLACIER
NUSHAGAK
NAKNEK
MILES & CHILDS GLACIERS
CHITINA
SELDOVIA
CORDOVA
DUTCH HARBOR
AKUTAN
SEWARD
PRINCE WILLIAM SOUND
UNALASKA
UNGA
KODIAK
WHITE HORSE
LAKE ATLIN
YAKUTAT
LAKE BENNETT
CARCROSS
ATLIN
SKAGWAY
GULF OF ALASKA
JUNEAU
TAKU GLACIER
DOUGLAS
SITKA
PETERSBURG
WRANGELL
KETCHIKAN
SERVICES OF "The Alaska Line"
Routes shown on this map designate services of the Alaska Steamship Company and connecting lines, covering the cruises and tours described in this brochure. Interior tours are made in connection with regular cruises of The Alaska Line.
ALASKA
PRINCE WILLIAM SOUND CRUISES
WESTWARD CRUISES
INSIDE PASSAGE CRUISES
TOTEMLAND CRUISES
GOLDEN BELT LINE TOURS
YUKON RIVER CIRCLE TOURS
BERING SEA ROUTE
ALASKA PENINSULA ROUTE
ALASKA STEAMSHIP CO.
THE ALASKA LINE
VICTORIA
PACIFIC OCEAN
SEATTLE

Wings for the World's Greatest Travel System...

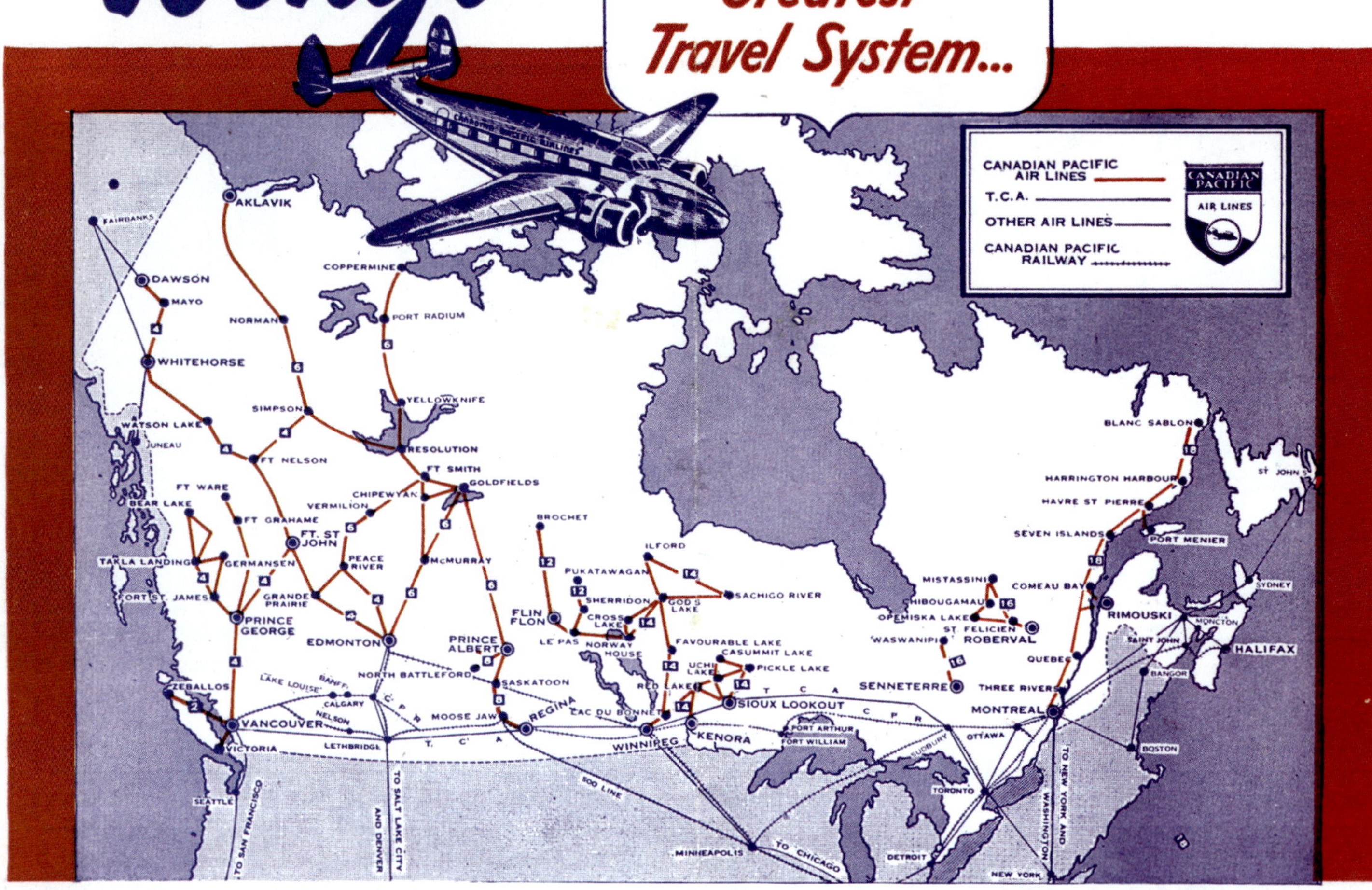

Canadian Pacific

AIR LINES

Half a century ago, the Canadian Pacific linked ocean to ocean across Canada by rail. Now it adds air transport to its rail and steamship facilities. Recently, it consolidated ten Canadian air transport companies running northward like arteries from the main east-west lines of communication...to the borders of the Yukon ...and the shores of the Arctic.

It now operates close to 100 planes, with a flying mileage of more than 5,000,000 plane miles a year. This makes it one of the world's largest commercial air operators. Its routes connect with Trans-Canada Air Lines and the leading American air lines.

Information, rates and reservations through any Canadian Pacific Railway agent.

PASSENGERS - MAIL - EXPRESS

— CHAPTER SEVEN—

RUSSIAN LEND-LEASE

A U.S. officer (second from right), and three Soviet pilots at Marks Field in Nome, AK, await the arrival of four twin-motored aircraft from factories in the U.S. They will then take them over and fly them to the battlefields in the Soviet Union. The flier in the heavy, quilted coat, is a Soviet ace holding many decorations. U.S. foreign Economic Administrator, Leo T. Crowley announced that up to May 1, 1944, the U.S. had supplied the Soviet Union with 10,000 aircraft with about half transferred through the Alaskan route by the 7th Ferrying Command of the USAAF. –US Army Air Forces photo, Aug. 7, 1944

The Alaskan Division, A.T.C.

Certificate of Commendable Service

Award of this Certificate is made to

T/SGT LYLE L. JOHNSON, 19072020

in appreciation for 21 months of commendable service under severe conditions peculiar to Canada and Alaska requiring ingenuity, perseverance and devotion to duty.

Eugene Stevens Name

Colonel, A.C. (Rank and Org.)

Commanding Officer
U. S. Army Air Base

1452nd AAF BU EDMONTON, CAN. (Location)

D. V. Gaffney
Brig. General, U.S.A.
Commanding

Flying planes over mostly uncharted territory from Great Falls, MT to Fairbanks and then on to Nome was very hazardous and many planes, such as this P-39 fighter did not make it. —Courtesy of Henry Hunt

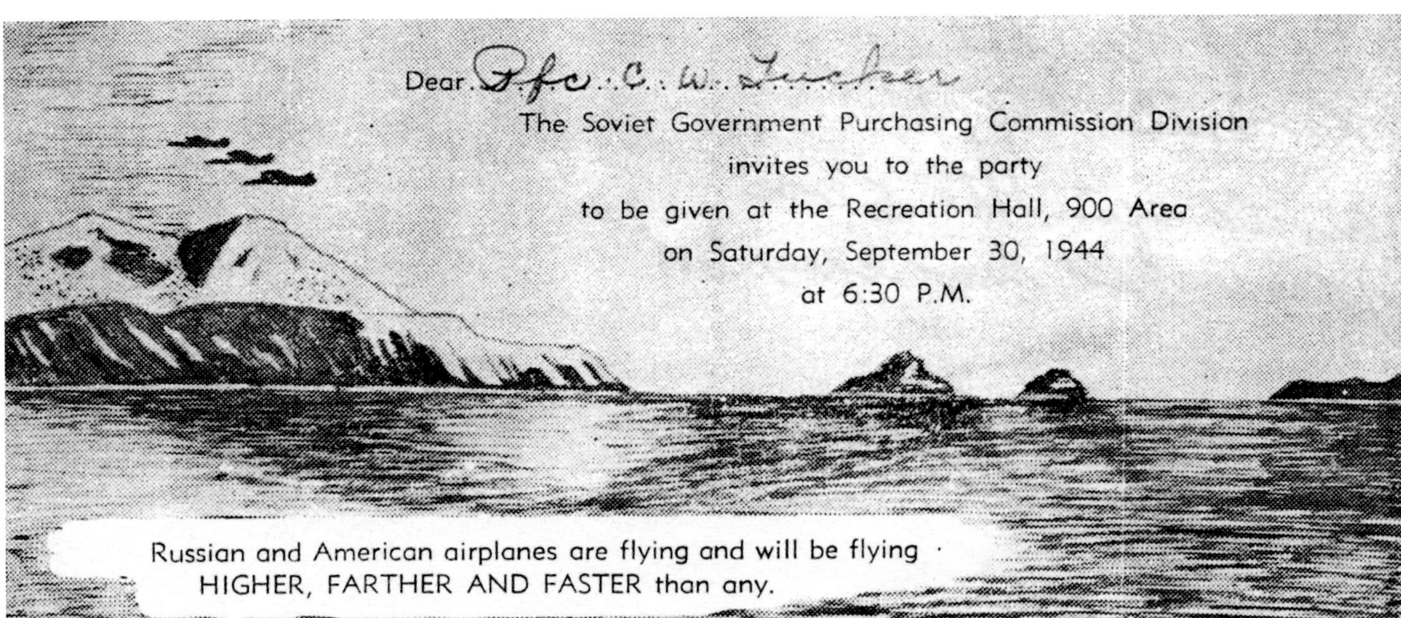

Dear Pfc. C. W. [illegible]

The Soviet Government Purchasing Commission Division
invites you to the party
to be given at the Recreation Hall, 900 Area
on Saturday, September 30, 1944
at 6:30 P.M.

Russian and American airplanes are flying and will be flying
HIGHER, FARTHER AND FASTER than any.

A party invitation to an American soldier in celebration of the 5,000th plane being delivered to Ladd Field in September 1944.

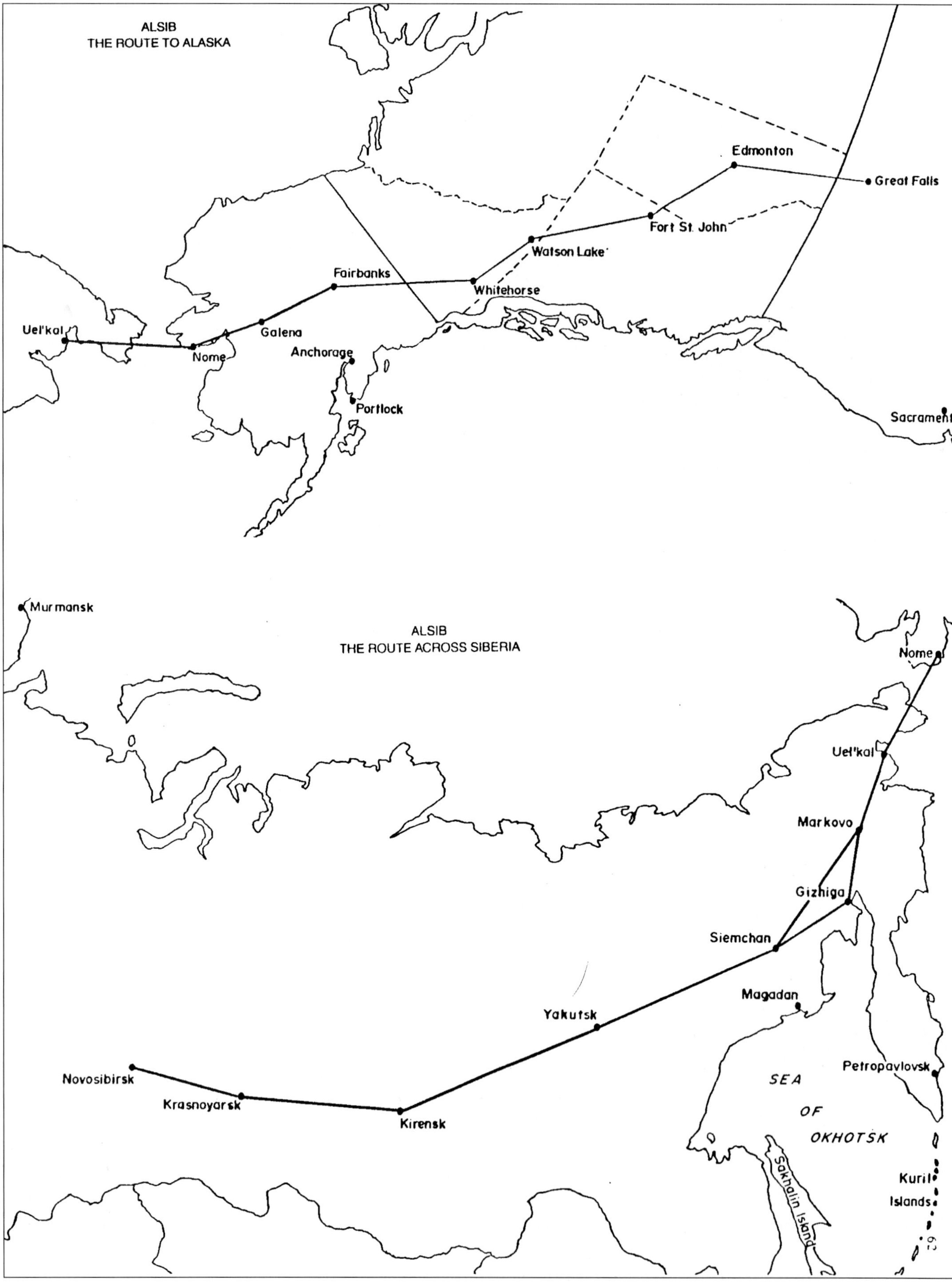

The flying routes from Great Falls, MT to Novosibirsk, Siberia for the Lend-Lease aircraft. –Courtesy of John X. Jamrich

HOTEL RAINBOW

Great Falls, Montana

•

Dinner Menu

HOT CONSOMME

SPLIT PEA AND MUSHROOM SOUP

1. BROILED SPLIT LOBSTER TAILS SHOESTRING POTATOES...$1.50
2. HOT VEGETARIAN DINNER...$1.15
3. SHIRRED EGGS WITH COUNTRY SAUSAGE...$1.25
4. COLD ROAST PRIME RIBS OF BEEF POTATO SALAD...$1.25
5. ROAST LOIN OF PORK DRESSING APPLE SAUCE...$1.25
6. BEEF TENDERLOIN STEAK VEGETABLE AND MUSHROOM CASSEROLE DINNER $1.60

BAKED OR OVEN BROWNED POTATOES CAULIFLOWER & PEAS

DINNER ROLLS

COMBINATION VEGETABLE SALAD RAINBOW DRESSING

DESSERTS

FRESH APPLE OR CHOCOLATE PIE

PINEAPPLE SUNDAE LIME SHERBET

ASSORTED CHEESE PLATE BENTS WAFERS

COFFEE, TEA OR MILK

* * * * *

SERVED FROM 5:30 TO 8:00 P. M.

MONDAY, JANUARY 18, 1943

BLUE POINT OYSTERS ON THE HALF SHELL.....75¢

BROILED FRESH MUSHROOMS—90c
Served on Toast with Bacon
Rolls and Beverage

COMBINATION BAKED HAM AND SWISS CHEESE SANDWICH—60c
Dinner Soup
Potato Salad and Drink

ONE LAMB CHOP GRILL—85c
Dinner Potato
Rolls Beverage

VEAL CUTLET TOMATO SAUCE—75c
French Fried Potatoes
Rolls and Beverage

RAINBOW COMBINATION VEGETABLE SALAD—75c
1000 Island, French, or Mayonnaise
Melba Toast Rolls
Beverage

CLUB HOUSE SANDWICH 90c
Saratoga Chips and Beverage

11TH WEATHER REGION
Office of the Regional Control Officer
APO #942, c/o Postmaster
Seattle, Washington

HLS/vmk

3 November 1943

SUBJECT: Staff Weather Officer for Soviet Military Mission.

TO: Lt. John X. Jamrich
AAF Weather Station
APO #938, U. S. Army

THRU: Commanding Officer
APO #938, U. S. Army

1. At a recent conference with Colonel Machin of the Soviet Military Mission, it was decided that a weather officer familiar with the Russian language be designated as the Staff Weather Officer for the Soviet Military Mission. It is, therefore, the decision of this office that Lt. John X. Jamrich act in the capacity of Staff Weather Officer to the Russians. His primary duties will be furnishing necessary flight weather information to the Russian pilots; conducting a briefing room which will include not only weather information pertinent to flights but will also include photographs, facility charts, and other flight information necessary for safety in flight; and keeping Colonel Machin and the Russian Staff advised at all times as to the best times for flight operations westward.

2. This change of duty status does not in any way involve transfer from the 11th Weather Squadron nor does it involve change of station. It will, however, be Lt. Jamrich's responsibility to see that the Russian speaking meteorological officers now stationed at Galena and Nome are performing their duties properly and that all needed information is furnished to the Russian pilots. This will involve travel between Fairbanks and the above mentioned stations and such inspection trips should be made upon request of Colonel Machin and other members of his staff.

3. Close coordination will be effected by Lt. Jamrich and the Base Weather Officer in order that all facilities may be utilized in carrying out this specific duty. Consultations should be had from time to time with Colonel Little, Colonel, Machin, and Lt. Drewes as to the best manner of presentation in the briefing room.

4. Lt. Jamrich's duties will begin immediately upon receipt of this letter.

H. L. Smith

H. L. SMITH
Colonel, Air Corps
Regional Control Officer.

CONFIDENTIAL Noted: Col. Keillor

JOHN X. JAMRICH

President Emeritus of Northern Michigan University tells the story of his time with the Russian Lend-Lease program in Alaska at a gathering at the university in 1954.

I had lived in Czechoslovakia between the age of two and nine and with my foreign language study in college, I was proficient in several European languages. I was a graduate of the University of Chicago Meteorology program, and commissioned as a 2nd Lt. in the U.S. Army Air Forces. Naturally, I fully expected to be shipped to the European Theater. To my surprise, I received orders to report to Seattle for transportation to Anchorage, AK. My indicated assignment was to the Aleutian Islands, but our commanding officer in Anchorage discovered that I spoke several languages, including Russian. Given my language ability, coupled with my meteorology training I was assigned to Ladd Field in Fairbanks. When I arrived, I was told that the Soviet pilots were experiencing considerable frustration with the weather forecast accuracy and the absence of U.S. Army Air Forces meteorologists with the ability to speak Russian.

The forecasts were being prepared primarily by the U.S. Weather Bureau. In the Russian's pilots view, the forecasts lacked the precision required for the flights from Fairbanks over into Siberia. I was appointed as the Liaison Weather Officer for the Russian Flight Group stationed at Fairbanks. I was to provide and coordinate the work of forecasting for their flights to Siberia; In addition, I was responsible for coordinating the development of acceptable "secret" weather codes for transmission purposes.

The Soviets were a suspicious lot. They were reluctant to even share their weather observations, taken in Siberia, with us even though their flights depended on forecast accuracy. They were intensely in the various installations we had throughout Alaska, keeping their bases in Siberia pretty much to themselves. But the pilots, for whom this temporary flight duty of ferrying planes was their rest and recreation from the battles of the Russian front, and I became very good friends and they developed an almost complete dependence and confidence in my forecasts.

I flew with them on many of their group flights to Nome and their first stop in Siberia, The short amount of daylight in winter, the extremely low minus 65 degree temperatures of the winter, the 18 to 20 hour daylight periods of summer, and the complex weather patterns of the area proved more than a minor challenge to us in developing accurate forecasts.

During the summer months, during the height of the war, they would fly two or more groups of planes from Fairbanks. During the winter--the sun rising at 10 a.m. and setting at 3 p.m.- -there was time for just one flight, so if they took off, there was no room for error in the weather forecast. And, with the 40 to 65 degree below zero readings on a typical morning, the decision to fly or not had to be made several hours before the 10 a.m. takeoff. The reason for that was that each of the 20 or 30 planes scheduled to fly that day had to be warmed up with a heater for about two hours. The oil viscosity in those days was not anything like we have today.

Complex weather patterns, indeed! We even manufactured our own fog at Fairbanks on very cold, winter mornings. The inversion was so strong, that the smoke from the power plant developed a fog layer that frequently covered the airfield like a blanket. Yet, with all of these complicating factors, we were most fortunate that during the almost three years of such flight activity, involving between eight and nine thousand aircraft clearances which were issued, there was not a single loss due to an inaccurate weather forecast. All told, it is estimated that they lost about 300 of the aircraft on the flights for reasons other than weather.

As I said, the Russians were zealous and intense about getting aircraft to the front. They preferred the P-39 and P-63 fighters; the A-20 low- level attack bombers as well as the B-25, probably their favorite action aircraft, although they always went back to the C-47 as the most dependable for transport. One should remember that many of these Russian pilots had never flown these U.S. –type aircraft before. They had to be checked out in them before taking them up. It was real interesting to work with these seasoned pilots and watch them being very casual as they were being checked out on the ground by our pilots—through interpreters.

Occasionally, a pilot would make a critical error. It was in one of these situations that I became acutely aware of the minimal care for the individual human life exhibited in their military. One of the new pilots had just been checked out; he taxied out and took off, He just forgot to close up his cockpit door properly. As he was taking off, the door flew off and evidently he became confused, resulting in his crashing into a hillside at the end of the runway. I was standing on the taxiway with their commanding officer—Colonel Machin. When I saw the smoke from the crash. I suggested to the Colonel we should probably take a Jeep and go with the emergency vehicles. His answer was: "Why bother, he's probably dead anyway. Let's proceed with the flight." With that we got into his B-25 and joined the flight to escort it over the Bering Sea, this being a particularly bad weather situation over that area.

I should explain that in certain weather situations the weather would be fine at Fairbanks and at Uel'kal their first stop in Siberia. In their zeal to fly as many planes to the front as possible, I had convinced them that, when the weather was bad at Nome, where they would normally stop, they could fly over the cloud deck, over the Bering Sea area. For this sort of flight, they needed the B-25 to lead them over the cloud deck.

Essentially, I lived with the Soviet pilots during the assignment even though my sleeping quarters were in our Air Force BOQ. It was an experience that enabled me to know the Soviet military personally. The pilots were much like ours—carefree, but loyal. As Russians, they had been schooled thoroughly in the Communist philosophy. And, this was a well-educated group of officers. In our frequent discussions at mealtimes, they would insist that they had a true democracy. After all, they would say, "we have elections and everybody gets to vote." They, of course, dismissed the "minor" fact that their ballot had only one candidate for each office.

They were generally heavy drinkers. Often, they brought over their own supply of vodka. But, they clearly had an eye out for the welfare of their country and the people back home. Payday for them was interesting to observe. They were paid in American dollars, so they would have a substantial roll of bills to dispose of. Two things happened: first, they would descend on the PX and buy what they could in the line of personal items such as watches and the like, to take back to Russia. Second, whatever money was left, they told me that they sent it back home to factories to build tanks and military hardware. They did not have "war bonds" to buy; they just gave money for those causes. They were friendly, but fraternizing between American men and the few Russian women they had in the group, as well as between them and our women was frowned upon.

This is a 1944 view of the "famous "or ("infamous") Fourth Street in Fairbanks.

View of the briefing room located in the Russian flight area. On the left is Lt. Gamov, a Russian flight leader. To the right is 2nd Lt. Jamrich. The blackboard always contained an updated cross-section of the Fairbanks/Galena/Nome/Uel'kal weather conditions. Jamrich had written on the board in Russian, "Flights not possible."

The 16th Weather Detachment, stationed at Ladd Field. John Jamrich is 3rd from the left in the front row.

The "lighter" side of service at Ladd Field.

In April 1945 a fire broke out in the WAAC's (Women's Army Auxiliary Corps) barracks at Ladd Field. One WAAC died jumping out of the second story window. Famous aviator and head of the WAAC program, Jackie Corcoran came to the field and gave all the "girls" new cosmetic bags. A new barracks was built in six weeks.
—Courtesy of Cecil Tucker

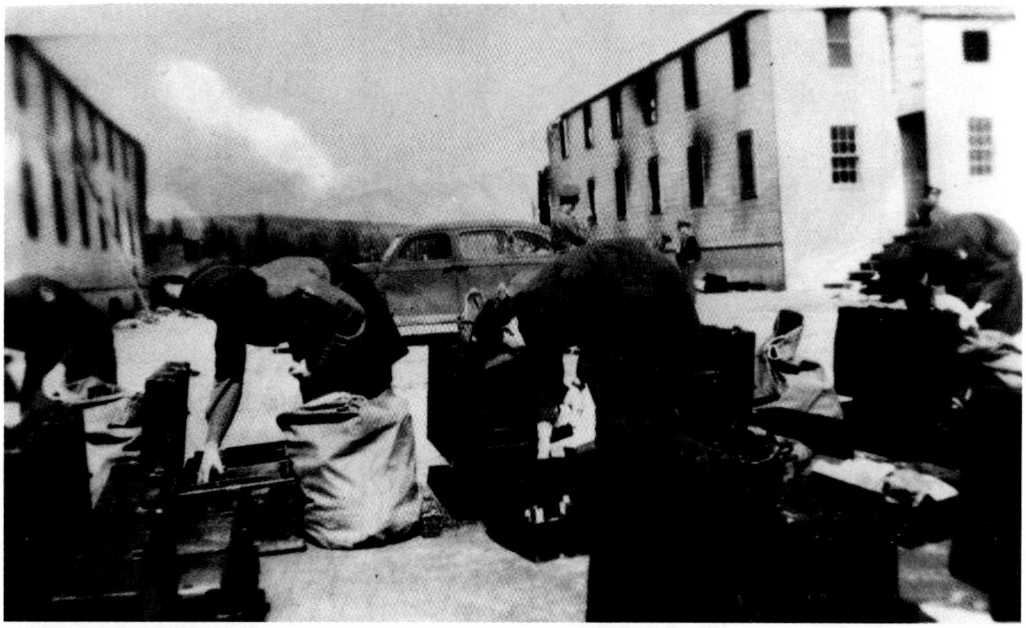

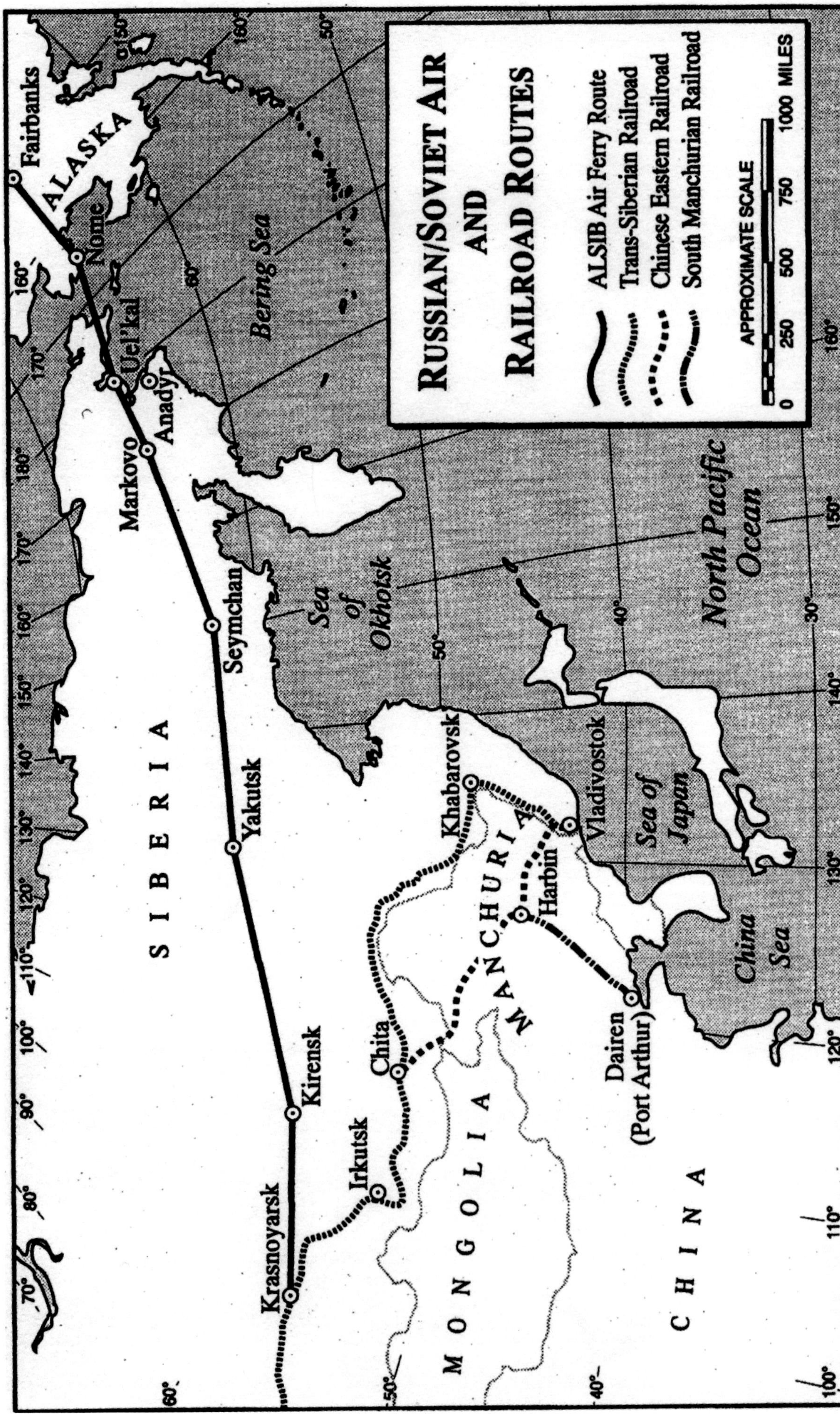
RUSSIAN/SOVIET AIR AND RAILROAD ROUTES
ALSIB Air Ferry Route
Trans-Siberian Railroad
Chinese Eastern Railroad
South Manchurian Railroad
APPROXIMATE SCALE
0 250 500 750 1000 MILES
ALASKA
Fairbanks
Nome
Uel'kal
Anadyr
Markovo
Seymchan
Yakutsk
Kirensk
Krasnoyarsk
Irkutsk
Chita
Khabarovsk
Vladivostok
Harbin
Dairen (Port Arthur)
SIBERIA
MONGOLIA
MANCHURIA
CHINA
Bering Sea
Sea of Okhotsk
North Pacific Ocean
Sea of Japan
China Sea

Captain Howard Hunt, 97, of Anchorage was a Lend-Lease pilot and a CB1 Theater veteran. He is the last World War Two pilot who flew the famous B-17 bomber, the Memphis Belle. *He stayed in aviation his entire career.* –Courtesy of Blaine Cornelison

Aerial photo of Marks Field with the city of Nome in the upper right. –Courtesy of Anne Millbrooke

This view of Ladd Field gives an idea of the huge amount of aircraft sent to Russia during the war. Over5,600 P-39 aircraft were sent up this route. –Courtesy of Anne Millbrooke

Both American and Russian troops manned the radio reception and transmission office. –Courtesy of Anne Millbrooke

In August 2006 officials from the United States, Canada, France and Russia participated in a ribbon-cutting ceremony in Fairbanks for a $600,000 bronze and granite Alaska-Siberia Lend-Lease Memorial. This project was started in 2001 by Alexander Dolitsky, chairman of the Alaska-Siberia Research Center. It was created by sculptor Richard Wallen and stone mason Alex Turner. Dolitsky was quoted at the ceremony stating: "From 1942 to 1945, the Alaska-Siberia Lend Lease program demonstrated that both nations could set aside different cultural values and principles to accomplish a common mutually beneficial goal to defeat Nazi Germany and its allies." It depicts both an American and Russian pilot. It is located at Griffin Park in Fairbanks.

Russia is In - - Looks Like We'll Be Busy

NORTH STAR

VOLUME 2 ALASKAN DIVISION, AIR TRANSPORT COMMAND, AUGUST 13, 1945 NUMBER 17

E. M. Speculate On Aldiv's Role

DIVISION HQ.—The long-expected and long-hoped-for declaration of war, loosing the titanic might of the Soviet Union against Japan, also loosed a flood of GI speculation as to the Alaskan Division's role against the one remaining Axis member.

At press time (Wednesday, Aug. 8) General Dale V. Gaffney, Division CG, was unavailable for comment, but two weeks earlier, at a press conference for Aldiv GI editors, he made the following off-the-record statement which can now be revealed:

"The future status of the Division depends upon developments in the Pacific. But in the near future we could be busier than ever."

When Lt. General Harold L. George, ATC's commanding general, visited the Alaskan Division last June he refused to predict the role the Division would play in the Pacific war; however, he told the NORTH STAR that "any increased activity along the Alaskan Division route will depend entirely on developments in the Pacific. A look at the map will disclose the possibilities of the route."

The Moscow radio announcement of the entry of powerful Russia into the Pacific war said Japan previously had appealed to the Soviet Union to act as mediator in the conflict.

Japan rejected the Potsdam ultimatum of July 26 by Britain

Division Dogfaces May Get

Editors Organize Press Association

CHAPTER EIGHT

AVIATION

A restored B-10 bomber at the National Museum of the US Air Force.

B-10 Army Air Corps bombers on a flight line for an inaugural flight to Alaska in the summer of 1934. The B-10 Martin bomber was designed and built by the Glenn L. Martin Company of Baltimore, MD in 1934 as the final improvement of several earlier prototypes. It was the first all metal monoplane bomber to be built and entered service in June 1934. It was the first mass-produced bomber, in total 348, whose performance was superior to the Army's pursuit aircraft of the time. It had two Pratt & Whitney engines and had a closed cockpit, rotating gun turrets, retractable landing gear, an internal bomb bay and full engine cowlings with a crew of three. Its maximum speed was 213 mph with a cruising speed of 193 mph, range of 1,240 miles, and a service ceiling of 24,200 feet. It had 3x30" Browning machine guns and a 2,260 pound bomb load. The only restored B-10 is on display at the National Museum of the US Air Force at Wright-Patterson AFB near Dayton, Ohio. It is painted in the original blue color that was used on the 1934 flight to Alaska.

General Henry "Hap" Arnold and Alaska

In 1934, Lt. Col. Henry "Hap" Arnold, later to lead the U. S. Army Air Forces during World War Two, won his second Mackay Trophy and a Distinguished Flying Cross for leading a flight of 10 Martin B-10 bombers from Bolling Field near Washington, D.C. to Fairbanks. The planes left the field on July 19th and landed five days later.

The purposes of the flight included identifying possible airfield locations and determining the possibility of deploying air units to Alaska in emergencies. The flight also demonstrated that flying over water between Seattle and Juneau, military aircraft could reach Alaska more directly and without flying over Canadian air space. The flight also showed the range of aircraft at the time had increased to the point that the United States could no longer depend on the Atlantic and Pacific oceans as barriers against foreign aggression.

The bombers were supported by Capt. Ross G. Hoyt of the War Plans Section of the U.S. Army Air Corps. He led two 0-38 aircraft flying in advance to Fairbanks and then later in July was dispatched to Nome to survey the potential for military airfields west of Fairbanks. Hoyt reported back that the only site suitable was at Nome. It would take until 1937 for land to be reserved for a field in Fairbanks, named Ladd Field and until 1941 for the CAA to begin construction of a field at Nome, later named Marks Field.

A rare restored B-18 on display at Castle AFB Museum in California. The medium bomber was designed in the 1930s by the Douglas Aircraft Company on their DC-2 model. It was to replace the Martin B-10 model which was flown in Alaska. By the early 1940s the B-18 was also obsolete. –Courtesy of Mark Strumsky

A Douglas B-18 Bolo bomber from the 73rd Bomber Squadron taxis up the landing strip, the first bomber to use the new facility at Yakutat, at the top of the Inside Passage. –Atwood Resource Center, Anchorage Museum at Rasmuson Center, b80-168-15

A Grumman Goose and a Stearman parked at the Juneau airfield in the early 1940s. –Courtesy of Robert Fleck

Headquarters Quonset hut in the foreground and the mess hall and tents in the background at the Kodiak Naval Air Base in 1943. –Courtesy of KHS, Joseph Bell Coll. P-453-6

The Canadian Para Rescue Service

During the war the RCAF operated #2 Air Observer School as part of the British Commonwealth Training Plan. Its general manager was former "bush" pilot, W.R. "Wop" May.

May was one of the most famous bush pilots in the North, primarily in northern Alberta, the Yukon and the Northwest Territories. He was born in 1896 in Manitoba and his family moved to Edmonton, Alberta in 1902. In 1916 he joined the Canadian Army, becoming a machine gun instructor but the next year he joined the Royal Flying Corps. In February 1918 he graduated as a First Lieutenant pilot and was posted to France. On April 1, 1918 "Wop" took part in the dogfight when Canadian pilot, Roy Brown shot down the famous German pilot, Baron von Richthofen.

May ended the war with 13 enemy aircraft downed and the Distinguished Flying Cross (DFC). He returned to Canada a hero and with his brother "Court "opened Canada's first registered aircraft company, "May Airplanes Ltd" in Edmonton. May flew all over central Alberta until 1924 when he got married and went to work for the National Cash Register Company, but he continued to fly and was president of Canada's first licensed flying club in Edmonton.

Five RCAF Pilots Lost in Unalaska

On July 26, 1942, while on route to Umnak from Cold Bay, the formation of seven RCAF airmen encountered bad weather and became disoriented –resulting in five of them killed when they crashed into a mountainside on Unalaska Island. An excerpt from the official debriefing report of P/O Eskil, one of the two surviving pilots from the formation:

After rounding Makushin Cape (Unalaska Island) and altering course to roughly follow the shoreline-weather became progressively worse. Fog banks and showers continually appeared to the north. We flew through several areas about 50 feet above the water. I could hear F/L Kerwin talking to Captain Fillmore (in an American C-53 support aircraft) intermittently but they seemed to be making very poor radio contact. I could not tune either one clearly....The air seemed clear near the water but visibility was very poor-much impeded by large areas of dense fog and showers. We were forced very near the water. ....we were forced right along the shore by a dense fog bank about 200 feet offshore. We were forced to about 20 feet from the water and I estimate the ceiling at about 50 feet. We were flying with the Wing Commander leading a "VIC" consisting of F/L Kerwin's section (with Maxmen) and Pilot Officer Whiteside's section (with Lennon) on the starboard of the Wing Commander, and my section (with Baird)) off the port. Sections were about three to four spans apart and ships in the sections slightly closer. F/Sgt Baird had overtaken me and slid over abruptly, forcing me to pass through his slipstream. We were very low and I dropped back slightly while righting my ship. As I was moving up to form on F/Sgt Baird's port wing, the Wing Commander ordered a turn to port. I was trailing the Wing Commander and Baird by 100 yards when the turn began. I was too low to drop into proper position for a turn and thus lost sight of all the other ships when I began my turn. I turned as tight and as low as I dared but sighted an aircraft well ahead of me cutting me off. Afraid that I would fly into the green beneath me I continued my turn and increased my throttle to about 37 Hg. My gyro horizon was out so I had trouble in maintaining a steep climb and turn. At about 500 feet freezing mist appeared on my windshield so I undid my harness and removed my oxygen and radio connections-intending to bail out if I stopped gaining height because of icing. At 4,800 feet I broke through between cloud layers, continued to turn and plugged in my radio....(After being momentarily disoriented by cloud and fog and making a couple of course adjustments). In a few minutes I ended up in what turned out to be the only hole in the area and sighted the Umnak air base....I phoned Captain Fillmore to clear me so I would not be fired on and preceded to land.

"Preflight Briefing" by Paul Goranson.
Image courtesy Canadian Armed Forces Collection

CAPTAIN ERNEST WALDO HICKOX joined the United States Army Air Corp in January of 1942 against the wishes of his family and over the objections that were inherent in his religion; he was a Quaker. He did so because Ernest was a patriot who was willing to make sacrifices in order to protect the freedoms he enjoyed and the country he loved. An excellent pilot, he became a flight instructor in Nov. 1942, serving at Mintor Field, Bakersfield, California. Assigned to the Aleutians in June 1944, he became a squadron leader who was trusted and respected by all who knew him. Captain Hickox loved his wife and daughter, and he loved flying his P-40 Warhawk; he called his plane the "Bonnie Kaye." A man of exceptional courage, loyalty, and conviction, he lived by his belief that "love is more important than fear." In July of 1945, after leading his squadron to safety in inclement weather, without landing, he continued flying to locate a lost flier and he completed a heroic rescue of one of the men in his squadron who had ditched into the sea. When attempting to return to base, Captain Hickox and his P-40 went down on the slopes of Mt. Makushin. He received the Soldier's Medal for Valor. Seventy years after the crash, Captain Hickox's P-40 Warhawk was recovered, salvaged, and restored. In January of 2017, it once again took to the air, and the epitaph he wrote as editor of the flight school yearbook for those pilots who had "flown west into the sunset" actually became a reality. He wrote:

> *"Your wings still shadow the earth and your engine's roar still fills the skies."*

Images this page courtesy Kaye Hickox

This article appeared in a wartime issue of *Cosmopolitan Magazine.*

Aleutian Patrol

How a young pilot and his Navy Patrol Wing accomplished an impossible task in the Aleutians

BY DONALD E. KEYHOE

FOR TWO hours, the big Navy Catalina had cruised through a gray murk that hid the Aleutians. It was four days since the Japs' first raid on Dutch Harbor. Somewhere beyond that curtain of fog an enemy surface fleet was still trying to land an invasion force.

In the pilot's cockpit young Lieutenant Bill Thies peered ahead through the mist. Every available plane from Patrol Wing Four was on the search. Twice contact had been made—and lost in the fog.

The ponderous PBY droned along under a fog-bank ceiling of barely two hundred feet. Suddenly a blur to starboard caught Thies' eye. He banked quickly, saw the long dark hull of a Jap submarine.

The Catalina was carrying 500-pounders that day. Safe release height, for a bomb that size, would have been at least 1,000 feet. But the fog was too thick. If he climbed, he would lose the sub. Thies nosed down, engines full on. He was less than 200 feet from the U-boat when a bomb went plunging down.

Thies zoomed just as the bomb hit. A terrific blast hurled the PBY upward, almost out of control. Fragments gashed the hull, tore a gaping hole in the port wing. Flame leaped out from ruptured gas and oil lines and the port engine went dead.

For an instant the plane seemed doomed. But by sheer luck a fragment had also cut the fire-extinguisher tube. Carbon dioxide streamed out and quenched the blaze. Flying on one engine, Thies and his crew nursed their crippled plane 400 miles back to Dutch Harbor.

Working night and day, the crew changed the port engine, repaired the wing and hull. In thirty-six hours, Thies and his men were back with Patrol Wing Four, searching for the Japs.

"Patwing 4" had been ready, flying armed patrols, on December 7, 1941. For months afterward, Thies and his comrades battled Arctic winter, trying to guard the Aleutians. They fought the blizzards, the williwaw—a freakish wind that can change direction in seconds, wrecking planes as they land or take off.

Finally the Japs came. Thies had been at Dutch Harbor on June third, when the Jap planes struck. Their calculations upset by strong Dutch Harbor defenses, the Japs had lost heavily, and the remaining planes had fled for their carriers. After them went Patwing 4.

But the Japs had chosen their weather too well. From fisherman-spies of prewar years they knew every vagary of the Aleutians. There was a vast blanket of fog over the area. Thies saw comrades fly into that gray murk, never to return. With others, he flew blind patrols, hour after hour, risking the fog-shrouded peaks in that desperate hunt for the enemy.

On one search with Patwing 4 he flew a sweep of more than a thousand miles in solid fog. The big Cats were armed with torpedoes and 1,000-pound bombs—a laborious job for ground crews with no loading equipment. The ceiling was less than fifty feet, and for 500 miles Thies flew ten feet above the water. There was no trace of the enemy fleet, and they turned back after searching at Kiska. For a while Thies and the other pilots kept an incredible formation through the mists, guiding on Aldis lights in the Patrol Wing leader's plane.

Official U. S. Navy Photos

Lt. Bill Thies and one of the PBY planes that fly the Aleutian patrol.

Then the ceiling closed down toward zero. Thies had to land, and quickly. He checked the map, made for a small bay of which he knew almost nothing. If he had climbed up, jettisoned his torpedo and bombs, no one would have blamed him, but torpedoes and bombs were too precious. Thies landed in murky blackness, with enough TNT under his wings to blow up a battleship. Next morning he took off and calmly went back to Dutch Harbor for another patrol.

It was not long in coming. Suddenly the radio at Kiska went dead. It could mean merely strafing—or it could mean invasion. Thies was ordered to find out.

There were low clouds above Kiska Harbor. Thies let down through them, and ran into a storm of antiaircraft fire. The sky was dark with flak. He took a swift look, saw five cruisers, eighteen destroyers and ten transports. With guns blazing at the Cat from every ship, he zoomed for the clouds.

Circling on top, he radioed a contact report to Dutch Harbor. Back came an order to bomb the enemy. Thies and his copilot looked at each other. The PBY's had never been designed for dive bombing. But horizontal bombing at that low altitude would be sheer suicide.

Thies found a hole in the clouds, dived through with wings howling. The PBY shuddered as the speed went up to 250 knots, and Thies breathed a prayer that the wings would stay on. Ack-ack fragments hit the wings, and bullets went through the plane. There was no time to use a bombsight. Four 500-pounders went hurtling down toward the nearest transport. Then both Thies and his copilot bent back on their controls for a four-handed pull-out.

The wings moaned, but held, and the Cat came out of its headlong dive. With more flak gashing the hull, the big plane climbed into the cloud layer.

The next day Patwing 4 began the "Kiska Shuttle." Every available plane was sent over with the brief order: Bomb the Japs. Thies and his crew made another trip that day. But when they came out below the clouds they ran into a swarm of Zero fighters. Thies pulled up on top of the clouds—and met another flight of Japs.

He ducked back into the clouds and made a measured run inside their protecting folds. At the precise moment he dived through, took aim at a Jap cruiser and let go the bombs. Again the copilot hauled back on the dual controls to help him pull out. The bombs struck near the cruiser, one apparently a hit. Thies had no time to make sure.

As they started back to Dutch Harbor, flying in the clouds, a radio message ordered Thies to evacuate five aerologists from Kanaga. The PBY's fuel was low, but he headed for the island.

When they arrived, the tide was out. Even at best, landing was difficult in the narrow bay. But Thies put down, took the five men aboard with their equipment. Battling a cross-wind, he got the overloaded plane off the water one second ahead of a crack-up on the rocks.

It was dark when they got back to their base on Atka. Thies found a tiny break in the clouds, made an instrument landing offshore and taxied into the harbor. But his troubles were not over. He still had to find a mooring buoy. And somewhere in the blackness of the harbor were jagged rocks which would sink them instantly. For three hours, Thies and his copilot taxied back and forth in the dark. At last they found the buoy.

But for the epic battle of Patwing 4 against overwhelming odds, Alaska might have fallen to the Japs. For his part in it, Thies was awarded the Navy Cross.

Others like Bill Thies were decorated for heroic action. But perhaps more valued even than their decorations was the message to Patwing 4 from the Commander in Chief of the Pacific Fleet which ended: "My personal thanks to all hands. I have every confidence you will continue to accomplish the impossible."

Accomplish the impossible. That was Patwing 4.

Buy U. S. War Bonds—$52.00 will buy 1 bombardier kit

C-O-N-F-I-D-E-N-T-I-A-L

HEADQUARTERS
FORT MEARS, ALASKA

July 19,1942

JAPANESE PLANE FOUND ON AKUTAN ISLAND

Nagoya Type Zero Fighter: Low wing, all metal, single seat monoplane, single engine, pronounced dihedral, flush riveting used throughout, well streamlined, shows excellent construction. plane nearly new. The plane is Zero type, No. 1, Carrier fighter plane, Model 2, put into service February 19, 1942.

FUSELAGE: About 23 feet long. Serial No. 4593.

WINGS: Pronounced dihedral, 40 feet wingspread, swept back on leading edge, about 24 inches of wing tips fold up for storage, split wing flaps, round wing tips; wings riveted solidly to fuselage. Wings 8 feet 3 inches wide where they join fuselage. Plane provided for bomb rack on each wing. When wing tips are horizontal, but not locked, a red tab projects to warn pilot. Much improvement is shown over our planes in the manner in which the lights on wings and tail are faired into the wing and tail.

TAIL: Horizontal tail fin has slight negative dihedral, and is placed above center of the fuselage. It is tapered on both edges, but mostly on the leading edge; about 6 feet 8 inches from fuselage to tip and 4 feet 9 inches wide next to the fuselage. The vertical fin is tapered about 45 degrees on leading edge.

ENGINE: Made by Nakajima, 14 cylinder, double row, air-cooled radial. Engine is fastened with four bolts. Quick change power plant assembly. Multi-explosion- type 12, No. 12885 (Nakajima). The engine has several improvements over our engines, namely drains, connections and engine mounting.

PROPELLER: 3 bladed, constant speed, spinner over propeller hub. Made by Sumitomo Metal Works Corporation, Propeller Manufacturing Plant.

LANDING GEAR: Retractable, hydralic system; when wheels are retracted, recess is covered with flaps; tire size, 600x175; tail wheel and arresting gear are retractable; tail wheel is solid rubber, about 6 inches in diameter.

ARMAMENT: Two 20 mm guns, one in each wing, about 60 rounds of ammunition for each; air-cooled, derived operating power by means of the Oerlikon method based on the "blow back" principle. Guns numbered serially, Gun No. 1464 differing from Gun No. 47 principally by change in types of ammunition chest mounts. Both guns similar to Navy Mk. IV, anti-aircraft type, 20 mm (Oerlikan), with the exception, the Japanese gun is considerably shorter in length and lighter. Operation is believed to be identical. The Japanese guns have a 30 inch barrel, pneumatic cocking device, pneumatic trigger motor, sturdy three-point suspension, a flash hider constructed as part of the barrel. Estimated muzzle velocity is 1800 fs. Ammunition stored in a sixty round container similar to ours. Ammunition was similar to our 20 mm, although the cartridge case was considerably shorter and the type of fuse was different. Several types of ammunition were known to be used. Although the guns examined were exposed to severe climatic conditions for almost five weeks, no signs of corrosion were evident. The guns gave every indication of precise workmanship and extremely careful maintenance, favorably comparing in design and construction with those used by our forces.

(1) Type: 99, No.1 Fixed, Revision 1. # 1464, Fukoka Arsenal.
(2) Type: 99, No.1 Fixed, Make 2. Toyo 47, January 1942, Toyokawa Arsenal, Toyo 47.

Two 7.7 mm recoil operated guns, synchronized to fire through propeller; 500 rounds per gun; guns are type 97, made by Nippon Manufacturing Corporation; fixed machine gun type 3, revision 2. 1942. Three sizes and shapes of 7.7 ammunition, loaded in the following manner: 1 tracer, 1 armor piercing, 1 incendiary, 1 armor piercing, 1 tracer. The tracer is semi-boat tailed. Others have square bases, but are not same size or shape. Cartridges are about 1/4 inch shorter than .3006, and wider at base. They are not rimless. The primer is much larger than ours, and is made with two firing points inside. The jacket is cupro-nickel. The cartridge will chamber in M 1, but will not fire because of rim and wide base. One bullet examined had flaw where jacket was incomplete.

Equipped with electric gun sight; No. 150; Showa 16, month 12 (December), 1941, manufactured Sendaida Optical Works Corp.

GAS TANKS: Detachable plywood belly tank, streamlined, about 18 inches in diameter and 6 feet long. It is divided into compartments with splash boards, and sets nearly flush against plane. It is fastened with one casting just aft of the landing gear. Apparently the belly tank holds only about half of its rated capacity of 160 gallons.

There is a gas tank of welded and riveted aluminum in each wing, believed not to be leakproof. Tanks were made by the Heavy Industries Corporation, Nagoya Aircraft Manufacturing Plant. Number of manufacture, 4468; Number of article, 2182; Weight, 9.5 kilograms; Capacity, 202.0 litres; Pressure, (?) 0.14 kilograms/ 2 centimeters.

ARMOR: No armor on any part of the plane.

COCKPIT: Single seat, pilot strapped to seat in three places, no armor; cockpit cover resembles plexiglass. No automatic flight control. Plate inside cockpit has following information: Place of manufacture--Mitsubishi (?) Heavy Industries Company, Nagoya Aircraft Manufacturing Plant. Name--Zero type, Model type A6M2. Engine--Nakajima Mk 1. Weight--1715.0 kilograms; carrying capacity, 650.3; entire weight, 2365.3 kilograms. Year, date, month of completion--1942, 19 February, and the inspector's stamp.
*(Note by CO VF-41, No XFC. Directional gyro and Art. bouyon only)

②

RADIO: Two-way radio; radio mast aft of cockpit is máde of streamlined wood, hollow, with copper wire inside. 96 Type air, No. 1, wireless voice transmitter, type 1. Receiver No. 976, 1942 January. Manufactured by Toyo Electric Corporation.

The radio compass was made by Fairchild Aero Camera Co., New York City. Aerial #429. Loop located in pilot enclosure, just in back of pilot's seat. Controls located on right side of cockpit. L or K meter located on instrument dash board. This equipment looked as though it had been used before it was installed in this plane. Frequency range, 170 to 460 and 450 to 1200 KC. Switch was in the 450 to 1200 KC position when gear was removed. The generator taken from the Fairchild Radio Compass was an Eclipse, made in the United States.

ENGINE OIL TANK: Manufacturer's No. 3452; Weight, 7.40 kilograms; Capacity, 60.0 litres; Pressure (?) 10.30 kilograms/ 2 centimeters.

AILERON: 130 inches long; 16 1/2 inches wide next to the fuselage, 8 inches wide at outside end. All control surfaces are of fabric.

BOMB LOAD: Place provided for bomb rack on each wing.

INSIGNIA: Insignia on top and bottom of wings; also on both sides of fuselage, these are much brighter than those on the wings; yellow stripe around after part of fuselage.

PARACHUTE: Type 97 (1937) parachute, model 2; No. of manufacturer, 1490853; Manufactured, 1939, September 9, at Fujikura Heavy Industries Corporation.

PILOT'S CLOTHING: Had registration No. 2475; Name, Yoshita, Chugi or Masao; Issued May, 1940 at Yokosuka Naval Supply Depot.

NCO Pilot Officer Tadayoski Koga, circled.

A16-3 (027)

United States Pacific Fleet
Patrol Wings
Patrol Squadron Forty-one

by

Comm. in Chief
U.S. Fleet
c/o Postmaster
Seattle, Washington
22 July,1942

CONFIDENTIAL

From: Commander Patrol Squadron FORTY-ONE.
To: The Chief of Naval Operations.
Via: Commander Patrol Wing FOUR.

Subject: Salvage of Japanese Nagoya Type Zero plane discovered at Akutan Island 10 July 1942.

Reference: (a) OpNav desp. 162214 of July 1942.
(b) Compatron 41 conf. ltr L21 (028) dated 22 July
(c) Compatron 41 airmailgram 181000 of July 1942/42

Enclosure: (A) Set 14 photographs showing salvage of plane and details of guns.
(B) Copy Fort MEARS G-2 report sent CGADC.

1. On 10 July 1942 a member of the flight crew with Lt. W.N. THIES, A-V(N), U.S.N.R. when returning from a tactical patrol sighted a small crashed Japanese plane on its back on the southwest side of AKUTAN Island. From its size it was believed to be a Zero type Navy fighter. Lieutant Thies returned, reported his discovery and immediately was placed in charge of a party to investigate and salvage such parts of the plane as were of intelligence value. The party was transported to the nearest beach on Akutan Island by YP-151.

2. After considerable struggle the plane was found in a high valley about a mile amd a half from the beach in a soft marshy land. It is believed that the crash occurred on or about 4 July 1942, the date of the last raid on Dutch Harbor. The pilot apparently attempted to make a normal wheels-down, flaps-down stall landing in the soft ground, skidded along for a short distance carrying away the landing gear, damaging flaps, and belly tank, and going over on his back, in which position he skidded somewhat farther damaging the wing tips, vertical stabilizer and trailing edge of the rudder. The plane was resting with the fuselage and engine half-buried in the knee-deep mud and water. The pilot's head and shoulders were submerged in water.

3. The pilot's body, in its decayed state, was first removed. This was very difficult owing to the boggy ground and the two safety belts and rudder stirrups which held him in place. With fifteen men assisting, it was possible to raise the tail of the plane only slightly. To release the safety belts it was finally necessary to cut through the side of the fuselage. Each time this was done unexpected equipment was encountered, making it necessary to cut again. Eventually the body was removed and carefully examined for insignia, markings, etc., of intelligence value. The label on the uniform was removed, as also were various other articles of clothing. Nothing was found in the pock-

ets. The local Japanese interpreter believes that the pilot was a Lieutenant Commander (air?) Yoshita (first name obscure but believed to be Masao or Chugi), the yellow band around the fuselage of the plane bears out the fact he was a group leader. He was buried with simple military honors and Christian ceremony near the scene of the accident.

4. In addition to the articles mentioned above, a transparent plastic folder of several leaves was found secured around the pilot's neck. This contained: (a) pictures of the latest U.S. Army and Navy planes, (b) simple Japanese Voice Code, (c) engine power curve, (d) simple graph for drift determination, (e) Japanese Panel Code (obscured). All had been submerged in water. The writing had been partially obliterated since the ink and photographic chemicals used in making them were soluble in water, apparently for security purposes. The cards were read by the local Japanese interpreter and forwarded with interpretation to the Office of Naval Intelligence via Commander Patrol Wing Four. It is believed that the plane was assigned to the carrier RYUJO.

5. The 20 mm guns, optical reflector gun sight and certain small articles were removed for immediate attention. It was then found that the condition of the plane warranted attempts to recondition and flight test it. It was also discovered that the wings were integral with the fuselage, making the salvage extremely complicated. At this time the press of other operations necessitated recalling the salvage party to Dutch Harbor.

6. On 12 July 1942 the second salvage party, with Lieutenant R.C. KIRMSE, A-V(N), U.S.N.R. in command, equipped with heavy salvage equipment and a heavy tractor started for Akutan Beach. In this second salvage party the Commanding Officer of Naval Air Station, Dutch Harbor arranged for the services of an experienced rigger, Mr. Jerry LUND, attached to the Siems Drake Construction Company. The services of Mr. Lund were invaluable, He was later placed in charge of the third salvage party. While attempting to unload the gear onto the beach, the "Mary Anne" carried away two anchors and was forced to return to Dutch Harbor without having landed the tractor. After working for two days under great difficulties in knee-deep mud and by working on plywood "islands", the salvage party managed to lift the engine of the plane partly out of the mud by means of a suitably placed "high lift". A prefabricated skid made of 6" x6" timbers was assembled on the spot, but it was found that the plane was too heavy to get onto the skid without a winch. It was again necessary to return to Dutch Harbor for more suitable equipment.

7. On 15 July the third party, Mr. Lund in charge, left in YP-72, taking a barge, medium-sized bulldozer fitted with a winch, a second and heavier prefabricated sled and with considerable gear and lumber. The "Mary Anne" was determined unsuitable for this trip. The plan was to land the bulldozer from the barge through the surf, bulldoze a sort of road a mile-and-a-half up a small riverbed to the plane's position. All material had to be dragged up to the spot and assembled. With the "high lift" in place the

(2)

engine was hoisted out of the plane and placed on a skid. The plane was then lifted, still in the upsidedown position, and placed on a similar skid. During these operations the tripods sank three to four feet into the mud. The two sleds were dragged laboriously down to the beach, fording two three-foot streams enroute. It was then necessary to drag the skids through the surf and onto the lighter. This difficult feat was accomplished without further damage to the plane.

8. On arrival at Dutch Harbor 18 July 1942 the plane was righted and carefully guarded while being cleaned. Certain additional parts were removed for preservation. In spite of special guards and precautions it was found almost impossible to anticipate every whim of souvenir hunters and for that reason the cleaning was kept to the minimum. Crating of the plane and parts was accomplished as rapidly as possible while awaiting suitable Navy transportation.

9. It was possible, however, to recondition the machine guns optical reflector, gun sight, the pilot's parachute, most instruments, radio equipment and landing gear aerol struts. The engine and propellor were carefully cleaned and all water removed from the engine cylinders, Several cylinders exposed to water show some rusting, but most are in excellent condition. It was found that the oil scavenger line had been severed by a bullet and considerable oil lost, however, the engine can be turned freely by hand. It is regretted that the pneumatic system used in conjunction with the 20 mm guns could not be removed for shipment with the ordnance gear since it would have necessitated considerable disassembly of the plane. This may be done by a better qualified agency.

10. The plane's construction with wings integral with the fuselage interposed a difficult problem of crating. The resulting crate dimensions are such that rail shipment will probably be impractable, Accordingly, it is recommended that reconditioning and reassembly be accomplished at the Naval Air Station, Seattle, Washington. Shipping details are given in reference (b).

11. The essential data concerning this plane has already been forwarded by airmailgram, reference (c), and additional data by enclosure (B). The fuel rating is given as 92 octane, power curves have not been interpreted. No leak proofing, armor protection, destructor devices, IFF or similar equipment was discovered.

12. The plane will necessitate considerable repair, but it is believed entirely pracable to rebuild and flight test it.

PAUL FOLEY Jr.

cc: Buaer
CinCus
CinCpac
Comnorweseafron
Comalsec
CompatwingPac
CompatplanerepronPac
NAS Dutch Harbor
NAS San Diego

VS-49 pilots in the Aerology room at Ft. Mears at Dutch Harbor getting weather reports.
–Courtesy of ASL-P338-1663. H. Marion Thornton photo

A B-29 bomber, apply named Klondike Kutey at Ladd Field in Fairbanks, Jan. 17, 1945. It was thought that possibly the Superfortruss could be used from the Aleutians to bomb mainland Japan, but by this time more Pacific islands had been captured or were ready for invasion, and they would be closer to the targets and not have to fight the variable weather conditions.

William Thies, Captain, US Navy Retired

On June 9, two days after our weather station went off the air at Kiska, I was ordered to fly out there to investigate. Jim Bowers has earlier reported unidentified ships in Kiska Harbor. When we arrived, we spent about an hour five miles east of the harbor, first sending an "enemy contact report," then a lengthy "amplifying" message. That done, we had nearly reached Amchitka on the way "home" when Wing Commander Gehres sent me a plain language radio messge from Kodiak to "bomb enemy shipping Kiska Harbor." We returned to Kiska and scored a hit on a transport under heavy AA fire, for which I was awarded the Navy Cross and all other crew members were awarded the Distinguished Flying Cross. Theis was also the first to find the crashed Japanese Zero (Koga's Zoro) on Akutan Island.

Reminiscences of W. H. Squires of VP-62

On May 30, 1944 I was on a patrol in my PBY 46V from my base on Amchitka out of VP-62, on a northwest sector into the Bering Sea when a fuel line broke in the superstructure of the wing. Fifteen hundred gallons of gas dumped into the interior of my plane.

I was several miles north of Kiska when this happned and immediately contacted my home base with an "O" and "May Day," giving them my position and then I dumped my depth charges and made a U-turn back toward Kiska. Then I ditched the PBY about a half a mile off of Srednie Point on the east coast of Kiska.

I made a poor landing and knocked out a few rivets in the hull and the plane slowly sank. I had a crew of 10 men and we crammed into a seven-man life raft. A second raft failed to inflate. We were discovered by a standby PBY and rescured by the seaplane tender, *USS Arocet.*

VP-62 was the first patrol squadron to get to the Aleutians before the Japanese invasion. A PBY was on patrol about 500 miles south of Amchitka on Dec. 6, 1942. The pilot found the "Lost Japanese Fleet" and reported it by radio to his home base. He made a "contact report" naming four carriers, six cruisers, a dozen destroyers and many other ships. Fifteen mintues later he reported the same, amplified, plus course and speed.

Of course, the whole thing was a case of "mass hysteria" and there was nothing there at all. When the plane returend to base it observed the American fleet, consisting of a couple of destroyers and mine sweepers. Later the FBI, military intelligence and other authorities nearly court-marshal the plane's commander and crew. The commander was sent back to Washington and the crew to other squadrons.

In 1922 Squires was returning from a Carribean cruise. He was standing in line waiting to go through customs when he noticed a man benind him wearing a baseball cap with the Navy wings on it. It turned out that the man was in VP-62 but with the original group before Squires arrived and was the radioman who sent in the report about the Japanese fleet.

Charles Fitzpatrick

Charles Fitzpatrick served as an aviator with Bombardment Squadron 136, Fleet Air Wing 4, flying a PV-1 Vega Ventura bomber from Attu to Paramushiro in the Kurlie Islands of northern Japan in 1944-45. The 800 miles each way was the longest over water bomber flight of the war.

On his way back to the lower 48 on March 17, 1945 his PV-1 had to ditch off of Kodiak Island near the village of Karluk. It was about 9:30 p.m. and there was a crew of six and one passenger. They would all have drowned in the icy waters if it had not been for a missionary who was walking across a bridge from the main island to a "spit" where the cannery was, and saw the aircraft sink beneath the sea, with the landing light somehow stuck and showing through the water. The plane only had a four-man raft on board. The missionary gathered some Native boys and managed with difficulty, through rough seas, to rescue everyone on board. —Courtesy Mrs. Charles L. Fitzpatrick, Baltimore, MD

THE ALEUTIAN CAMPAIGN'S BIGGEST AIR BATTLE

TOLD BY ROBERT H. MURRAY, SEATTLE, WASHINGTON

During the Battle of Attu, Japanese twin-engine "Betty" bombers from Paramushiro attacked the American forces on the island on May 22-23, 1943, the first such raid of the war. Fighter patrols were sent out soon afterwards to intercept the enemy aircraft if they should try it again. I was on one of the May 23 flights, a formation of six P-38s of the 54th Fighter Squadron led by Col. Watt of the 11th Air Force Fighter Command.

"We were not completely surprised when the command post aboard the battleship *Pennsylvania* gave us vectors to an incoming flight of enemy planes upon our arrival over Attu, 260 miles west of our base on Amchitka. As was frequently the case in those days, my VHF radio wasn't working and I learned all the radio conversation from the survivors after the fight. Although I missed out on the radio chatter, I knew something was up when the drop tanks fell away and Watt went to full stick, pulling his nose into a steep climb. The use of full throttle tended to break up what had been a tight formation. When I spotted the flight of "Bettys" high overhead I guessed that they were at about 20,000 feet and as I struggled to get my oxygen mask on I fell farther out of formation."

"It was a fine spring day in the Aleutians with a nearly solid overcast at about 5,000 feet around Attu which became broken to scattered to clear as we flew west of the island on our pursuit of the enemy. I passed through a cloud in the climb and when I emerged the "Bettys" were hightailing it to the west and left of my position. The other P-38s, except for Hyde who was unable to keep up with the action because of engine trouble, were to the left of the "Bettys."

"During the chase I saw the remarkable sight of the entire jettisoned bomb load of the Japanese formation exploding in the water. The pattern of the geysers was identical to the formation of the bombers which was generally lined abreast. I charged my guns and, firing a test burst, was dismayed to find my 20mm was taking the day off. We carried HE (high explosive) rounds in the big gun and were told never to charge the piece in flight since forcing a round behind a jammed round could result in blowing the nose off the aircraft. I ignored the advice and made several attempts to charge the 20mm in the tail turrets and I was pretty unhappy that it was going to be my .50 caliber against their 20mm. (20mm had about four times the energy of .50 caliber)."

"As I made my first pass I found out why they were lined abreast. As I sucked in behind the enemy formation in my curve of pursuit, 16 20mm guns picked me up and fired those huge tracers right at my frail body. Warren Banks later described the tracers as being bigger than basketballs! As I learned later, Watt was shot down and lost in his first pass and shortly after Geddes became hors de combat but ditched and was rescued by the Navy."

"It was pretty exciting and my memory isn't clear about all the passes I made except for the first and last. I do recall seeing a P-38 in a big barrel roll during the heat of the battle and I thought that there was a guy who was really enjoining himself! (Probably Warren Banks). The Japanese were slowly descending to increase their speed and take advantage of what clouds they could find. I recall seeing one of the bombers in a slow spiral with dense smoke trailing one nacelle."

"My last pass was spectacular. The flight had moved far to the west (we had probably flown into the next day since Attu is only about 100 miles east of the International Date Line), and into nearly clear air with a few fair weather cumulus. As I tried to work forward for a high side attack the formation disappeared into a cloud. I continued climbing and entered the cloud. After flying needle-ball-and-airspeed for what seemed an hour I broke out directly above the Japanese formation. I rolled over and dove on the leader, getting in a long burst and then finding myself in a screaming dive with the North Pacific looking awfully close. After I recovered I took a look around and counted 12 "Bettys" and no P-38s. There had always been a lot of controversy about numbers of aircraft in this engagement. For example, I counted 16 "Bettys" before we got our shots off."

"At this point I was feeling very lonesome and far from home. I was then 350 miles from the nearest strip and I had been at full throttle on internal fuel for more than half an hour. I waved goodbye to my friends in the "Bettys" and turned to the east. I climbed up to cloud base and scanned the horizon for an island but there wasn't any. Oops, which way is home?"

"We had two navigational aids besides dead reckoning at that time: we could call ground control for a radar steer using our IFF (Identify Friend or Foe) transponder but my VHF was inoperable; we also had a Detrola set which was a receiver for the low frequency radio range. I turned up the Detrola and got nothing but static; it turned out that the people in charge of the air operations had commanded radio silence during the air raid."

"At this point I remembered getting the sun in my eyes on the first pass so I put the sun on my right wing and flew along for a while leaning out the engines a little more every time I thought about it. My efforts were rewarded by Attu coming up over the horizon and as I came up to Massacre Bay with the North Pacific fleet lying safe at anchorage I spotted our great big B-24 aircraft circling and waiting for me. I neglected to mention that the third navigational aid the 11th Air Force provided its fighters was a B-24 navigational escort for missions thought too difficult for the limited navigational skill of the fighter pilot."

"There was no sign of any P-38s. I thought maybe the other guys had got turned around and were wandering in the Pacific with no way to find home. So I headed back to Amchitka without waiting for the B-24 knowing that I could make much better time alone and maybe get the radio range stations back on the air in time to help my friends find their way home. As it turned out, Banks and Moore got back safely without my help. Unfortunately, Warren Banks was killed in a weather situation flying out of Alexi Point on Attu later that year."

"We were told in 1943 that a U.S. Navy submarine lying offshore at Paramushiro had witnessed the departure of the "Bettys" and radioed that information to Amchitka which led to our scramble. We were also told that the sub had observed the return of only four bombers to their base which led to the award of seven probables to the squadron in addition to the five victory credits awarded. I was surprised that I was given credit for a kill. All I had told the intelligence people in S-2 was that I had seen a bomber burning and descending-I never said that this was the result of my fire. I was pretty badly scared during the engagement and somewhat demoralized at not having the big gun working. All my firing was at pretty high deflections once I had got a taste of the Japanese tail cannons. Go look at GSAP (gunsight aiming point camera) and you see that most definite kills were made from dead astern. After my first pass I made every effort to avoid that position."

Information of the other four-ship flight was related by Dan Lange of St. Louis, MO. "I was involved on a small scale which I'll not forget. It started when I was awakened about 4a.m. by a flashlight in my face. Harley Tawlks, gave me 10 minutes to meet down in operations saying, "A large flight of Japanese bombers is on its way to attack our ships and men on Attu." No time for help from our mechanics, and my plane was an older P-38 without a climb –on ladder. The only other way to get up to the cockpit was to pull the tail down and walk the boom, now wet and slippery from the dew and fog. I fell off twice, but finally made it on the third try! I remember our flight of four included our C.O. Harley Tawlks and two other pilots. We circled Attu for about an hour until relieved by Higgins' flight which included Col. Watt, John Geddes, Fred Moore and Bill Banks."

Higgins

CONFIDENTIAL

FIELD HEADQUARTERS ELEVENTH AIR FORCE
APO #980, c/o Postmaster
Seattle, Wshington

GENERAL ORDERS)
:
NUMBER 82)

July 1, 1943

COMMENDATION AND VICTORY CREDITS

Under the provisions of AR 600-55, the following commendation is published:

1. On May 23, 1943, a flight of six P-38's of the 54th Fighter Squadron, led by Lieutenant Colonel JAMES RICHARD WATT, 0361717, the Commanding Officer of the 343rd Fighter Group, while flying a defensive patrol in the vicinity of Attu Island in support of friendly occupation forces, engaged a force of sixteen enemy Mitsubishi 01 medium bombers (Bettys), during the period 1630 to 1700 bering War' Time. Commencing over Attu, the combat continued southwest of that Island as the enemy formation fled desperately toward Paramushiru.

2. As a result of the running combat, at least five of the enemy planes were seen to burst into flames and fall into low hanging clouds out of control. Seven additional planes were seen to go into the clouds in uncontrolled dives, smoking, and were probably destroyed. Lieutenant MOORE, the last pilot to break off combat reported that only four enemy planes were left in the enemy formation when he left it and turned back toward Attu.

3. One P-38 had supercharger failure on one engine and was unable to enter the combat. The five remaining planes were piloted by Lieutenant Colonel JAMES RICHARD WATT, 0361717; Second Lieutenant FREDERICK (NMI) MOORE, 0663076; Second Lieutenant WARREN BURNETT BANKS, 0736071; Second Lieutenant HARRY CLARK HIGGINS, 0732246; and Second Lieutenant JOHN KENNEDY GEDDES, 0662642. Lieutenant Colonel WATT is credited with one of the five enemy planes definitely shot down, First Lieutenant MOORE with three and Second Lieutenant Higgins with one. The remaining seven "probables" can be credited to no one pilot since the engagement was purely flight combat and all five pilots contributed to the resultant victory.

4. As a result of the enemy's defensive fire, one P-38 piloted by Second Lieutenant GEDDES was damaged and forced to land in the waters of Massacre Bay, Attu. He used his one man life raft and was rescued shortly thereafter by a Navy Kingfisher float plane. Lieutenant Colonel WATT broke off combat about twenty-five minutes Southwest of Attu, was heard to say that he had been hit and was turning back, and was not again seen or heard from.

5. The 54th Fighter Squadron and the 343rd Fighter Group are deserving of the highest praise. From May 23, 1943 until this date the enemy has not again dared to take offensive air action against our forces at Attu.

By command of Major General BUTLER:

JOHN V. HART,
Colonel, G. S. C.,
Chief of Staff.

OFFICIAL:

s/ ORVAL A. KORF
t/ ORVAL A. KORF,
Major, A. G. D.,
Adjutant General.

A TRUE COPY: Abraham Peskin
ABRAHAM PESKIN,
1st Lt., Air Corps,

CONFIDENTIAL

Lt. Colonel John S. Chennault, son of the well-known Claire Z. Chennault, commander of the famous "Flying Tigers" of the China-Burma-India Campaign, was the original commanding officer of the 11th Fighter Squadron as a 1st Lieutenant. Within a seven month period he was promoted three times, to Lt. Colonel and commander of the 343rd Fighter Group. –Courtesy of KHS OP-608-14-1

Warhawk fighter, of the 11th Fighter Squadron, with the famous tiger reproduction, as was used in the CBI Theater, sits on the apron at Adak in 1943. –Courtesy of KHS OP-608-15-2

Flying officers of the 11th Fighter Squadron sit and stand on and by a P-40 Warhawk, Adak, 1943. –Courtesy of KHS OP-608-18-1

A Martin B-26 Marauder bomber at Adak. The bomber came on line in 1942 and was used in every theater of operations during the war. It had a crew of seven, a maximum speed of 317 m.p.h., a ceiling of 23,000 feet and a range of 1,159 miles with six machine guns and 3,000 pounds of bombs. –Courtesy of Daniel P. Faas

Beachcraft C-45 used for surveys on the Alaska Highway 1942.

Restoration of a U.S. Army Air Forces B-26 Marauder Bomber

Three B-26s took off from Edmonton, Alberta on Jan. 16, 1942 for a thousand mile flight to Whitehorse, Yukon. The final destination was Elmendorf Field in Anchorage where they would be used for the defense of Alaska. The planes carried a full allotment of fuel, but exhausted most of it after running into foul weather. Knowing they couldn't make it to Whitehorse the pilots agreed to a forced landing in a shallow valley near the Smith River and the headwaters of the Grayling River in northern British Columbia, about 90 miles southeast of Watson Lake, Yukon.

Two planes crashed on their bellies, ripping the underside of the aircraft, but not injuring the crews. The third aircraft put down its landing gear to slow its air speed, but the gear snagged a clump of bushes as it was heading to a semi-flat area. The plane, swing at a 90-degree angle to the left and crashed nose first into the ground. The two pilots were injured, but the rest of the crew survived.

On January 18 a flight of P-40s, led by 1st Lt. John S. Chennault, going north spotted the downed crews, The next day a 1920s high-wing Fokker aircraft landed at the crash site and took out the two injured pilots. The rest of the crews had to wait for days until they were guided down to a frozen lake where they too, where picked up and flown to Alaska.

In April 1942, the Air Force retrieved all the parts that could be stripped from the three B-26s and transported them to Elmendorf Field for use as spare parts. At this early stage of the war, crews had to fly with shorter daylight, no maps other than some pencil sketches and the wartime restrictions that prohibited the use of operating radio beacons, radio ranges of navigational aids. This was due to the widespread fear that the enemy might use them for bombing purposes. The flight had no weather reports and the sextant used by a celestial navigator soon proved useless. All these things would add up to a potential dangerous situation if bad weather was encountered, which did happen.

The crash site was in an area known as the "Million Dollar Valley" because of all the aircraft that crashed there during the war. In September 1971 a group from the Military Aircraft Restoration Corp. of Chino, CA went to the valley to retrieve the three B-26s and bring them out by helicopter with what was left of them. It was a tough job to take apart the remaining pieces, especially since they had landed in a frozen swamp. It took about three weeks to get the planes ready for lifting by a huge Sikorsky S-58T helicopter out to a deserted airstrip along the Smith River. Trucks hauled the parts down to Fort Nelson, BC and finally put on railroad cars for the long journey down to Ontario, CA and then on trucks again for the final 15 miles to the restoration shop in Chino.

Crews would work on the three aircraft as time and resources permitted for the next 19 years. On May 2, 1991, #40-1464 flew again. One of those on hand to watch was Howard F. Smiley, its co-pilot on its last flight. Sections of the other two eventually were sent to the MAPS Museum in North Canton, OH.

A Douglas SBD-5 Dauntless. The plane still has its tail hook stripes on its tail which was used by the carrier landing signal officer to line up the wings on approach to a carrier landing.

Russian-built PBY Catalina flying boat over Nome in September 1941. These were used to ferry Russian pilots to Nome from Siberia to pick up Lend-Lease aircraft.

B-17B and a Grumman G-44 Widgeon, five passenger, twin-engine amphibious plane at Adak, 1942. The Widgeon was a "little brother" of the Grumman family of flying boats-the Goose, the Mallard and the Albatross.

B-18 bomber flying to Juneau.

Members of Scouting Squadron VS-48 of the Fleet Air Arm returning home in September 1945. They are on the USS Teal AVP-5. Its normal capacity was at 65 but about 100 were on board. There were cots on the fantail and men slept wherever they could find room.

NORTH AMERICAN SETS THE PACE
...in the Aleutians
(One of a series describing North American planes in action on the battlefronts of the world)
MITCHELL BOMBERS SINK ALEUTIAN JAPS
ATTU and Kiska were a costly speculation for the Japs, thanks in large measure to North American B-25 Mitchell bombers and other hard-hitting Army and Navy planes.
On this front—as in Africa, China, the South Pacific and over Europe—"North American Sets the Pace"—with damaging blows at enemy ships, planes, land installations. In desert heat or Aleutian fog, the Mitchell has proved its versatility and striking power with each passing day of global air war.
We're proud of this record, but prouder still that we're building better, more deadly Mitchell bombers in greater numbers every day. It's our way of helping to win this war—sooner.
NORTH AMERICAN AVIATION, INC.
INGLEWOOD, CALIFORNIA
DALLAS · KANSAS CITY
Member, Aircraft War Production Council, Inc.
P-51 MUSTANG
B-25 MITCHELL
AT-6 TEXAN
Army-Navy "E" Flag awarded to California and Texas Divisions
NORTH AMERICAN
Sets the Pace!
ARMY E NAVY

— CHAPTER NINE—

NAVAL ACTIVITY

The USS Pensacola *CA-2 in Massacre Bay, Attu on June 9, 1944. The ship was a heavy cruiser, the lead ship of the Pensacola Class built at the New York Navy Yard and launched in 1939 at a cost of $11 million and commissioned on Feb.6, 1930. It went west to the Pacific Fleet in 1943 and took part in several island battles until April 25, 1943 when it set sailed for Alaska and arrived at Kulak Bay on Kodiak Island on May 27. On June 13, 1943 it joined the cruiser-destroyer task force for duty bombarding the Malsuwa airfield in the Kurlie Islands of northern Japan. It continued to patrol Alaskan waters until departing Kulak Bay on Aug. 8, 1943 for Hawaii where it took part in the battles for Iwo Jima and Okinawa, then back for overhaul to Mare Island, CA. It sailed again for Adak in the Aleutians where it was at the end of the war. The ship was decommissioned on Aug. 25, 1945 and was part of Operation Crossroads, the Atomic bomb tests in the Pacific and survived, finally sunk off of the Washington State coast in 1948.* –Courtesy of USN 97839

HMCS PRINCE ROBERT

HMCS Prince Robert united with other Canadian warships at the Esquimalt Naval Base on Vancouver Island, British Columbia for modernization, plastic bridge armor, elementary Asdic (anti-submarine equipment), primitive radar and several Oerlikon 20mm guns. Its mission was to guard focal shipping points in the Northwest Pacific, particularly off of British Columbia; to patrol sheltered waters where enemy vessels might hide along the coast; to reassure the public by their presence in the absence of other warships; to obviate American pressure on the sparse Canadian Naval forces in the area and to make credible publicized threats against the enemy.

Whatever the potential dangers of the program, the appearance of success is that no enemy patrols were detected off the British Columbia coast for the rest of the war except for a Japanese submarine surfacing near Nootka lighthouse and getting off a few rounds at some isolated cabins. In June 1942 the ship was ordered to cooperate with U. S. forces being transported to Kodiak, which served as a base for the recapture of Attu and Kiska. In August she sailed for Dutch Harbor. For two months the escort duties covered the 350 miles of the open sea between the islands. No enemy forces were encountered. She returned to patrol duty in mid-November.

REMEMBRANCES OF MIKE HYRAWAY OF THE CANADIAN NAVY

It was in the spring of 1942–there were three ships–*Prince David* (flagship), *Prince Robert* and *Prince Henry*. All three were auxiliary cruisers with 6" guns, anti-aircraft and depth charges for enemy submarines. We were sent to Dutch Harbor and moored across from the other ships in the harbor. We did a lot of convoy work-the most visual recollection was in convoying some American supply ships and I believe one of the worst storms came upon us with waves over 50 feet. All doors were locked, including watertight ones and no one was allowed out. We lost our convoy and not sure what happened but it wasn't until two days later that we pulled into Dutch Harbor. They had a floating dock yard and repairs were made to the ship.

We were there for two months but not allowed any shore leave except for the local base-we had to line up for beer at the canteen-two bottles at 10 cents each and then stand in line again for another go. While aboard the *Prince David* we did encounter some Japanese subs off the coast of British Columbia, Washington and Oregon and dropped a lot of depth charges. I cannot say for sure if we hit anything, but did see oil slicks and debris-but who knows. While we were in Dutch Harbor we heard Tokyo Rose's broadcast. She knew we were there, probably from our garbage, which was thrown overboard. That was stopped in a hurry when we figured it out.

U.S. Naval Armed Guards

The U.S. Armed Guards were the gunners on the merchant ships that supplied the military throughout the world during the war. Most of the gun crews on Alaska bound ships sailed out of Seattle, WA and Portland, OR. Raymond F. Barba relates a couple of stories: "I remember a story about a new Liberty ship that left Seattle for Dutch Harbor and in route it cracked in half and the Captain with his crew abandoned the ship but the Navy gun crews stayed on board, some on the forward part and the rest on the aft section of the ship. When the Captain noticed that the ship did not sink, he ordered the crew to return and they were towed back to Seattle. And then there was the story about the Japanese landing craft that thought this Liberty ship was its mother ship only to find out that the forward gun crew opened fire on them. Never learned what happened to that landing craft.

THE *USS WORDEN* DD-352

The destroyer, the third named after Rear Admiral John Lorimer Worden, who was the commander of the famous Union ironclad Monitor that battled the Confederate ironclad "Virginia" (Merrimac) in Hampton Roads, VA on March 9, 1862 and Superintendent of the US Naval Academy. He died in 1897.

The ship was a Farragut Class destroyer, built at the Puget Sound Navy Yard and commissioned on Jan. 15, 1934. She was sent to Pearl Harbor in 1939 as part of the Hawaii Department, then part of the Pacific Fleet in 1940. Was stationed at Pearl Harbor at the time of the attack and later was on patrol and scout duty in the South Pacific,

The only memorial to the gallant USS Worden *and her crew, seen inside the Alaska Veterans Museum.*
–Courtesy of Alaska Veterans Museum

The USS Worden *beached in Constantine Harbor.* –Courtesy of USN N-4125

but missed the Battle of the Coral Sea. During the Battle of Midway she screened the *USS Enterprise* and *Hornet* and took part in the invasion of Guadalcanal in November 1942. After the *USS Saratoga* was damaged, the *Worden* screened the carrier back to Pearl Harbor and the mainland.

On Dec. 27, 1942 she left San Francisco for the Aleutians to support the occupation of Amchitka Island. On January 12, 1943 while guarding the Army transport *Arthur Middleton* (AP-65) as it put the preliminary Army security unit on the shores of Constantine Harbor, it maneuvered into the rock-edged harbor and stayed there until the last man had landed, then turned to the ticklish business of clearing the harbor.

A strong current, however swept the ship onto a pinnacle that tore her hull beneath the engine room and caused a complete loss of power. The *USS Dewey* passed a towline and attempted to tow her free, but the cable parted and the heavy seas began moving the ship, without power towards the rocky shore, where it was broached and began breaking up in the surf. Comdr. William G. Pogue ordered to abandon ship but was swept overboard. Luckily he was hauled back on board unconscious, but 14 crewmen were lost. *Worden* was a total loss and was struck from the Navy list on Dec. 22, 1944. She won four battle stars up to this time.

The US Gunboat *Charleston PG-51 was the second of two Erie-class gunboats commissioned at the Charleston Navy Yard on July 8, 1936. She is pictured at Seward, AK and took part in support of troop landings at Attu in May 1943.*

The only memorial to the Battle and defenders of Wake Island in the United States was dedicated in Bristow, OK. Former Bristow mayor, Leon Davis along with members of VFW Post 3656 provided a park site next to their post along with other war monuments. Among them was a deck gun off the Charleston. *The park was accepted by the U.S. Marine Corps and defenders of Wake Island on June 17, 1978*

US SUBMARINE OPERATIONS IN ALASKA DURING WORLD WAR TWO

After 1937 the defense of Alaska and the northwest Pacific area took on new importance. Seaplane bases were established at Sitka, southwest of Juneau, Kodiak Island and Dutch Harbor in the Aleutians. The last two were also provided the support facilities for basing six submarines each, and by late 1941, they were ready for operation under a newly-formed Alaskan Naval Sector, part of the 13th Naval District headquartered in Seattle. When the war began, the sector commander controlled a small force of hand-me-down gunboats, two World War One destroyers and a few Coast Guard cutters and improvised patrol craft, plus 10 PBY Catalina flying boats. Two older submarines, S-18 (SS-123) and S-23 (SS-128) were sent from the West Coast, arriving at Dutch Harbor on Jan. 27, 1942. Within two weeks, they had departed on their first war patrols, defensive sweeps south of the Aleutian Islands and easterly toward Kodiak island. Although no contact was made with the enemy, the two S boats were the first to experience the full rigor of the weather and ocean conditions that characterized Alaskan submarine warfare for the next two years. An entry in S-23's deck log for Feb. 13, 1942 notes:

Shipped heavy seas over bridge. All hands on bridge bruised and battered. Officer of the Deck suffered broken nose. Solid stream of water down the hatch for 65 seconds. Put high pressure pump on control room bilges; dry after two hours. . . . Barometer 29.60, thirty knots wind from northwest.

Rear Admiral "Fritz" Harlfinger, who served on S-boats in the Aleutians, later described how dreadful it was:

The conditions those boats endured up there are simply indescribable. It was God awful. Cold, dreary, fog and ice glaze. The periscopes froze. The decks and lifelines were caked with ice. Blizzards. You could never get a navigational fix.

Moreover, the tides, currents, and weather throughout the region were often unpredictable and frequently treacherous, and the rocks and shoals of the island-studded archipelago posed a constant danger under the usual conditions of poor visibility from driving snow and rain, practically during the long northern nights.

After their relatively brief patrols S-18 and S-23 returned to San Diego for an overhaul that included superstructure modifications and additional internal heating in accordance with the "lessons-learned" from their first Alaskan experience. Simultaneously, a division of six additional S-boats-originally intended for Australia-was redirected to Dutch Harbor. These submarines-S-30 through S-35 (SS-135 through 140)-arrived in the theater between April and August 1942, to be augmented by S-27 (SS-132) and S-28 (SS-133), which headed north from San Diego in late May. Thus, when S-18 and S-23 completed their overhauls and returned to the theater at that same time, a total of 10 S-boats had been assigned to Alaskan waters. In April, on the first Dutch Harbor war patrols into Japanese territory, both S-34 and 35 penetrated as far as Paramushiro in the Kurlie Islands, but despite several attacks on merchant ships, they scored no successes.

Before the historic Battle of Midway, which our intelligence had found out the Japanese intentions, CINCPAC Admiral Chester Nimitz assigned two heavy cruisers, three light cruisers and 10 destroyers to a North Pacific Force under RADM Robert Theobald, who also assumed command of the "Alaska Navy" including the Dutch Harbor submarines. Since Theobald expected an enemy attack against military facilities on the Alaskan Peninsula and the eastern Aleutians, he deployed his main surface south and west of Kodiak during the first days of June. Four subs were sent to patrol off the approaches to the expected objectives in the east and two as far west as Attu in hopes of intercepting the enemy.

The surface fleet made no contact with the enemy fleet. Japan had no designs on the eastern Aleutians, and all along had planned to occupy Attu, Kiska and Adak well to the west. After the disastrous, for the Japanese, Battle of Midway, Admiral Yamamoto had nearly decided to cancel the land invasion but he was persuaded to at least occupy the two westernmost islands of Attu and Kiska. Only S-34 and S-35 were in any position to oppose the landings but neither had sighted the enemy by the time they were ordered back to Dutch Harbor. The Japanese had formed a task force to deliver supplies to their new territory but withdrew in August to support the Guadalcanal campaign. Seven U.S. fleet boats had made sorties into the northern theater including *Growler (SS-215), Triton (SS-201), Finback (SS-230)*, *Grunion (SS-216), Trigger (SS-237), Tuna (SS-203)* and *Gato (SS-212)*.

Of these S-boats only *Growler*, *Triton* and *Grunion* scored sinkings. The most spectacular success was achieved by Growler under LCDR Howard Gilmore-later to be awarded the Medal of Honor posthumously. The boat came upon three enemy destroyers anchored off Kiska and in his first attack of the war loosed torpedoes at all three, scoring hits on all three. *Growler* went deep to avoid two torpedoes fired back at her, but when the smoke cleared, one of the destroyers had sunk and the other two were so seriously damaged that they had to be towed back to Japan. The day before this attack, *Triton* sank another destroyer off the island of Agattu, and *Grunion* destroyed two patrol boats near Kiska on June 15th. Unfortunately this same patrol ended tragically, because contact was lost with *Grunion*, and after July 30 she was never heard from again.

The Alaska-based S-boats did even less well in the months after the Japanese invasion. In a total of 14 war patrols from Dutch Harbor targeted on Japanese shipping in the western Aleutians between July and September, no enemy sinkings were credited. S-27 was lost to grounding on a reconnaissance mission to Amchitka, when an undetected current carried her onto the rocks while she was charging batteries on the surface during the night of June 19, 1942. The entire crew made it to shore and were sighted by a PBY and rescued after six days. This is an edited version of this story written by Dr. Whitman, senior editor of Undersea Warfare magazine.

Built to a World War One design based on early submarine technology, the S-boats assigned to the Aleutians were 20 years old, largely worn out, and clearly regarded as "second-line" submarines. Powered by only two 600-horsepower diesel engines, they could make 12-14 knots on the surface-perhaps 10 submerged on battery-and with a test depth of 200 feet, there was little margin for error. Moreover, their surface displacement of somewhat less than 1,000 tons and their low freeboard made operating in the stormy, northern waters of the Aleutians and the Bering Sea a grueling daily challenge. Despite the electric heaters that had been installed for the northern climate, life below decks was dispiriting, cold and wet, not only from seawater sloshing down through the conning tower, but also from the condensation of atmospheric, moisture on all the metal surfaces inside.

In preparation for the retaking of Attu and Kiska, seven more S-boats (S-40, S-41, S-42, S-44, S-45, S-46 and S-47) were ordered north in the spring of 1943 and trickled into Dutch Harbor between May and December. Until August, the boats concentrated on the supply lines between Japan and the western Aleutians, but after the re-conquest of the islands, the emphasis shifted to more general hunting expeditions in the northern Kurlies. Again little was achieved. The 24 war patrols mounted from Dutch Harbor between May and the end of the year-generally about a month long but as much as 40 days-produced only four enemy victims totaling about 13,000 tons, all enemy merchant ships sunk near Paramushiro. S-44 (SS-155) was caught on the surface by a Japanese destroyer on October 7 during her first war patrol and lost with all but two crewmen, who survived to become prisoners of war.

At the end of 1943 with the credible threat from Japan ended the navy ordered the remaining S-boats withdrawn from Alaska and for the most part assigned to training duties. In the very last war patrol from Dutch Harbor, S-45 left the base on New Year's Eve and returned to Attu at the end of January 1944, before departing for San Diego and a general overhaul. Only nine confirmed kills were scored in over 80 war patrols and four of these were claimed by Pearl Harbor based fleet boats. Two S-boats-S-27 and S-44-and one fleet boat, the *Grunion* were lost, two with virtually all crewmen.

USS GRUNION (SS-216)

The *USS Grunion* (SS-216) was a Gato-class submarine, built by the Electric Boat Company in Groton, CT and commissioned on April 11, 1942 with Lt. Cdr. Mannert L. Abele in command. She arrived at Pearl Harbor on June 20, 1942, reporting for duty from the West Coast. The boat was ordered to proceed to the Aleutians and patrol westward from Attu on routes between the Aleutians and Japan. On July 10 she was reassigned to the area north of Kiska, and made her first report on July 15. Dutch Harbor received her message that, attacked by an enemy destroyer, she had fired three torpedoes at it, but all missed. Shortly after this message was received *Grunion* sent another relating that she had sunk three destroyer-type vessels on July 15. The message was garbled to the extent that details of the attacks were never learned (Japanese information reveals that *Grunion* sank patrol boats 25 and 27 and damaged a third). On July 19 *Grunion, S-32, Triton* and *Tuna* were assigned areas of approaches to Kiska, all to be there by daylight on July 22.

There was a strong concentration of enemy vessels at Kiska, this time being only a month and a half after the island was taken. The vessels patrolling there were told to watch particularly on the afternoon of July 22 for departing enemy naval vessels, since our own surface forces were scheduled to bombard Kiska that afternoon. The bombardment did not take place in accordance with the original plans, but our forces did stage the operation on July 28 and *Grunion* was told to guard the exits from Kiska during darkness on this date. On this day *Grunion* reported an attack on unidentified enemy ships six miles southeast of Sirius Point, Kiska. She had fired two torpedoes, made no hits, and been depth-charged, but sustained no damage.

Grunion's last transmission was received on July 30. She reported heavy antisubmarine activity at the entrance to Kiska, and that she had ten torpedoes remaining. On the same day, *Grunion* was directed to return to Dutch Harbor. She was not contacted or sighted after July 30, despite every effort to do so, and on August 16 was reported lost. Planes observing the approaches to Kiska for indications of enemy salvage operations in connection with the sub reported negatively. Japanese antisubmarine attack data available records no attack in the Aleutian area at the time, and *Grunion's* fate remains an unsolved mystery. There were no enemy minefields in the area: thus her loss may be presumed to have been operational or as a result of an unrecorded enemy attack. Her name was struck from the Naval Vessel Register on Nov. 2, 1942.

The mystery of the loss came to light in 2007 when a website put up by Yutaka Iwasaki, a Japanese model ship builder had translated a report written in the 1960s by a Japanese military officer who served in the Aleutians at the time. It described a confrontation between a U.S. submarine and the officer's freighter, the *Kano Maru*, on July 31, 1942, about 10 miles northeast of Kiska in the *Grunion's* patrol area. The sub dispatched six or seven torpedoes. All but one bounced off the freighter without exploding, or missed, the officer wrote, although the one hit knocked out the engines and its communications. The freighter returned fire with an 8-centimeter deck gun, and believed that it had sunk the sub. However, it has been determined that the sixth torpedo was a circular run which hit the shears but did not explode. It created and opening into the control room that made it impossible to control the rear dive planes to get out of a hard dive. The sub plummeted downward to approximately 1,000 feet where it imploded.

Now with a possible area to look which might be the sunken sub, the sons of the commander, who all lived in the Boston area took it upon themselves, rather than involve the US Navy, to hired an experienced marine survey company, Williamson and Associates to do a sonar scan of the area. The *Aquila* a Bering Sea crab boat spent more than two weeks towing a sonar cable from east to west and back again inside a 240-square-mile-grid that the survey crew had plotted, using information from naval archives and the *Kano* Maru officer's account. In mid-August 2006, the sonar picked up a 290-foot object with the sharp angles and jutting shadows of something manmade wedged into a terrace on the steep underwater slope of a volcano.

The *Grunion* was 312 feet long. However, so it is thought that the bow may have plowed beneath a mat of thick sediment, hence the apparent shortage of about 20 feet. Skid marks show the vessel slid to rest about 1,000 meters from the surface. Over the years earthquakes could have piled on more debris. The sub is the only known sunken vessel in the area and sonar picked up the distinct outline of a submarine conning tower. In August 2007 a second expedition was mounted using a high definition camera on a remotely operated vehicle which yielded high defination video footage of the wreckage. The Navy has confirmed that this is the missing submarine. No further action will be taken on the recovery of the vessel.

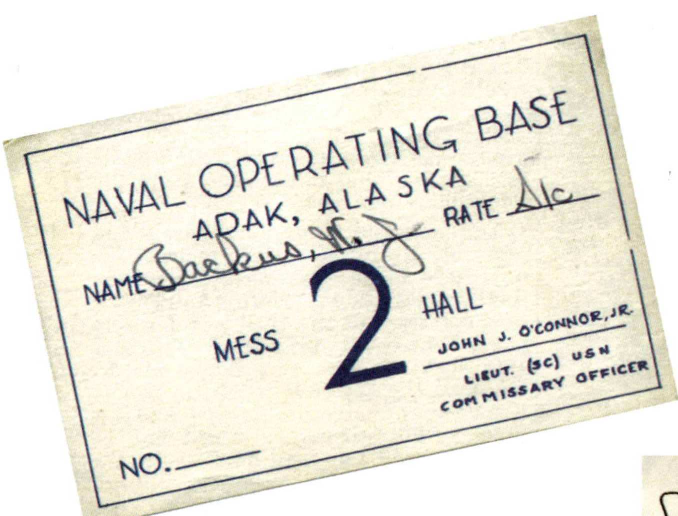

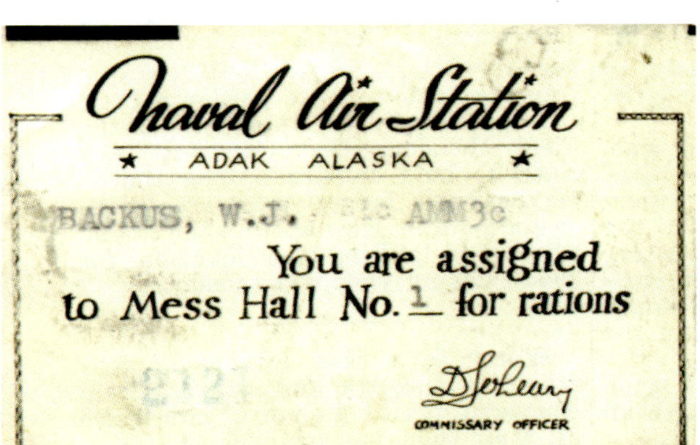

Volumn I June 11, 1944 No. 8

WINNERS REWARDED

The Chapel was the scene of the skill and luck competition last Wednesday evening, when the winners of the recent Pool, Ping-Pong, and Rifle competition were awarded the fruits of their efforts.

On hand to issue the awards and his personel congratulations was the Commanding Officer of the base, K. E. Brimmer, who in addition to presenting the awards stressed participation in the fishing contest now in progress. The Commanding Officer stressed the point that all fish regardless of size should be entered in the contest.

The presentations were made before a fairly filled house and all hands enjoyed the ceremony.

Highlight of the evening were the winners of the consolation prizes, which were compacts. Laughs a many were furnished the crowd when the winners stepped forward to receive them.

The winners were: Walfrid Forsten, Don Flikied and Fred Bloch in the Ping-Pong contest; A. J. Nichles, J. W. Schulte, Joe Amaral andJimmy Harkins in the Pool, and G. L. Stewart, H. W. White, F. Jenkofsky, H. D. Sinclair and Disalvo were the winners of the Rifle competition.

The Welfare and Recreation Department wishes to thank all competitors for the fine spirit shown throughout these tournaments. We take this last opportunity to again congratulate the winners.

o

FAST WORKER

A lawyer came to London to locate a young woman who had fallen heir to a large fortune. The police were called in to aid in the search, and placed the case in the hands of a clever and personable young detective. Several weeks passed by without any information, and the lawyer was beginning to feel deeply concerned over the matter, when the young detective appeared and smilingly informed him he had located the heiress.

"Where is she?" asked the lawyer.

"At my place," replied the detective. "I married her yesterday."

DISSERTATION ON A SACK

by: I. Sleep Well and U. Should Too

The sack, according to Webster, is a bag or pouch, especially a large course bag for holding grain. The "SACK," however, according to the finest Naval traditions, as promulgated in the BuPers Manual, Chapter Umpty umph, corresponds to Webster's definition of the humble bed-an article of domestic furniture upon or within which one rests or sleeps. To achieve full usage thereof, one must "hit the sack."

Therefore the sack is an integral and necessary part of Naval life and is standard gear from which one may "back the attack." To the civilian it is known as a commonplace bed, to the Army it's a particularly odoriferous type of sack, to the zoomies it's the hangar, but to the sailor it's THE SACK.

It is the considered opinion of the writers (who are experts and authorities in the proper use of the sack) that to maximize satisfaction from the sack, it must be properly approached and mounted. There are many different ways of doing this.

Some mount the sack with an arc-like movement comparable to and resembling a dive, abandoning themselves completely to the sweet arms of Morpheus.

Some approach the sack with an air of reverence and humility as they welcome a brief respite from the humdrum nature of everyday life.

There are those who punctilliously approach the sack with meticulous preparation. (They are as likely to break a leg or an arm on entering the sack as any other type.)

An then there is the drunken type, and we daresay that some of the more adventurous of you have had experience in this condition (Oh, for the good old days). This type of mounting the sack frequently results, in complete clearance thereof, and in snuggling alongside the sack, flat on the deck, and dead to the world.

Also there are those who fall upon the sack in utter exhaustion, with all

(continued on page 2)

THE FIELD MARSHAL'S LATEST COMMUNIQUE

by L. D. Girod

It's here—the invasion of Europe! Along with the invasion of Europe comes the announcement that every thing is going according to schedule, with much better results than had been hoped for. Please excuse a personal remark but the Field Marshal is pleased to report that he guessed that the invasion was to take place on the 6th of June; that the casualty rate would be far lower than any of the given estimates; and that it was to be successful beyond any doubt.

Without doing any phophesying about future operations let it be sufficient to say that the action for June won't be limited to the Western front as Russia will open on the Germans with both barrels, as some more big events are coming immediately and as all heck is going to break loose in the Pacific any day now.

The war isn't over and there's lots of fighting and work left to be done, but there is no question but that the final round of the European war is now on and that the enemy is not only badly beaten but also groggy. Whether this fight is to be a knockout or whether the towel is to be thrown in depends not only on Adolph and his stooges but also very much on the German public as well as the military leaders.

Anybody who feels that he has tough duty, try imagining that he is the head of the German propaganda department. What a headache that must be.

In conclusion please pardon a little advice. Don't be too optomistic as the Field Marshals that Germany is a cinch to hold out for a long time—maybe even longer than six weeks or six months. How about some of you who were picking the invasion for 1945 revising your war schedule?

o

Worry is a thin stream of fear trickling through the mind. If encouraged, it cuts a channel into which all their thoughts are drained.

THE P-510 TAKES TO THE AIR USING THE 10TH EMERGENCY RESCUE BOAT SQUADRON

The P-510 was an 85-foot plywood boat built in Seattle in 1942 for use by the 10th Emergency Rescue Boat Squadron operated by the 11th Air Force in Alaska. Its main purpose was to rescue downed pilots in the rough Aleutian flying conditions. This story was related by former radioman crewmen, Chuck Cloudy of a rescue in the Attu area.

"We monitored a Rescue Director to a Navy 63' crash boat regarding a P-38 which had crashed in the vicinity of Nevidiskov Bay at Attu. This must have been around noon, because our cooks had roasted a turkey for an early 1945 New Year's Day dinner and the turkey was about done. The sea was running 10 to 15 feet which wasn't bad for the 510, but which would be murderous for the 63 foot Navy boat. Our sense was, when we started out, that we were going to overtake the Navy and have the rescue to ourselves. We caught up with the Navy and when our boat was aside her stern, we took off into the air on a big 15 foot swell, and when we hit the water again our stern was aside her bow. Eventually the Navy turned back because they were taking quite a beating."

"Arriving in the bay, we put a shore party on the beach to hike up the hill behind the harbor. On the way up, they met the pilot on his way down. Other than his pride, he was not injured. By the time the shore party and the pilot were aboard, the turkey was done so we made a leisurely return to Casco Cove on Atka Island. According to him, his squadron had enjoyed a hell of a New Year's Eve party. His first thought the next morning was to go flying so he could clear his head. He requisitioned his wing commander's P-38 and went on a joy ride over Attu. During the course of the flight, he intended to

The P-510 at Adak.

Two boats tied up at their base. P-510 is on the left.

Crew of the P-510 in 1942.

P-150 and P-510 in Aleutian waters.

shoot down the steep valley behind Nevidiskov Bay and out over the bay. As he was approaching the ridge, he noticed something loose on the floor of the cockpit and reached down to pick it up. When he has successfully rescued a dried piece of mud, he looked up and noticed that he had lost both his propellers (apparently ground them up going over the ridge), and wisely decided that all he could do was to set the plane down, which he did on the first flat spot he saw, badly dinging the plane as he bellied in. He left the wreck and started walking down the valley where he met the shore party."

"Later on, shocked as the enormity of what he had done began to bear down on him, he was almost distraught. He managed to eat most of our turkey dinner on the way back to base and worried out loud about a court martial, loss of pay for loss of the aircraft, etc, etc. Air Force personnel were waiting at our tie-down and took the pilot away and we never heard anything further from or about him."

"The P-510 was sold after the war and converted to a luxury yacht certified for 149 passengers and 10 crewmen. It is operated out of Los Angeles by Adventures At Sea Yacht Charters."

Remembrances of Maurice L. Mayper of Walnut Creek, CA Crewman on the *USS Rapidan AO18*

The ship was commissioned on Jan. 1, 1922. "Our ship made about five trips from San Pedro, CA to Kodiak and then would continue on down the Aleutian Chain. I made brief visits to Cold Bay, Adak, Dutch Harbor, Kiska and Attu. Along with our sister ship the *USS Salinas* we carried high test aviation gasoline to the islands and occasionally to aircraft carriers." The *Salinas* was torpedoed but fortunately did not sink." Mayper was eventually transferred as an Aerologist to Weather Air Central at NAS Kodiak. He was stationed at Adak when the war ended.

I graduated high school in January 1943, and volunteered for the US Army in February, 1944. I was soon transferred from the infantry to the Transportation Corps, Harbor (Craft) Detachment and was sent to Alaska Defense Training in Seattle and assigned as a signalman to LT 144 in January 1944. We left that month for Alaska, with a crane-barge in tow with a crew of 21 for Seward, Kodiak, Dutch Harbor, Adak, Kiska. Shemya and Attu.

The Alaska Detachment was no small unit. The Harbor Craft had more than 150 vessels assigned to our unit. Crews consisted of between 15 and 30 soldiers. This was the US Army's "Navy." There were equal numbers in the South Pacific theater, including small tugboats, large deep sea tugboats, LT's, ST and BSP's freighters, cargo ships and more. We supplied equipment, materials, food, clothing, ammunition, weapons, replacement parts and more to the islands along the Aleutian Chain.

We arrived at Attu after most of the fighting was over, but there was still gunfire and grenades heard. Our job was to clean up the island and to supply needed ammunition, guns, clothing, food and medicine for the troops. Also to supply gas, oil and supplies to the islands by barges, BSP's. tugboats or Harbor Craft in the area. I was transferred in May 1945 to Cape Spenser, north of Nome for seven months and discharged on Feb. 2, 1946.

—CHAPTER TEN—

THE INVASION AND BATTLE OF ATTU

Japanese war art entitled "The Landing in the Aleutian" (7–8 June 1942). Artist Tomoharu Mikami. –Courtesy of WAPA 231

American troops land on Attu with the American flag waving on a captured Japanese landing boat at Massacre Bay. –International News photo

COMBINED FLEET OPERATIONAL PREPARATIONS

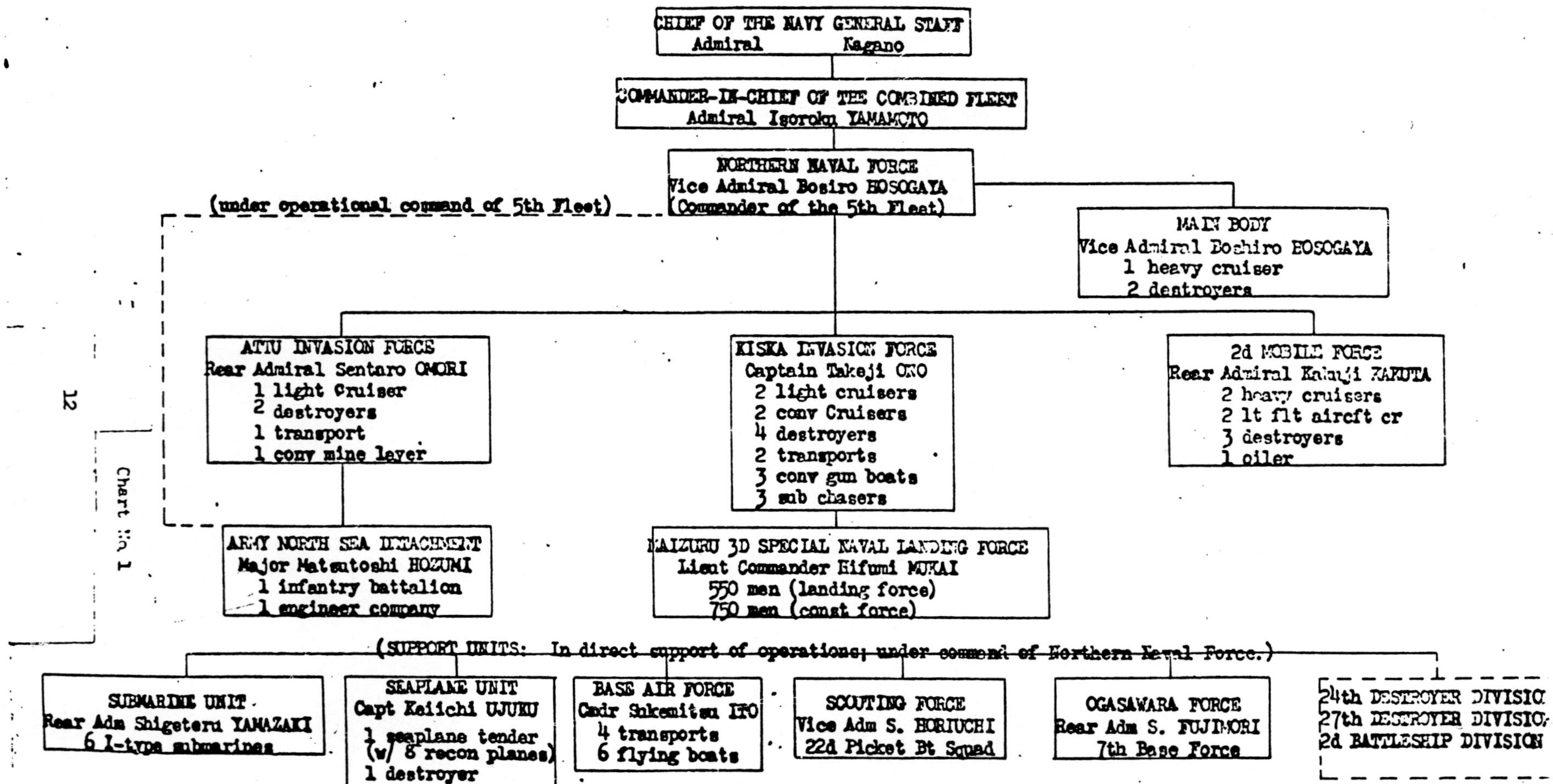

* To support the operation if situation requires.

C62830

Chart No. 1

12

Attu is the westernmost and largest island in the Near Islands group of the Aleutians Islands, making it the westernmost point of land relative to Alaska and the United States. It is nearly 1,100 miles from the Alaskan mainland and 750 miles northwest of the northernmost of the Kurlie Islands (formerly part of Japan, now part of the Russian Federation). Attu is about 20 miles by 35 miles in size with a land area of 344.71 square miles. The name Attu is a transliteration of the Aleut name of the island. Aleuts lived on the island long before World War II.

The early June attack on the Aleutian Islands was a part of the Battle of Midway which, according to many historians was partially prompted by the April 18, 1942 Doolittle Tokyo raid with 16 B-25 medium bombers attacking Japan from the carrier *USS Hornet*, the missed sinking of the US carriers at Pearl Harbor and the idea that capturing the island of Midway and three islands in the Aleutians would extend the eastern range of the Japanese defenses and protect their northern fishing grounds and as a bulwark against the use of American forces to invade the Kurlie Islands, the northern most part of the Japanese islands. The intention was to bomb the US military installations on Amaknak Island (Dutch Harbor), occupy Attu, Kiska and Adak and possibly divert part of the US carrier force defending Midway. All this using two carriers and occupying troops. As it turned out the Battle of Midway was a complete disaster for the Japanese navy, losing all their carriers and aircrews and forcing them to retreat back to Japan. It was decided, however to carry out the attack on Dutch Harbor and occupy only Attu and Kiska to provide bases for anchoring the northern part of their defensive line. Sixty-two light bombers and fighters off the carriers carried this out on June 3-4, 1942. (There are several different postulations as to the exact intent of the Japanese Aleutian plan among historians).

On June 6 the Japanese began landing their elite Navy 3rd Landing Force on Kiska, capturing a ten-man Navy weather team on the island and started building the defense structure. Concurrently Major Matsutoshi Hpzumi landed the 1,143 man North Sea (Hokkaido) Detachment, consisting of the 301st Independent Infantry Battalion and 301st Engineer Company at Holtz Bay on Attu, 190 miles west of Kiska.

On June 6 the Japanese invaded the island. Much of the native populations of other Aleutian islands had been forcibly evacuated before the invasion and interned in camps in the Alaska Panhandle, where many died of chronic disease. The 42 inhabitants who remained on Attu were taken to a prison camp near Otaru, Hokkaido, Japan where 16 of them died by the end of the war. The remaining natives were returned to other islands in the Aleutians or to mainland Alaska after the war.

During the winter of 1942, the Japanese reinforced and fortified both Attu and Kiska and had removed a small force from Agattu Island, moving some troops among the two occupied islands. A naval force under Admiral Charles McMorris was charged with interdicting enemy supply ship convoys. After the Battle of the Komandorski Islands, Japan was forced to use submarines for their resupply runs and eventually both islands were virtually cut off from the outside world.

The bronze Attu Village Memorial designed and fundraised by the Alaska Veterans Museum with four partners. It was placed at the village site in 2002.

–Courtesy of Aden Winkelman Papers (Alaska scout)

Photos of Japanese troops on Attu. –Courtesy of Jim Backus

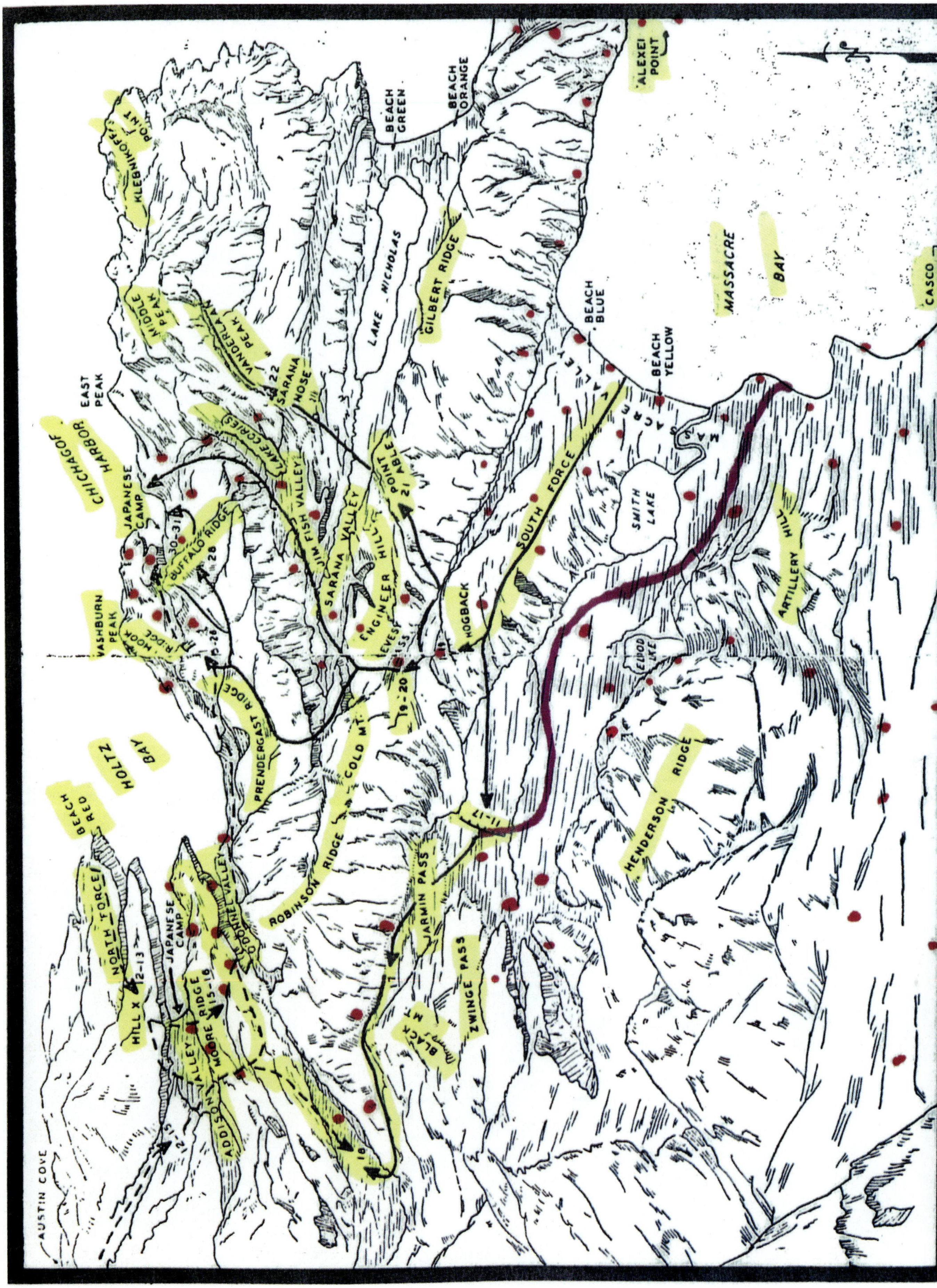
ALEXEI POINT
BEACH ORANGE
BEACH GREEN
KLEBNIKOFF POINT
LAKE NICHOLAS
GILBERT RIDGE
MASSACRE BAY
CASCO
BEACH BLUE
BEACH YELLOW
MIDDLE PEAK
VANDERLAAN PEAK
SARANA NOSE
22
EAST PEAK
CHICHAGOF HARBOR
LAKE CORIES
POINT ABLE
21
MASSACRE VALLEY
JAPANESE CAMP
30-31
BUFFALO RIDGE
28
JIM FISH VALLEY
SARANA VALLEY
ENGINEER HILL
SOUTH FORCE
SMITH LAKE
ARTILLERY HILL
HOGBACK
WASHBURN PEAK
HOOK RIDGE
19-20
PRENDERGAST RIDGE
HOLTZ BAY
BEACH RED
COLD MT.
ROBINSON RIDGE
HENDERSON RIDGE
11-17
JARMIN PASS
NORTH FORCE
JAPANESE CAMP
O'DONNEL VALLEY
HILL X
12-13
ZWINGE PASS
BLACK MT.
MOORE RIDGE
15-18
VALLEY
ADDISON
18
12-15
AUSTIN COVE

Photos from the John Hertenberger collection. He was in the 159th Infantry Regiment of the 7th Division.

THE BATTLE

On May 11, 1943, 12,500 troops landed at several sites on the island of Attu: Beaches Red, Scarlet, Yellow and Blue and Goltsov Point, Austin Cove and Massacre Bay. They had been assembled at Adak along with a large invasion fleet. This would be the first amphibious landing by U.S. forces during the war and the Army would learn much about amphibious landings and Japanese tactics from the battle. The landing force was the motorized Seventh Division, which had being training in the desert area of California for use in North Africa. But by this time the African campaign was over and this division was on the west coast, the closest to Alaska. Because of their location and that they were ready to go, the army called them up. Most of the troops had never even heard of the Aleutians and the Army had little intelligence or knowledge of the situation on the island-especially the harsh weather conditions. In May, one would think that winter was behind them--but not in the Aleutians. They sailed north with totally improper gear and equipment, especially leather boots only good for desert warfare. Also involved was a 30-man detachment from the Alaska Defense Command's 1st Alaska Combat Intelligence Platoon, know as the "Alaska Scouts" or "Castner's Cutthorats."

What little intelligence the Army had placed the enemy force at about 500 second-rate troops but came to find a heavily dug-in force of 2,500 holding the high ground. And of course it was still winter conditions-snow, cold and wind, typical of the islands in the chain. The troops went ashore with no opposition and were to advance inland, up the passes and assault the enemy along the heights of Fish Hook and Moore Ridges. The terrain was tundra, very hard to walk on where there was no snow and very hard to move artillery and mechanized equipment. Snipers caused havoc on the troops with officers, communications linemen, machine-gun bearers being the targets.

For days the Americans were on the ground without adequate boots, clothing, sleeping gear and even food and ammunition was hard to supply. Anything that would burn was ignited to try and keep warm but the worst problem was the leather issued boots which contributed to hundreds of frozen-foot problems. When enemy positions were taken, cold-weather gear was stripped off the dead and put on, with the chance of being shot as the enemy. It took days of fierce fighting in the rugged mountainous areas to finally push the enemy to their last stronghold at Chichagof Harbor. The Japanese also suffered, with little to eat and running out of ammunition. The commander, Colonel Yasuyo Yamasaki gathered together as many of his men that were still able to fight and on the evening of the 29th climbed from the harbor up to the American positions on what is now known as "Engineer Hill" to try and get enough supplies to continue the fight. The area was also a makeshift field hospital and the Japanese attacked and were repulsed three times before their last final Banzai attack which was deadly for both forces. Many American wounded were killed as they lay on their cots and there was much hand-to-hand combat. About 500 enemy troops made the last attack and at the end all but 28 had either been shot down or committed suicide, mostly with their own hand grenades rather than surrender.

Thus ended the 19-day battle, one of the bloodiest battles of the war for the Americans with 619 troops killed and hundreds wounded, and all but 28 Japanese killed.

7th Division Patch

THE *USS NEVADA* BB-36

The *USS Nevada*, a survivor of the Pearl Harbor attack left the San Pedro area on April 7, 1943 and sailed into the fog-bound, treacherous Massacre Bay at Attu on May 11. It began firing the next day in support of the landings and fired support missions through May 14, expending 248 rounds of main battery and 46 rounds of five-inch ammunition. At no time was it possible for the target area to be seen from the ship. Even the ship's own planes were unable to observe firing results. Visibility never extended beyond 1,000 yards.

Navigational hazards were at least as great as the combat hazard. No reliable chart of Massacre Bay was available. The leadsmen were on duty every minute the ship was in the fire support area. The depth ranged from 40 to 10 fathoms in less than the length of the ship. Radical changes of course and speed were necessary to keep the ship out of shoal water.

On May 13, as she was completing the last of a series of firing missions, the following radio colloquy took place between the Nevada and the shore fire control party. It was recorded elsewhere and subsequently published in an official combat narrative of the Attu operations.

1814 Nevada from Shore Control . . . "Commence firing."

1845 S.C. from Nevada . . ."For information, how are we doing over there?"

1847 Nevada from S.C. . . ."Observer says there are a lot of yellow fellows there and you are not wasting ammunition."

1859 Nevada from S.C. . . . "You fired one shot short, endangering our troops. Unless some correction is made, cease firing."

1900 S.C. to Nevada . . . "We think we can correct. We nearly ran into a rock and had to maneuver. How far short was the shot?"

1908 Nevada to S.C. . . . "Observer not sure, but it was about 900 yards short."

1910 S.C. from Nevada . . . "That shot may have been unseated shell. Will correct."

1918 S.C. from Nevada . . . "We have one loaded turret and would like to fire."

1921 Nevada from S.C. . . . "Commence firing!" (A pause, during which the Nevada evidently fired.) "Those babies went clear over the ridge!"

2013 S.C. from Nevada . . . "Reason those babies went over the hill. They had hot pants sitting too long in a warm gun."

2015 Nevada from S.C. . . . "Observer says all salvos but four have been very effective. You have hit machine guns, mortars, artillery positions and entrenchments..."

The *Nevada* then retired for the night.

THE *USS NASSAU* (CVE-16)

The ship was commissioned in August 1942 as CVE-16 or Escort Carrier, also known as "jeep carriers."

On April 23, 1942 the carrier sailed from San Diego bound for the coming battle of Attu. Its complement of 24 aircraft had less than one week of training before reaching Cold Bay for a short stay and then on to Attu. On May 11 the first launching of F4-F Wildcats was made in support of the troops. Some of the planes inadvertently caused some tense moments for one landing party. A few hours prior to the main landings, an advanced force had paddled ashore in rubber boats from submarines *Narwhal* and *Nautilus*. Moving inland, the soldiers left their rafts on the rocky shore. As the rising sun began to burn away the fog, several fighters spotted the beached rafts. Frustrated by the weather and the apparent lack of targets on the island, the pilots were quick to take advantage of this opportunity to attack the "enemy." Several strafing runs rendered the rafts useless, leaving the soldiers in a spot, since the rafts were their only means of escape if they ran into trouble. Luck was with them as the rafts were not needed again.

VC-21, the fighter squadron on board continued to support the ground troops but the one big deficiency of the ship's operation was the lack of TBFs (torpedo bomber) for real bombing attacks. The ship seldom operated more than 40 miles from the island and often was within 10 miles of Holtz Bay. Because of the lack of wind around Attu, notwithstanding the williwaws, almost all of the sorties were launched by catapult. Considering VC-21's lack of training, the nature of the operation, and, of course, the treacherous Aleutian weather, the loss of five pilots was thought to be low.

After the battle the Nassau was sent to the Pacific to transport aircraft. She was decommissioned in October 1946 and scrapped in 1961.

THE *USS TEAL* (AM-23/AVP-5)

The *USS Teal* (AM-23/AVP-5) was a Lapwing-class minesweeper commissioned as Minesweeper No. 23 in 1918. In November 1919 it was modified as an auxiliary aircraft tender. It was re-designated a small seaplane tender AVP-5 in 1936 and saw duty with Pat-Wing 4 in the Pacific Northwest and Alaska areas. Until the end of the war it plowed the icy waters between the Aleutians and along the Alaskan coast but was also pressed into service as an escort and sometimes as a resupply transport. She was decommissioned in 1945 and scrapped in 1948.

THE 383RD COMBAT INFANTRY BATTALION, SEVENTH INFANTRY DIVISION

Combat Port Company "A" of the Battalion was the only black unit that landed on Attu. The approximately 200 troops were trained as stevedores for off-loading from the ships and keeping the trucks filled with supplies. The two photos were supplied by former Staff Sergeant Benjamin M. Woods of Bronx, NY who would work on the *Adaken* newspaper and become a well-known illustrator after the war.

Japanese artifacts collected by Aden E. Winkelman

Sergeant Aden E. Winkelman

Winkelman (1914-1968) enlisted in November 1941 in the Alaska Defense Command's Combat Intelligence Platoon, more popularly known as the Alaska Scouts or "Castner's Cutthroats." He was with a 16-men detail, led by Capt. Robert Thompson, which left the transport ship J. Franklin Bell on the morning of May 11 aboard two landing craft and then transferred to 25-foot dories to silently paddle ashore near "Red Beach" north of Holtz Bay. A company of the 17th Infantry soon followed. Sgt. Winkleman and the other scouts found no Japanese defenses at the landing site and secured the area in advance of the main landing on the beach later that afternoon. After the main forces came ashore, they slowly fought their way past Hill X and into the West Arm of Holtz Bay.

During the early fighting Sgt. Winkelman found two different Japanese dog tags (pictured). They were introduced into the Imperial Japanese Army in 1894. While American tags included the soldier's name and other personal information, Japanese tags simply showed en enlisted soldier's number within the unit, requiring reference to a written roster for full indemnification. This decision was based on the fact that the Japanese writing system included over 2,000 characters for recording names, making the use of metal dies to stamp individual names impractical.

After the battle Sgt. Winkelman and his discharge from the Army in 1945, remained in Alaska. He married in 1948 and got his pilot's license and flew for a time with Alaska Airlines and later worked as an aircraft mechanic and an airport manager. He also attempted to establish a guiding business on several occasions. He died in 1968.

This handbook belonged to 28-year Sergeant Yanagihara, a native of Izume Village, Aomori Prefective who served with the headquarters company of the 303rd Independent Infantry Battalion on Attu and who was killed during the battle. All Japanese soldiers received a copy of this small handbook titled Guntaitecho (Military Notes) into which they recorded their transfers and pay. Every handbook begins with Emperor Meiji's 1882 message about the nation's military code of conduct on loyalty, courteousness, bravery, integrity and frugality. All soldiers were expected to memorize and recite this 20-page book. –NA via Ephriam D. Dickson III

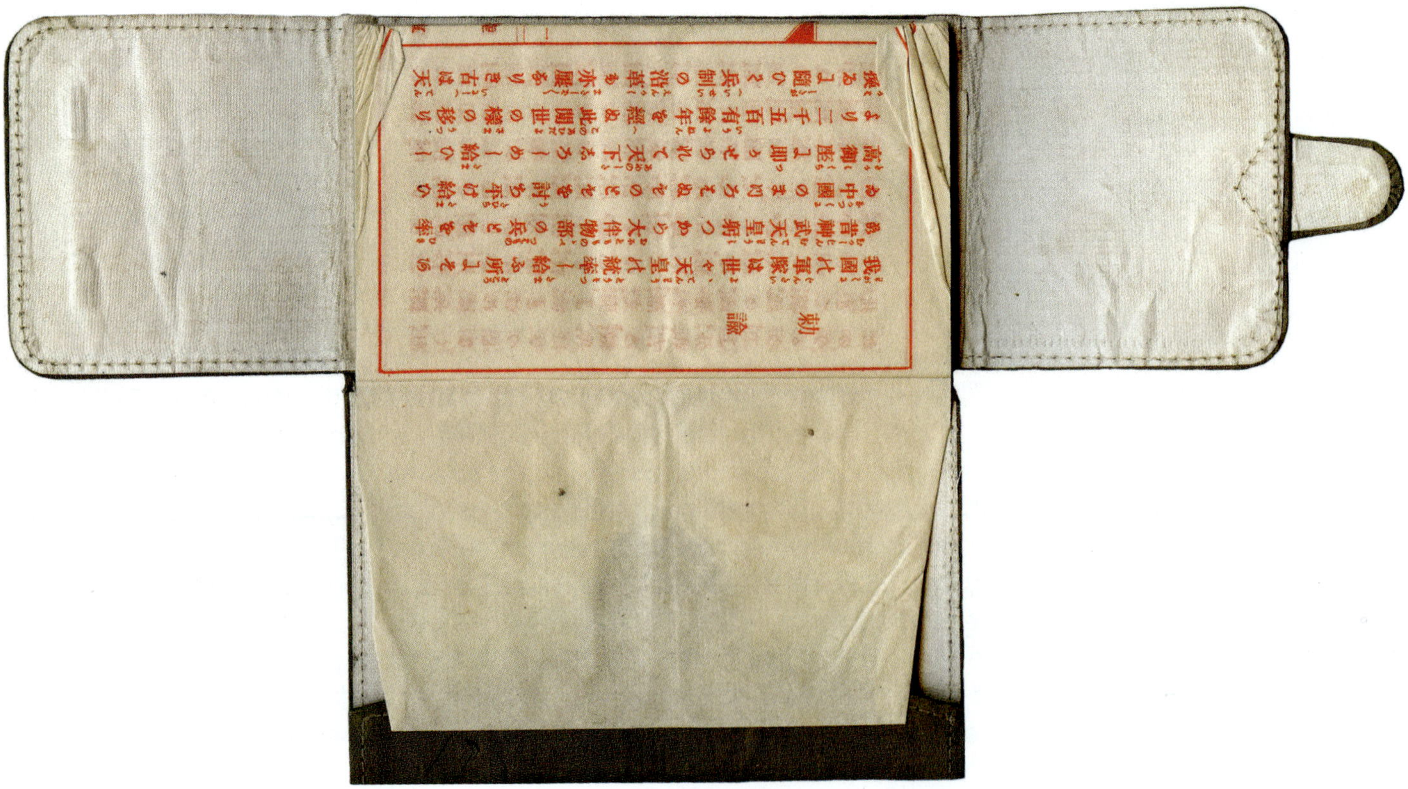

THE ALASKA COMMUNICATIONS SYSTEM

The (ACS), also known as the Washington-Alaska Military Cable and Telegraph System (WAMCATS), was a system of cables and telegraph lines constructed in 1900 by the US Army Signal Corps. The lines were to serve both military and civilian needs in the territory of Alaska. By 1904 some 2,100 miles of undersea cable, 1,400 plus miles of land lines, and a wireless segment across at least 107 miles were in place. WAMCATS was renamed the Alaska Communications System (ACS) in 1936 and remained under control of the army until 1962. It provided a vital lifeline to the many remote and almost inaccessible communities across Alaska.

The ACS Station members at Attu in 1945. Harold Smith who was the station chief is in the lower right. Aden Winkelman is on the top left. –Courtesy of Blaine Cornelison

Digging out the ACS hut, one of the many harsh conditions the men faced in the Aleutians. –Courtesy of Blaine Cornelison

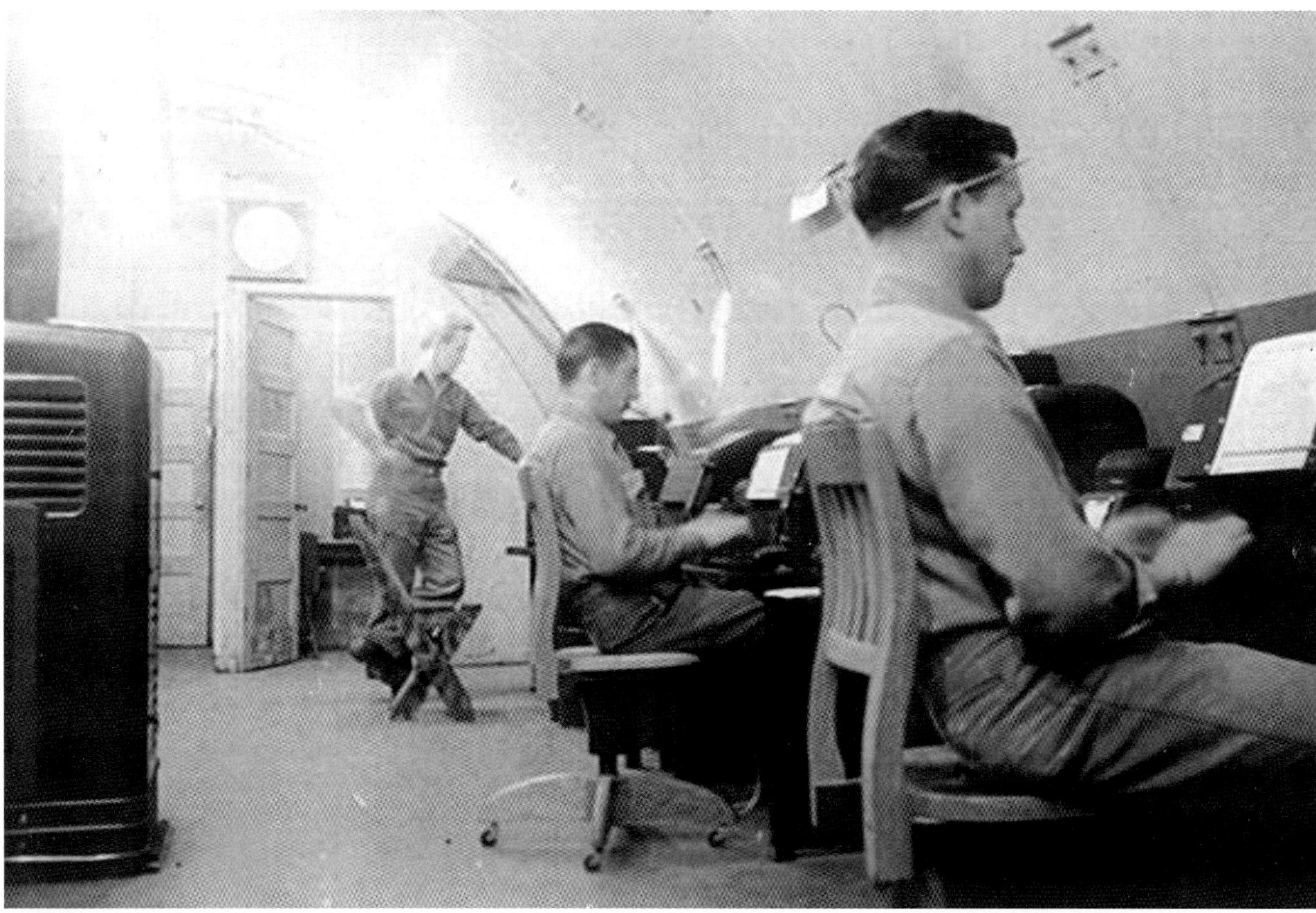

ACS personal at their stations, providing a valuable service to the military and civilians in remote Alaska. Harold Smith is the operator in the very front of the photogaph. –Courtesy of Blaine Cornelison

"Get The Message Through!"

ACS NEWS BULLETIN

VOL. 2 NO. 8 | AUGUST 1943 | 8 PAGES

FELLA, CAN YOU SPARE A GLARE? ACS MAN OUTSTARES BEAR

CORDOVA--"Look 'em in the eye," the animal-trainer's basic manual says--and PFC Darwin Pitz followed instructions to the lètter on a recent exploring expedition among the hills back of Cordova.

Pitz was sitting on a log alongside the trail

when his eyes were jerked back from their contemplation of Nature's beauties by the appearance of a big brown bear ambling toward him.

Reaching futilely for the side-arms he wasn't wearing, Pitz decided he'd rather try to outstare the beast than try to outrun him.

He eyed Mr. Bruin with what he hoped was a steely stare...the bear stared right back. Some moments of this exchange failed to bring about any change in the status quo.

Trying to remember how Svengali did it, Dar finally must have projected the old lightning into his glance--because the bear turned around and ambled back the way he'd come.

CURIOUS BRUINS TAKE SECOND LOOK AT SARGE

NORTHWAY--ACS wolves have been on the friendliest of terms with local wild life here.

On his way to the kitchen one recent evening, OIC T/4 Donald LaDuke came face to face with a black bear. After one quick look, the bear left.

However, he evidently couldn't believe his eyes --as he returned next night for a second look--and brought a companion with him. The two put on quite a show for the grinding movie camera with which PFC Jack Cogeshall came rushing from the bunkhouse.

"Ferdinand," a semi-tame squirrel, has moved right in on the boys--accepting food from their hands. Pvt. Lew Botting nursed a sore thumb for a few days after "Ferdie" peevishly bit him for not letting go of a slice of bread rapidly enough.

BEAR LOSES DECISION TO STEELE

JUNEAU--Hunting a taxidermist, S/Sgt. Blair Steele is now busy explaining to the boys how he takes the monotony out of life in the North country. An old-timer around Juneau, Blair recently made his annual trek to the woods and came back dragging a big, black bear. The bruin measured seven feet, two inches.

SARGE SAVES THREE FROM DIP IN CHILLY TONGASS NARROWS

KETCHIKAN--M/Sgt. Lawrence A. Burrows was working on his homestead five miles north of town that sunny afternoon of Aug. 1, when he heard an outboard motor sputter, spit and stop out in Tongass Narrows.

From where he was, he couldn't see the boat, but he could hear the cries for help.

He headed for the beach on the run. There, he saw two heads bobbing around the sides of the overturned speedboat about 100 yards offshore.

Burrows quickly shoved his own $10\frac{1}{2}$-foot skiff into the water and headed for the scene. Enroute he saw another head appear in the icy Narrows.

Reaching them, he discovered they were three Ketchikan business men. Harry Creighton, garageman, owned the boat and was accompanied by Howard Youngman, archery instructor, and W.M. Wilkins, barber.

The boat had started to ship water and Wilkins, in attempting to lighten the load, had jumped overboard, but this only caused the boat to swamp.

Burrows had a difficult time keeping the trio from capsizing his own boat. He finally persuaded two of them to hold to the stern and the third amidships while he laboriously rowed them to shore. Bucking a strong tide, it took him 20 minutes.

The men were exhausted after the experience, but hot coffee from Mrs. Burrows and dry GI clothing from Larry soon lifted their spirits.

So, after the Army performed the major part of the rescue, Larry called the Coast Guard, and the salt water boys bailed the boat out and towed the rescuees back to town.

Burrows has no idea what may happen next. He

at sea until 1930 when he joined ACS and went back to sea again as chief op on the cableship Dellwood.

Transferred to Nome in late 1930 and stayed there three years, getting glimpses of Lindbergh, Jimmy Mattern and Post and Gatty on their round-the-world flights.

Was OIC at Candle in 1933, and when the station closed down, an ACS plane flew him to Nome to help keep communications open after the disastrous fire there of that year. He then served in Seattle and Sitka before coming here in 1936.

He's chief op here and went from corporal to M/Sgt. in the last two years. He has his own home in Ketchikan where he resides with his wife and four children. Hobbies: clearing ground at his homestead and raising a garden.

ACS MEN GUESTS AT KISKA NO-HOST PARTY

KISKA--Social note: A score of ACS men, in company of 2nd Lts. Gene Young and Clare Hanawalt, were guests at a no-host party on Kiska's scanty beaches Aug. 15.

What had been touted as the International Dateline's battle of the century turned into an Aleutian rubberneck tour.

The late inhabitants of this capital of the Rat Islands had left the doors open, threw the keys away and migrated south, presumably with the salmon.

SOME RELATION TO "ANON." WE'LL BET

SWEATING OUT A FURLOUGH? NEW FORMUL

A new policy on furloughs, independent of t
laid down by ADC, has been initiated by the AC
but don't let that give you hot pants.

Applications will be considered the 1st and
15th of each month by Hq Division heads, and
be dealt out sparingly according to the variou
factors involved, including:

1. Applicant's length of service.
2. Length of time since his last furlough.
3. Whether a replacement will be needed.
4. Whether a replacement can be obtained.
5. Whether an "outside" or territorial furl
is requested.

Some observations by one of the men behind
move to grant furloughs where possible may giv
you an idea of the picture:

"In the first place, a furlough in wartime
strictly a luxury. In most theaters--like Afr
or England or the South Pacific--furloughs are
'out.' When a man is sent overseas it's more
less understood that he's there until the busi
is all cleaned up.

"Well, in Alaska, it isn't quite so tough,
it isn't quite so easy, either. Transportatic
the big bottleneck, but it isn't as big a bott
neck as it is in the more distant theaters.

"We stress that the man's OIC state whether
replacement will be needed. What often happe
that the men get together and agree to work a
couple of extra hours a day to take up the sl
for the furloughed man. They figure on a 15-
basis.

"But what they don't figure on is that the
may lay over as long as two months in Seattle
ter his furlough is over, awaiting return tra
tation. Consequently, after three or four we
we start getting frantic requests for replace

"So the OIC must consider whether he can g
along without the man--not for a two week per
but possibly for as long as two and a half mo

"It's obvious we can't grant all furlough
plications. If we did, we'd just have to clo
shop.

"Most applications probably will come from
erations, since they have more than half of o
personnel. But it won't be possible to grant
loughs wholesale in any one station or statio
because we can't train replacements any more,
since the radio school is virtually empty, an
can't send student ops out to a station to re
a veteran operator without hurting our whole
ation.

"However, we will give consideration to ea
and every furlough.

"If a man does get one, he should consider
self lucky, and shouldn't go around bragging
it as it will only create ill feeling and may
timately result in calling off the whole deal

It is suggested that men apply for the ter
torial rather than "outside" furloughs. Then
there's more chance for them to return to the
jobs on conclusion of the furlough and give s
one else in that station an opportunity to go

The Mt. McKinley Park setup is recommended
It's one of the swankiest resorts on the enti
continent.

All this applies to applications for ordin
furloughs. Emergency furlough requests will

(Continued on Page 4, Col. 2.)

R-E-S-T-R-I-C-T-E-D

–Courtesy of Harold Smith

Strafed and sunk in Chichagof Bay, this zero-type reconnaissance "Rufe" seaplane was raised and taken to Adak for examination by technicians. It had folded wings, a plywood tail, a Mitsubihi engine, one free machine gun and its bomb bay had two live bombs in it when it was raised from the water.

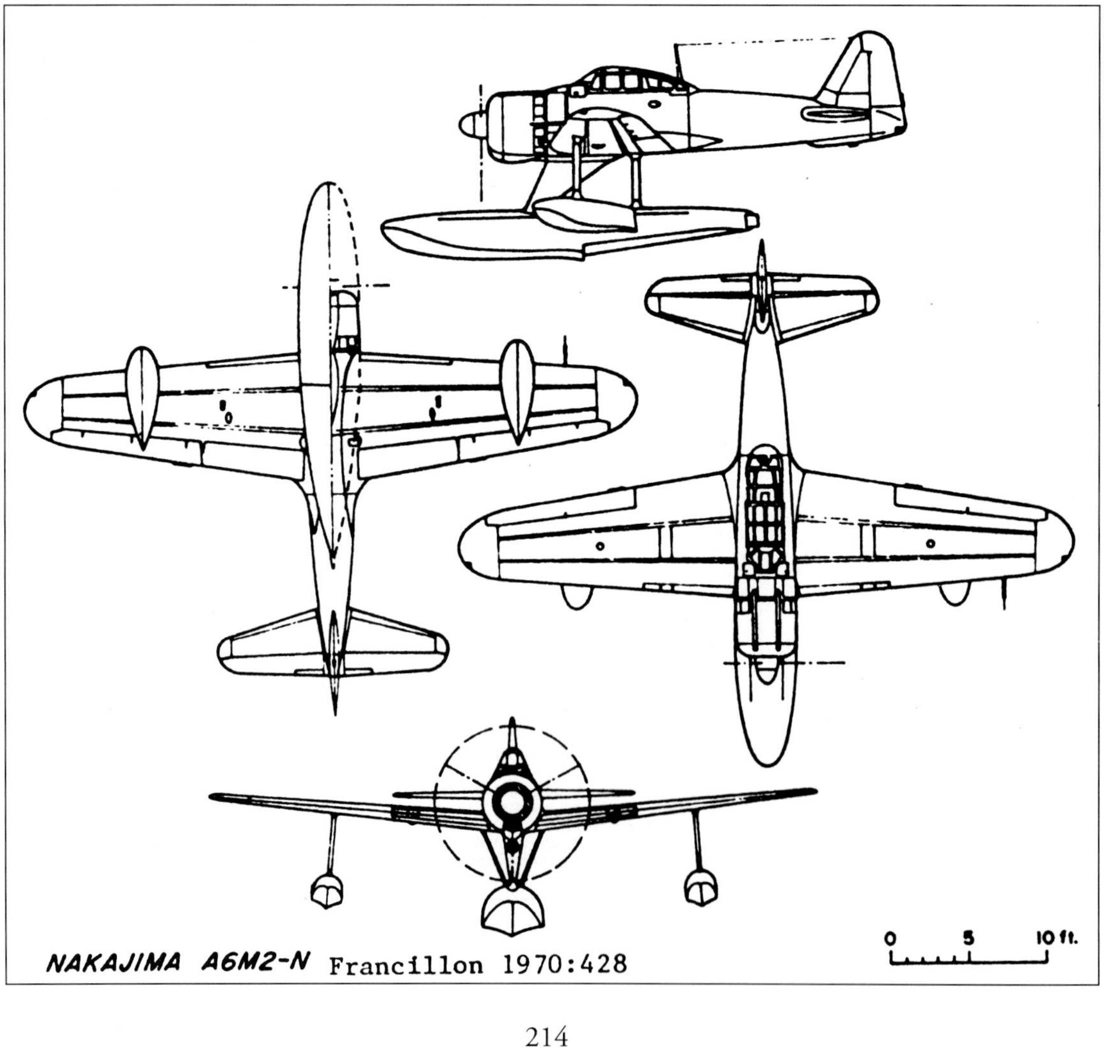

NAKAJIMA A6M2-N Francillon 1970:428

The Japanese occupation force on Attu lived in harsh conditions and it became even worse once the naval blockade tightened around the island.

A large tunnel, 3,000 feet deep was dug into a mountain side on Attu by Army engineers to house munitions, supplies and even huts as a precaution against a possible return of the Japanese in force, which of course never happened. –Courtesy of Blaine Corneilsen

–Courtesy of the University of Montana Media Service

A GENEROUS GIFT

In 2017 Barbara O'Donnell's estate donated two million dollars to the University of Montana Foundation for the Thomas Barton O'Donnell Endowed Scholarship to be awarded to students with financial need. She and her husband were both alumni of the university in 1941 and 1942. Her husband Tom joined the Army and was a captain with the 7th Infantry Division on Attu. He was wounded in the neck and shoulder but three days later he returned to his company to resume action. Six days later on May 26 he was wounded again and died. He was posthumously awarded the Distinguished Service Cross for his grit, leadership and courgage.

Attu, 1944.

Housing quarters.

B-25 on the Marsden Matting airfield.

Leisure time, tents in the background.

A hangar with the mountains in the background.

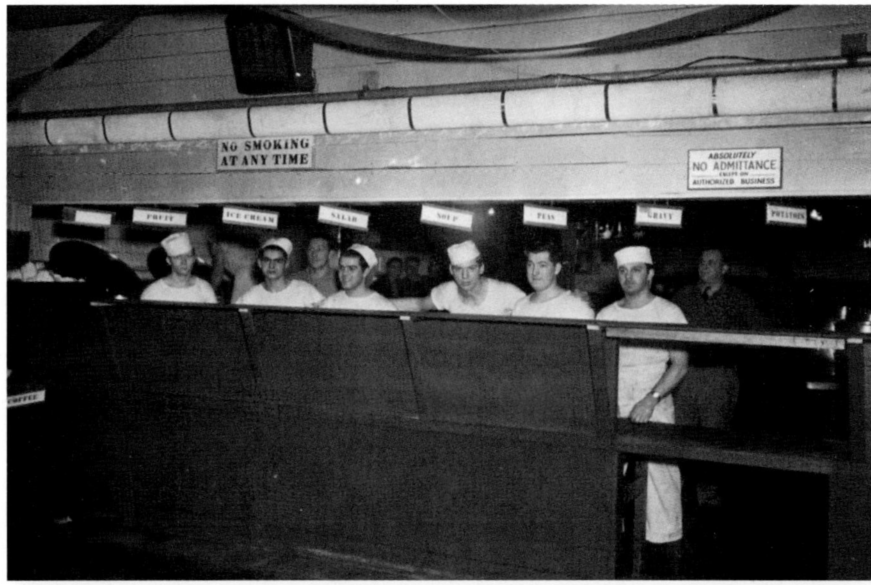

Christmas dinner at the Naval Air Station, Attu 1944. –Courtesy of Jim Backus

THE ATTU MORNING SUN

Vol. 2 Thursday, January 6, 1944 No. 26

REDS TAKE NAZI RAIL HUB

NEWS SUMMARY

Pacific War:

Two new raids on the Marshall Islands were announced by the Navy. One American fighter was lost over Mili. The second raid was made on Jaluit. Jaluit is generally regarded as the center for Jap shipping in the Marshalls. Its lagoon is 30 miles long and 12 miles wide. American airmen have spotted more Jap ships in the Jaluit lagoon than anywhere else in the Marshall atolls.

The Japanese bombed American positions in the Gilbert Islands 300 miles south of the Marshalls. Tarawa, Makin and Abemama were hit without damage to our installations, the Navy said.

Japanese bombers raided the headquarters of the U.S. Fourteenth Air Force in China, but were driven off.

Tank led Marines on New Britain, taking the offensive after smashing Japanese counterattacks, are advancing against stiff resistance towards Borgen Bay. The Marines are supported by heavy artillery.

Yugoslavia:

Marshal Josef Broz Tito announced Wednesday that the prolonged German offensive in eastern Bosnia had been smashed and that Yugoslav forces had regained enemy occupied territory including the important town of Vlasenica, 30 miles northeast of Sarajevo, where huge stores of war material were captured.

BERDICHEV FALLS AFTER 5 DAY BATTLE

Russian units of the Red Ukrainian army captured Berdichev, transfer point for the Leningrad to Odessa railroad and the Odessa to Warsaw railroad. The city was formerly the headquarters for Nazi armies in the Ukraine. Berdichev was taken after five days of battle, the Russian communique said.

Red army units to the north, in White Russia, advanced along the railroad from Veliki Luki toward Riga, capital of Latvia. Heavy fighting was developing in the swamps and lake country between Nevel and the Latvian border.

Berdichev was Hitlers headquarters when he was directing the Nazi push toward the Caucasus mountains in southern Russia. Military observers are pointing out that the Russian strategy seems to be to trap and destroy the German Army rather than pushing them back. The fall of Berdichev threatens the Nazi forces in the Dnieper Bend with encirclement.

AIR OFFENSIVE AGAINST GERMANY CONTINUES

American heavy bombers, plowing ahead through defenses which included rocket planes and ME110s towing what appeared to be a new type of anti-aircraft bomb, struck the Kiel shipyards Wednesday for the third time in three weeks and ranged across a record 800 mile front to blast airfields at Bordeaux and Tours in France and other targets in western Germany. Never before in a major operation has the U.S. Eighth Air Force been able to attack targets so far apart as Kiel and Bordeaux or been able to execute so many diversionary thrusts. The airline distance

—CHAPTER ELEVEN—

AMPHIBIOUS TASK FORCE 9 THE INVASION OF KISKA

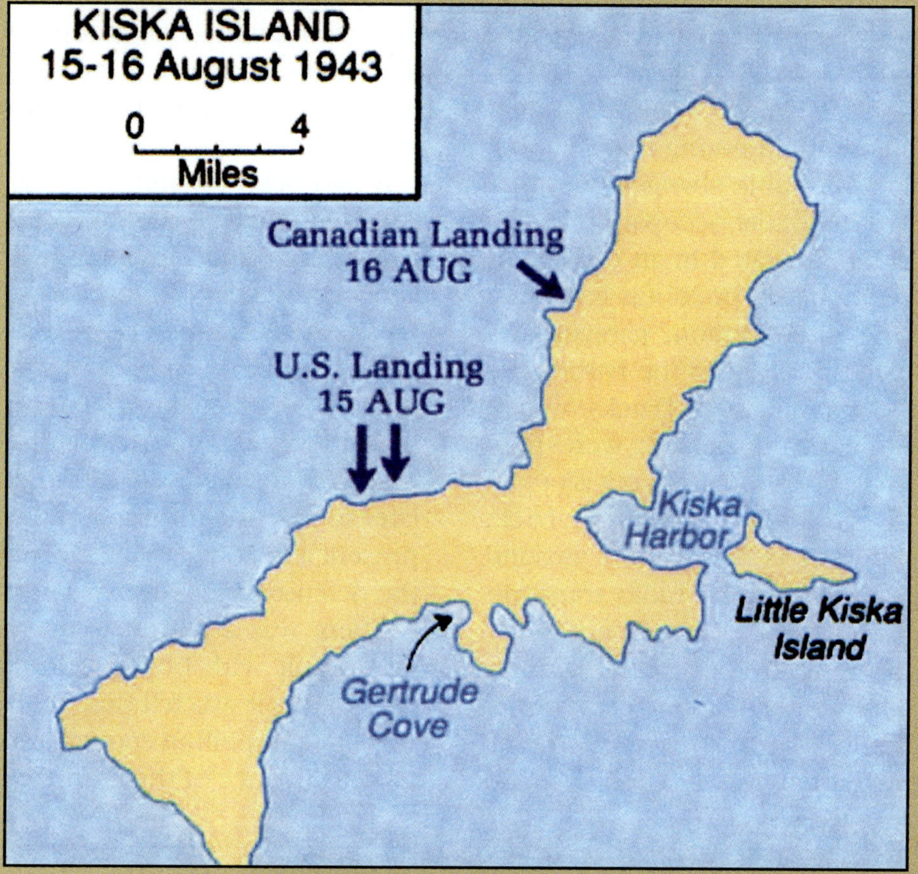

The Canadians landed on both August 15th and 16th.
—Courtesy of U.S. Army Center Military History

BEFORE THE ALLIED OCCUPATION

The Japanese had left Kiska 18 days before the Allied forces invaded. How did U.S. Intelligence at Adak not detect their absence?

Aerial reconnaissance revealed that many of the buildings were destroyed and that many barges, formally present were missing. On Aug. 4, 1943, Admiral Kinkaid's intelligence officer handled the Admiral a memorandum noting that the photographs showed "remarkable changes" and that "never before since the initial occupation has so much destruction been created in an equivalent period of time. " Twenty-six buildings had been destroyed including radio station, garages and barracks. Of a score of barges in the harbor the week before, only one remained. Trucks, which the Japanese customarily dispersed, were now clustered near the harbor shore. Radio Kiska had gone off the air on July 28 and never came back. However, returning pilots did report ground fire. Even though there was no radio transmissions from the island and its radar was not working, there were some reports of fresh diggings. Repeated naval bombardments drew no reply. It may seem remarkable that this evidence revealing a possible evacuation was not followed up on; but in 1943 the Japanese had a reputation for being talented when it came to the deception of troop movements; so it was thought that they had moved the bulk of the force into the hinterland in order to fight in small groups. It was thought that the enemy had moved into defensive battle positions and were using the barges to redistribute its forces.

It had been thought that the enemy may have left behind a rear party to fire AA weapons at Allied aircraft and naval observes; and then were later removed by submarine. Information from a Japanese source, Captain Arichika Rokuji, Chief of Staff of the 1st Destroyer Squadron which conducted the evacuation, said in 1945, " There was no one left ashore except three dogs, however, timed explosions were left to detonate a few days later to give the impression that troops were still present and going about the business of changing the defenses.

There was a plan to scout the island prior to the assault with boat parties, but this idea was dropped as it was felt that the Japanese resistance was not compelling enough to require an advance reconnaissance of the island, except by air.

"Patrol" on Kiska. In 1943 Lt. Edward John Hughes of the Canadian Forces was posted to Kiska, apparently Canada's only official artist in the Aleutians. He had been in England and Wales previously and proved to be one of the most prolific artists of the war, producing over 1600 drawings, watercolors, and oils.

Japanese roads, huts, and airfield. –Courtesy of Blaine Corneilsen

The invasion of Kiska (code named Operation Cottage) consisted of a major naval task force and 15,000 troops of the US Army's 7th Division, some of them veterans of the Attu battle, 2,500 troops of The First Special Service Force (US and Canadian), 5,000 troops of the 87th Mountain Infantry Regiment and 5,300 troops of the 13th Canadian Army Brigade. It took place on August 15, 1943. A few weeks before approximately 6,000 Japanese troops evacuated the island, using fog as a cover; destroyers sailed into Kiska harbor and brought every man out and back to Japan. Only on New Guinea and Guadalcanal in the South Pacific did the Japanese evacuate their troops, the rest of the battles they fought to the death. Unfortunately friendly fire in the darkness killed 24 troops and four more were killed by booby traps. Fifty others were wounded. In an island cove, the destroyer *U.S.S. Abner Read* was damaged by an enemy mine with the loss of 71 men and 24 injured. It took another few days to secure the island and make sure there were no enemy troops left. Most of the troops left shortly afterwards but the Canadians stayed on for occupation duty for four months.

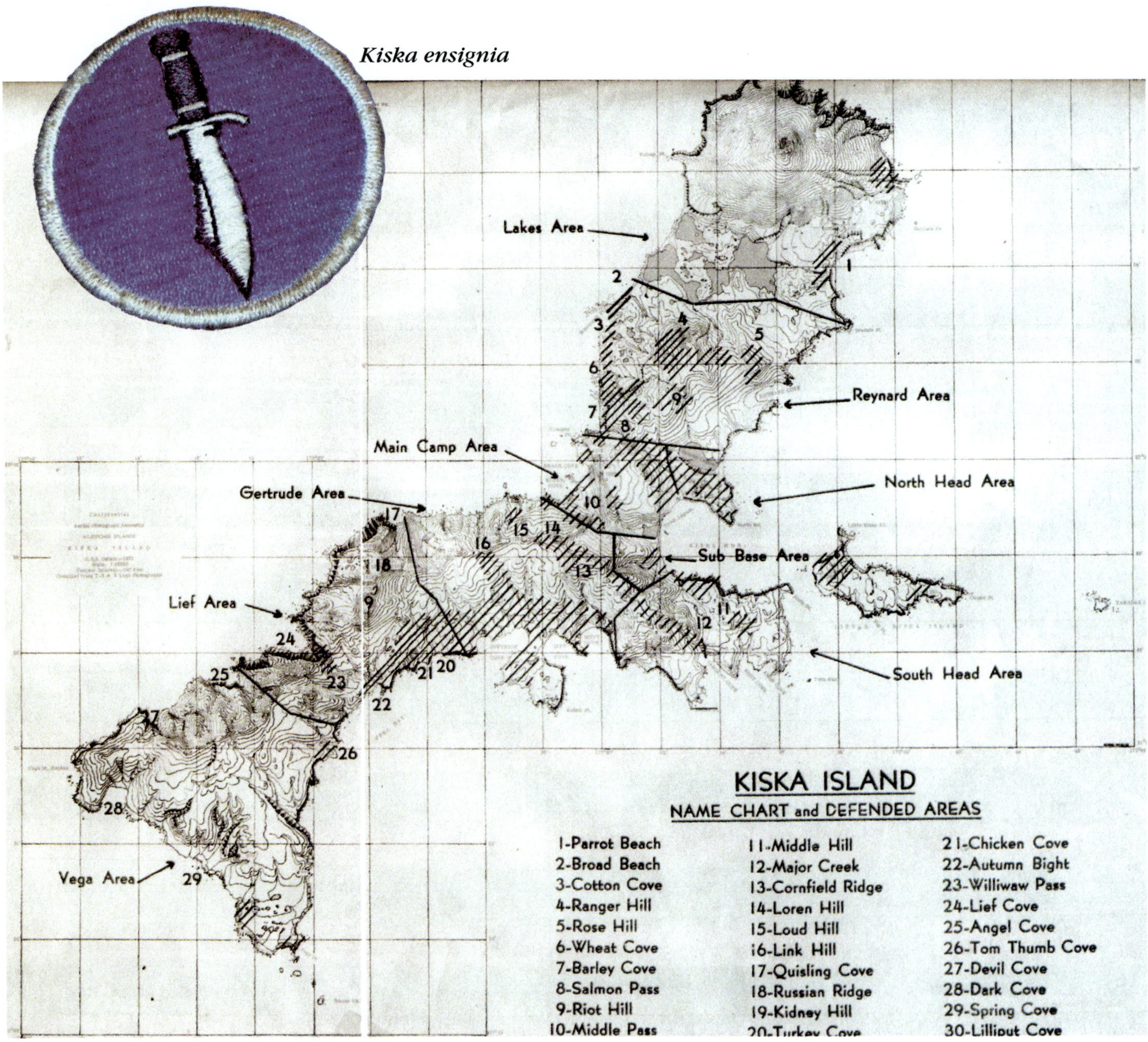

Kiska ensignia

HEADQUARTERS ELEVENTH AIR FORCE
APO 942, c/o Postmaster
Seattle, Washington

December 27, 1942

INTERPRETATION OF "ALEUTIAN FLYER #1"

Titlex: So Sorry for You.

Remarks: The themes in the text were suggested from Alaska. The language has been kept direct, simple and unliterary, and no necessity has been seen for an excessive degree o f piliteness.
The inscription on the front of the flyer, "So sorry for you," is the everyday Japanese expression covering a situation like that summed up in the text. In pre-war years, it was the stock response, tinged with irony, to complaints about violation of American rights in occupied China.

Front.

(The large inscription means "So Sorry For You." The place names, from left to right, are "Japan," "Kiska" and "Alaska." The distance from Japan to Alaska is given as 3,600 kilmeters.)

Back

GRAVEYARD OF THE NORTH PACIFIC FOOLISH VENTURE

You are isolated completely, your lines to the homeland cut, How futile the death awaiting you on the lonely, barren Aleutians!

Your warlords have given up execution of the Aleutian attack. They have stopp ed sending reinforcements far across the storm-swept Northern Pacific to resist American might, which grows daily, for the sacrifices of p ast months have been too great. How many ship s have been bombed and sunk before your eyes? How many more have gone down without your knowledge? Airpl ane losses have been heav y. How many men have been drowned, killed and wounded? Such is the enormity of the sacrifices that they dare not announce them at ho me.

Now that winter is here, your warlords cannot even send you food and other supplies. Rescue of you is out o f the question. You have been abandoned.

As you well know, the might of the United States forces advancing by means of bases in the chain of islands from the American Continent, is approaching you like an ever-rising tide. Since landing, not once have you been able to take the offensive. Now even your means of defense are vanishing. Pitiful are your straits! As your are dying in vain, your families far across the sea deserve great sympathy.

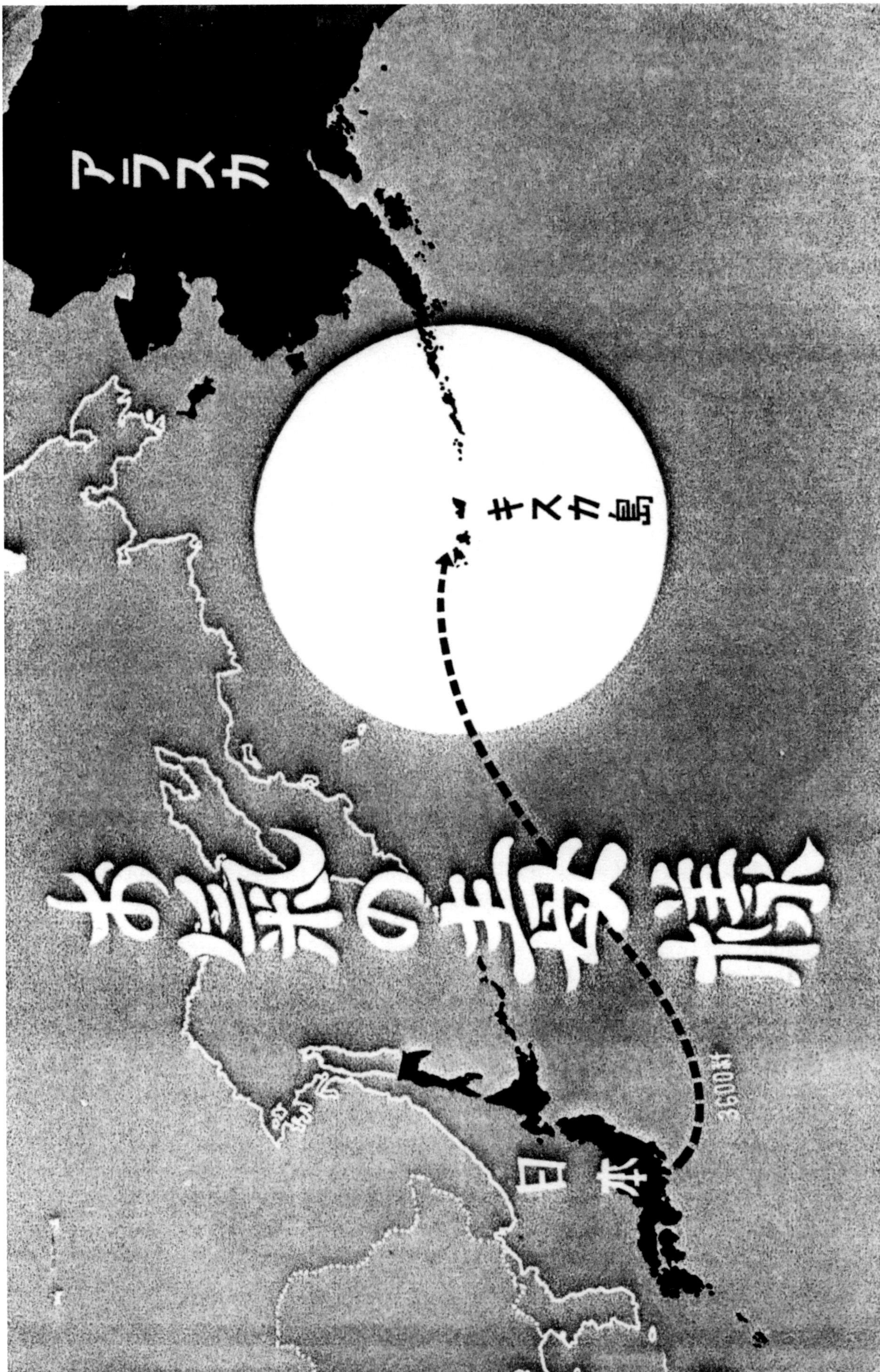
お氣の毒様
アラスカ
キスカ島
日本
3600粁

北太平洋愚策の墓地

本國との連絡を遮斷された諸君は今や全く孤立の狀態に在る諸君の今日の憂目、荒涼たるアルーシャン列島の絕島に無意味な最期を遂げたることは、何たる無駄死だ。

諸君の督軍連は既にアルーシャン攻擊遂行を全く斷念してゐるのである。　日に其の威力を增す米軍に對抗する爲め、遠く嵐吹く北太平洋の孤島に援軍を送る事を諦め、諸君を見殺しにしてゐるのだ。　何故ならば過去數ヶ月に於ける犧牲餘りにも多大であつた爲めである。　諸君の目前で爆沈された船のみで幾艘あるか？　而して諸君に報道されずに擊沈された數はそれより如何程多いことか。　航空機の損害は餘りにも多かつた。　溺死者、戰死者、或は負傷者の如何計り多かりしか？　此の犧牲の餘りにも多き爲め、本國では發表する事さへ出來ぬではないか！

今や極寒來たりたるに諸君の督軍達は諸君に食量其他の補充品さへ送る事が出來なくなつてゐる。　諸君等を救出する等は思ひも及ばぬ。　諸君は全く見放されて居るのである。

周知の如く、米軍の威力はアメリカ大陸より列島に點在する基地を經ていやが上にも增大する潮の如く諸君に切迫してゐるのである。　諸君は全く米軍の爲すが儘の窮狀に在るのである。　上陸して以來一度として諸君は攻勢を取る事が出來なかつたではないか。　而も今や防禦の手段さへ無くなりつゝあるではないか。　みじめな窮狀とは諸君の事だ。　遙か大洋の彼方にある諸君の家族こそ氣の毒の至りだ。　何故なら、諸君が何等爲す所なく死んで行きつゝあるからである。

SPECIAL MEMORANDUM NUMBER 2

S E C R E T

3

OFFICE OF THE COMMANDING GENERAL
Amphibian Training Force 9
Fort Ord, California

5 July 1943

SUBJECT: Battle Identifications.

TO : All Officers and Non-Commissioned Officers, ATF 9.

1. On the battlefield, fighting sometimes finds enemy and friendly troops mixed up at close range and in quick, desperate action. To provide identification in these hectic moments, every member of ATF 9 will wear two (2) Blue Bowie Knife shoulder patches, one on each shoulder of:

- a. Alaska Field Jacket (sewed on).
- b. Rain Jacket (glued on with canvas cement).
- c. One OD shirt (sewed on).
- d. Parka (sewed on).

These shoulder patches will be emplaced after leaving the continental United States; patches will be issued aboard ship and sewed and/or glued on by all individuals.

2. Each member of ATF 9 will have a daylight identification panel, an 18-inch black and white cloth checkerboard with him at all times in combat for distant identification. These panels have the tie-tape for ease in securing on the back or chest. Those will be displayed whenever U. S. or Canadian troops wish to recognize each other, or whenever U. S. airplanes fly over front lines strafing the enemy.

3. As an additional aerial recognition, each squad will carry two 19" x 31" fluorescent panels, either red or chrome yellow (orange). These panels are extremely visible from the air and must be displayed only when U. S. planes are overhead.

4. For patrol identification at night a small 7-inch by 3-inch fluorescent panel is provided. This panel is made active by sunlight; it must be exposed during daylight to store up a flourescent glow for night use. It is easily recognizable at a distance of 20 yards at night. Do not expose this headlight to the enemy.

5. The black and white checkerboard, the red or chrome yellow air panel, and the fluorescent night panel will be issued in the staging area. Everyone is cautioned to watch for these panels and withhold fire when they are displayed. The Jap cannot reproduce them and can only obtain them from us by careless loss or capture.

CHARLES H. CORLETT
Major General, U. S. A.
Commanding

S E C R E T

4

SPECIAL MEMORANDUM
NUMBER 3

S E C R E T

OFFICE OF THE COMMANDING GENERAL
Amphibian Training Force 9
Fort Ord, California

5 July 1943

SUBJECT: Individual Camouflage.

TO : All Officers and Non-Commissioned Officers, ATF 9.

1. It is my earnest desire to furnish each officer and soldier everything possible to protect him from getting hurt on the battlefield. In the past, the American soldier has been notoriously careless about camouflage, and it has unquestionably caused men to be killed or wounded.

2. We have secured excellent material for personal camouflage in the nature of paint and nets. The paint is absolutely harmless, in fact it can be eaten without injury, and while it is not easily washed off with plain water, it removes very easily with soap and water.

3. The human face is very easily seen at great distances. Duck hunters know how important it is to hide the face in the duck blind. To prevent surprise our faces must be exposed and our eyes alert for any enemy action. We therefore must paint our faces in the proper way and utilize natural grasses in our helmet nets and clothing to keep the enemy from seeing us.

4. Every effort should be made to camouflage our persons, our gun positions, and to avoid making paths that will give the enemy information as to our location.

5. Dummy positions to draw enemy fire may be desirable. Defilade from artillery fire for command posts, ammunition dumps, message centers and aid stations should be secured.

6. We must not be too close together at any time. This, coupled with movement, will save many lives. When you hit the ground, roll over several times. Keep moving forward by crawling so they cannot mark you down for mortar or machine gun fire. Deceive the enemy every way you can. USE YOUR HEAD.

7. Attached are some suggestions for putting on war paint and for concealing yourself with grass or moss that you may find wherever you are.

CHARLES H. CORLETT
Major General, U. S. A.
Commanding

S E C R E T

6

SPECIAL MEMORANDUM
NUMBER 5

S E C R E T

OFFICE OF THE COMMANDING GENERAL
AMPHIBIAN TRAINING FORCE 9
Fort Ord, California

5 July 1943

SUBJECT: Souvenirs, Straggling, Booby Traps and Looting.

TO : All Officers and Non-Commissioned Officers, ATF 9.

Many Americans are great souvenir-hunters. In peace time, it is an interesting hobby, but in war it may be very dangerous for many reasons.

It has been found in past engagements that some men drop out of their squads to collect souvenirs or loot when the battle is in progress.

This is, of course, against military law. Every squad or other military organization is a team. If one or more men drop out of it at any time it weakens the team and endangers the lives of the men who continue the fight.

Other men drop out because they are tired or possibly a little bit yellow. This endangers and risks the lives of the rest of the men of the team.

It is felt that all men in this Force will have the guts and determination to stand by and protect the men they are with who are their friends and buddies.

It is hoped that all men have been eliminated who will not do this.

Sometimes, this straggling or souvenir-hunting has been caused by thoughtlessness by perfectly fine, brave men, so you are reminded here to do your share on all occasions so that you will not be suspected of carelessness of your teammates or of cowardice.

Frequently, tempting pieces of loot hide booby-traps that may blow not only yourself but others to atoms if they are picked up. Especially this may be true in deserted buildings.

When the fight is over, there will be plenty of time to search for souvenirs without exposing your comrades to danger.

Charles H. Corlett
CHARLES H. CORLETT
Major General, U. S. A.
Commanding

The USS Abner Read *lost its stern after hitting a mine—but survived. The stern sank in the pitch-black water.*
—Courtesy of the USN, via Steve Harding

Admiral Thomas C. Kinkaid leader of the Kiska task force.

General view of Kiska Harbor showing American alligator transport craft on the beach and ships in the harbor. The alligators brought supplies from the ships to the shore, September 5, 1943.

U.S.S THUBAN AKA-19

The ship was named after the primary star in the constellation Draco. It was an Andromeda-class Attack Cargo Ship and was commissioned at the Brooklyn Navy Yard in June 1943 and then headed to Adak, arriving on August 5 and anchoring off Quisling Cove with the Kiska invasion fleet on August 15. It won seven battle stars in World War Two in the Pacific Theater and served in Korea and other areas and was decommissioned in October 1968 and disposed of in September 1984.

Memo to All Hands 13 August 1943

We are now embarked to take the Island of Kiska from the Japs. This will require the coordination of all our efforts and the cooperation of all hands. There will be a lot of hard work, long hours and a certain amount of danger, but we must drive the Japs out of the Aleutians, and I know that each and everyone of you on this ship will do your best.

The folks back home will be reading about you in the newspapers and they will know that you were in on this job, I'm sure they will feel proud of you.

Our ship has been in commission only a short time and it has been a hard grind getting everything whipped into shape, but let me say now that I am very pleased with the results. Now we are ready for anything, and I know that you will all do your duty and your very best in this coming scrap.

GOOD LUCK AND GOD BLESS YOU ALL
J.C. Campbell commanding

U.S.S. ABNER READ (DD-526)

The Fletcher-class destroyer was commissioned at San Francisco, CA on Fed.5, 1943 and named after Lieutenant Commander Abner Read. Along with Task Group (TG) 51.2 she sailed to Attu to support the invasion. After shelling the island she sailed back to San Diego on May 16 and went into dry dock. She again sailed for Adak to join TF 16 for the invasion of Kiska, and began her patrol duties around the island. While patrolling off of Kiska on the night of August 17 the destroyer was shaken by an explosion aft at 0150 and it was thought that she had hit a Japanese mine. The concussion tore a huge hole in her stern and ruptured her smoke stacks. Men sleeping in aft compartments suffered from smoke inhalation. In the darkness, a few men fell through holes in the deck into fuel tanks below. A total of 71 sailors were lost. Then the stern broke away and sank. At 0355 the destroyer was taken under tow by the *USS Bancroft* and further repairs in various Alaskan ports and then towed to the Puget Sound Navy Yard for extensive repairs. In late 1944 the destroyer was part of the Leyte invasion in the Philippines but was struck by a kamikaze aircraft attack and sank with the loss of 22 men.

The exact location of the stern had always been a mystery until July 2018, when searches on a team funded by NOAA, using modern sophisticated equipment, a ROV, found the 75' long and about 18' high stern encrusted with sea life. The stern and remains will remain in place as hallowed ground. See photo on page 227.

AIR OPERATIONS IN THE ALEUTIAN CAMPAIGN

Canadian Air Operations

The men of the Home War Establishment (HWE) did not expect they would ever fight beyond Canada's borders. In 1942 the U.S. fearing an attack on the northernmost point of the Pacific Coast enlisted Canada's help in its defense. The RCAF, well aware of the weaknesses in the Prince Rupert area, agreed to post No. 115 (fighter) Squadron to the US Air Base on Annette Island near Ketchikan in southeast Alaska, some 100 kilometers north of Prince Rupert.

In June two additional RCAF Squadrons, No. 8 (Bomber-Reconnaissance) and No. 111 (Fighter) were already on their way to support the 11th Army Air Forces in Alaska. Transiting by Annette Island then by Juneau and Yukutat they landed at Elmendorf Field in Anchorage on June 8th. Meanwhile No. 118 (Fighter) Squadron left Dartmouth, Nova Scotia and flying clear across North America reached Annette Island. The airmen soon realized how dangerous flying such long distances between air bases could be, and how unpredictable was the foggy and stormy weather under these latitudes. In addition it soon became evident that the lack of spare parts for the British designed Bolingbrokes bombers would result in the aircraft being grounded for extended periods of time.

In August the Bolingbrokes of No. 8 Squadron and the P-40 Kittyhawks of No. 111 Squadron were transferred to Nome and Umnak island. On Sept. 25, 1942 The U.S. and Canadian Air Forces attacked Kiska. Squadron Leader K.A. Boomer commanded No. 111 Squadron. They bombed the Japanese installations on Kiska and strafed the fleet. The enemy had only two fighter planes in flying condition, Rufe fighters (Zeros converted into hydroplanes). Both took part in the response and during the skirmish, the lead Rufe was shot down by Boomer while the other Rufe was shot down by Major Jack Chennault of the 11th Fighter Squadron. Claims included the two Rufes as well as five to eight larger flying boats in the harbor. All the Canadian and American airmen were awarded US Air Medals for this "hazardous 500 mile over water flight' in single engine aircraft. Squadron Leader Boomer was also awarded the DFC; he had won the only air victory by a member of the HWE.

Despite these raids. Both occupied islands remained in enemy hands. The Canadian squadrons remained on the remote bases to take part in patrols and defense operations. After the end of the Aleutian Campaign in August 1943 the Canadian airmen were withdrawn back to Canada.

The US 11th Air Force started attacking Kiska as early as June 11, 1942, just after the Japanese landing. From then on Kiska was hit frequently and once new bases were established further west than Umnak; Attu could also be attacked. The new bases were established at Adak (occupied on August 30th) and Amchitka (occupied on January 12, 1943). Pilots and navigators waiting in their hut before going out in the B-24s to bomb Kiska from their base on Umnak Island. The men read, sleep, play checkers, or just take it easy. –Courtesy of USAF

–Courtesy of USMC

–Courtesy of USMC

JAPANESE PLANES KNOWN TO BE OPERATIONAL AROUND KISKA

At no time during the occupation did the total effective plane strength exceed 30 or 40 planes.

Seaplanes-six "Mavises" were reported moved into Kiska on June 8, 1942. Twelve were spotted in Kiska Harbor near Trout Lagoon on June 12. Three of the "Mavises"were lost to Allied bombers in June 1942. Nakajima "Rufe" also called "Float Zeros" appeared in June 1942. Of 18 delivered, six were shot down, two or three were destroyed by bombing and all but two of the remaining were lost to surf and weather by the end of June. Two or three were found after the reoccupation. Salvage piles at the end of the Kiska Camp contained nearly 40 different planes including "Rufe" Nakajima floatfighters and "Jake" Watanabe float reconnaissance planes, which dominated the wreckage. Other types included a "Mavis" Kawanashi 97, "Pete" Mitsubishi observation float plane and possibly one Aichi reconnaissance float plane.

ALLIED PLANES OPERATIONAL IN THE ALEUTIAN CAMPAIGN

Four B-17s were initially involved in 1942, including two prototypes and two LB-30s, which were B-24s converted for transfer to the RAF, B-24s, B-26s, PB4Y-2s. P-40s, P-38s P-39s, B-18s, C-45s, SBDs and an SCO, a cruiser-based catapult observation plane.

Bombs dropped on a dock and storage area on Kiska. –Courtesy of KHS OP 608-17-2

THE ESCAPE OF THE JAPANESE GARRISON FROM KISKA

WRITTEN BY KARL KAORU KASUKABE

I have been lucky for being a mountaineer! Before the war, among other workers at the Mitsubishi Nagoya Aircraft Works. I climbed three thousand-meter peaks in the Japan Alps in midwinter–a natural laboratory for experiments in low-temperature science.

We experienced the effects of high altitude at minus thirty to minus fifty degrees Celsius and gathered experimental data for the pilots of our country's Zeros and Flying Dragons.

My studies in meteorology and the experience I had with the Chukyo Alpine Club made it possible for me to understand complex weather patterns and eventually, by taking advantage of thick fog as cover, to help my garrison slip out of Kiska Island without the Americans knowing it.

The Japanese forces on Kiska were ever on alert, constantly trying some way to get out of the Americans' tight encirclement by PBYs, submarines and coastal torpedo boats escorted by destroyers–in effect, a triple blockade.

From July 24 to 29, 1943, many coded fleet operations telegrams (and many not coded at all) flooded into our communications corps on Kiska. We were aware of the fact that the large American fleet was pulling ships and planes off the blockade and lining up in the waters west of Kiska. The aim, obviously, was to intercept any Japanese rescue fleet. And so both fleets engaged in the game of cat-and-mouse in the foggy Aleutian waters.

American radar operators, perhaps through frustration and nervousness, reported what they thought was radar contacted with the Japanese fleet. The result was an all-out attack on "radar blips" (The Battle of the Pips, which turned out to be no battle at all).

At 1920 hours on 28 July, a Japanese Army sentry on the outpost at Vega Point observed the dim light of the American fleet some one hundred kilometers away, on a compass heading of 160 degrees.

The American force's uncoded messages flooded in and Japanese navel intelligence was thereby able to pinpoint the position of the U.S. fleet. We focused on transmissions from portable telecommunications equipment and took note of the slang spoken among the immigrant rank and file on Amchitka, 134 kilometers away. We were able to determine that PBYs were engaged in refueling operations and that the task force itself was refueling and rearming.

The Japanese were able to determine areas around Kiska where engagement seemed unlikely to occur and to identify a window of ten to twelve hours when dense fog would most likely provide cover for the rescue operation. Garrison headquarters had to carry out the evacuation operation within that limited amount of time.

After considering the PBYs' three hundred- to five hundred-mile radius patrolling area and their range from bases on Shemya and Amchitka, Kiska headquarters decided to make the attempt.

The approach to Kiska Harbor would take four hours; loading fifty-three hundred men, one hour; and departing from Kiska would take another four hours. Originally, the arrival of the fleet at the Kiska anchorage had been scheduled for 1800 hours. In order to put it four hours ahead, that is, at 1400 hours, Kiska headquarters transmitted the single Japanese Kana-letter code, "Yu, Yu, Yu" at five minute intervals, ordering the Japanese rescue fleet to approach at the earlier time. This pre-arranged, one-time code was unbreakable. The Japanese rescue fleet anchored at Kiska Harbor at 1340 hours on 19 July 1943.

Two light cruisers and nine destroyers had replaced their usual cargo of seaplanes and torpedoes with a total of twenty landing craft. These were unloaded at sea and, along with the nineteen boats berthed at the Kiska garrison, made for a formidable armada indeed!

The rope ladders aboard the cruisers and destroyers were hung down, and they covered both sides of the ships. Many landing craft, large and small, sailed right alongside the large vessels as men from the garrison threw their rifles and bayonets into the sea and climbed the ships' rope ladders to safety. The shuttles to and from the rescue fleet, employing thirty-nine landing craft, had made it possible to complete the embarkation of fifty-three hundred men within fifty-five minutes! Thus did the Japanese garrison make its escape from Kiska.

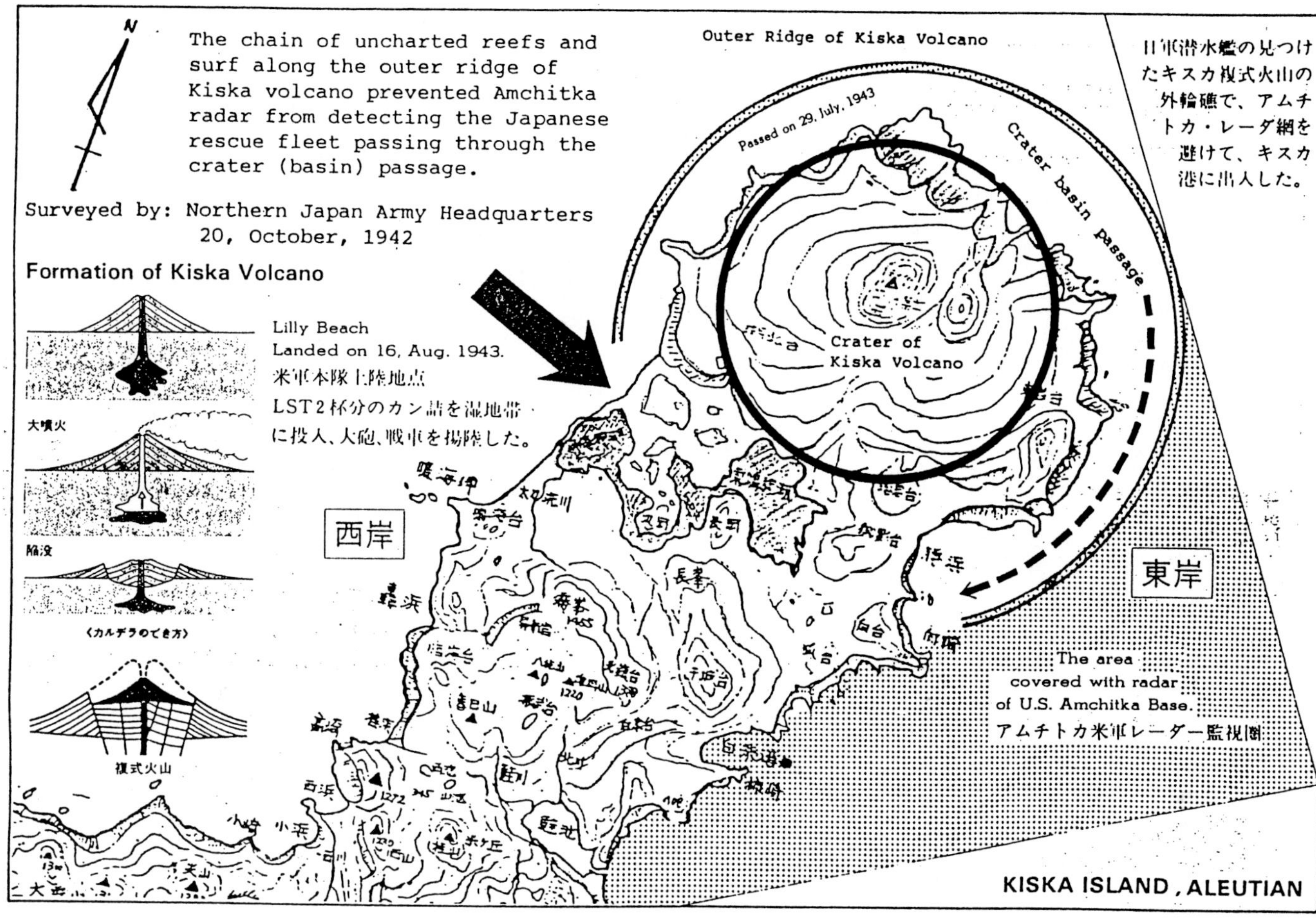

The garrison radar had been installed on the crater ridge above Kiska Harbor and commanded a 360-degree view. Originally it had been salvaged from the British battleship "Prince of Wales" and in fact had been the first radar seen in Japan. Thanks to British ingenuity, Japanese operators had been able to discern objects as far away from Kiska as three hundred kilometers.

Now, oddly. This example of the very latest in technology would become part of a simple and solemn observance.

At a pre-arranged signal—the explosions signifying the destruction of the radar installation—the whole garrison, now aboard the rescue fleet, prayed silently for those American and Japanese who had been killed in action.

From 1942 to 1943, the American Campaign had consumed as many lives as were now safely aboard the rescue ships: 2,638 Japanese had perished on Attu, and another twenty-five hundred men had died on and around Kiska Island and on the rough waters of the Aleutians. In addition, there were the thousands of American causalities in the Aleutian theater.

The thirty-nine landing craft were scuttled and, along with the rope ladders and weaponry, sent to the bottom of Kiska Harbor. The rescue fleet made for Paramushiro, at the northern edge of the Kurlis, at full speed—thirty knots.

If things had happened differently, we would have butchered each other to the last man on the beaches and, in the underground fortress where I sat with others of the intelligence corps, I would have been doomed to die. The dead would have been left on the lonely tundra wilderness forever, the landscape of which is bleakness itself.

The American forces massed for the invasion of Kiska numbered ten thousand (actually 35,000 thousand American and Canadian troops) and would have faced the Japanese garrison of nearly six thousand. The latter were disciplined troops, poised like rattlesnakes, ready to strike, and well-suited in the fortified holes on the lava ridges around Kiska Harbor.

Very likely that tundra wilderness would have turned scarlet with the blood of fifteen thousand American and Japanese troops.

EVACUATION OPERATION OF JAPANESE KISKA GARRISON (29 July~31 July, 1943.)

日本北洋艦隊・キスカ島守備隊撤収作戦図 （7月29日~31日、1943年）

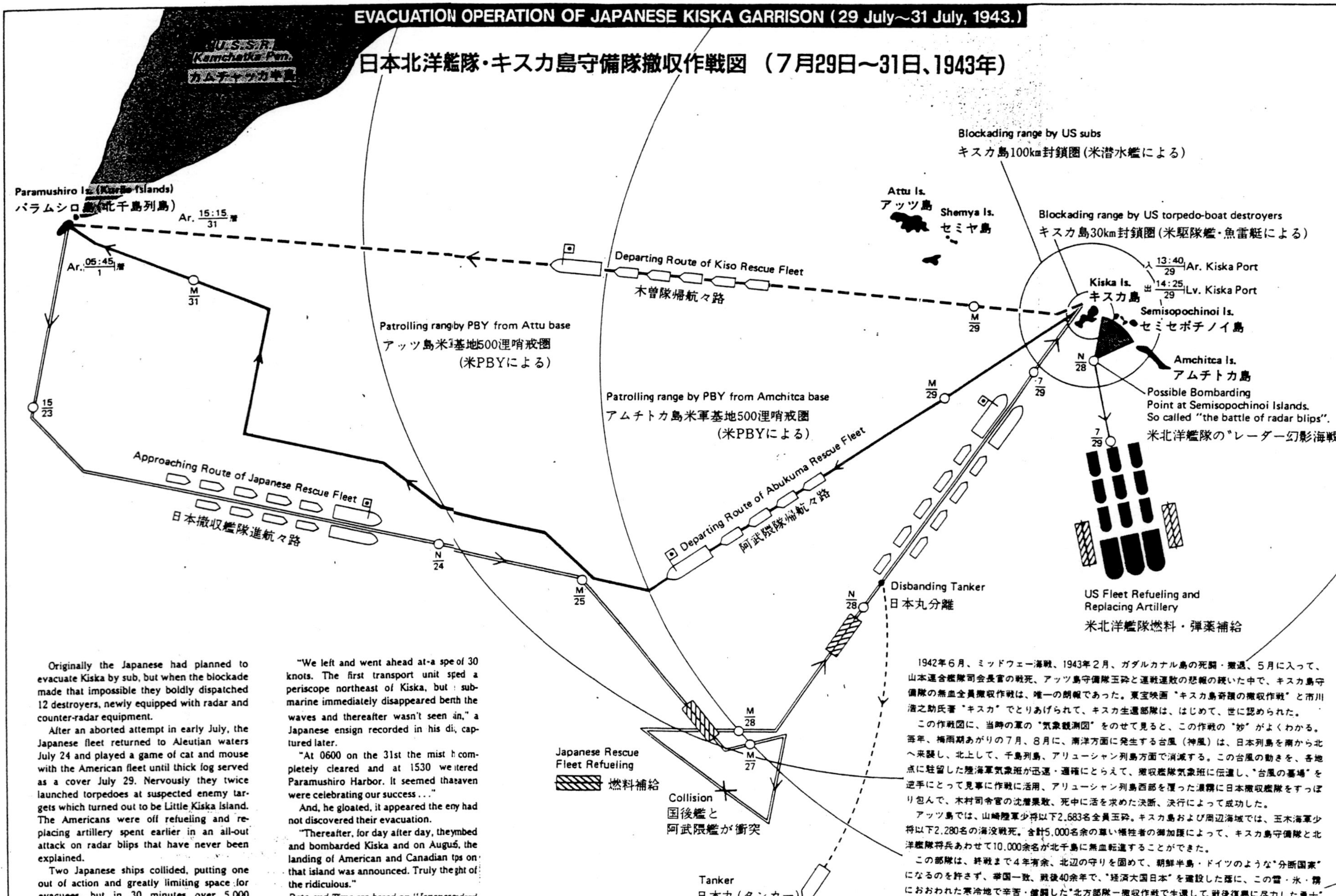

Originally the Japanese had planned to evacuate Kiska by sub, but when the blockade made that impossible they boldly dispatched 12 destroyers, newly equipped with radar and counter-radar equipment.

After an aborted attempt in early July, the Japanese fleet returned to Aleutian waters July 24 and played a game of cat and mouse with the American fleet until thick fog served as a cover July 29. Nervously they twice launched torpedoes at suspected enemy targets which turned out to be Little Kiska Island. The Americans were off refueling and replacing artillery spent earlier in an all-out attack on radar blips that have never been explained.

Two Japanese ships collided, putting one out of action and greatly limiting space for evacuees, but in 30 minutes over 5,000 Japanese soldiers managed to clamber aboard, the fleet upended anchor and made a dash for home.

"We left and went ahead at a spe of 30 knots. The first transport unit sped a periscope northeast of Kiska, but sub-marine immediately disappeared benth the waves and thereafter wasn't seen ain," a Japanese ensign recorded in his di, captured later.

"At 0600 on the 31st the mist h completely cleared and at 1530 we itered Paramushiro Harbor. It seemed thaeaven were celebrating our success . . ."

And, he gloated, it appeared the eny had not discovered their evacuation.

"Thereafter, for day after day, theymbed and bombarded Kiska and on Augu5, the landing of American and Canadian tps on that island was announced. Truly the ght of the ridiculous."

Date and Time are based on "Japanesendard time". $\frac{7}{29}$ = at 7 o'clock on 29th, July $\frac{I}{8}$ = at night on 28th. $\frac{M}{29}$ = at mid-night on 2

1942年６月、ミッドウェー海戦、1943年２月、ガダルカナル島の死闘・撤退、５月に入って、山本連合艦隊司令長官の戦死、アッツ島守備隊玉砕と連戦連敗の悲報の続いた中で、キスカ島守備隊の無血全員撤収作戦は、唯一の朗報であった。東宝映画〝キスカ島奇蹟の撤収作戦〟と市川浩之助氏著〝キスカ〟でとりあげられて、キスカ生還部隊は、はじめて、世に認められた。

この作戦図に、当時の軍の〝気象観測図〟をのせて見ると、この作戦の〝妙〟がよくわかる。毎年、梅雨期あがりの７月、８月に、南洋方面に発生する台風（神風）は、日本列島を南から北へ来襲し、北上して、千島列島、アリューシャン列島方面で消滅する。この台風の動きを、各地点に駐留した陸海軍気象班が迅速・適確にとらえて、撤収艦隊気象班に伝達し、〝台風の墓場〟を逆手にとって見事に作戦に活用、アリューシャン列島西部を覆った濃霧に日本撤収艦隊をすっぽり包んで、木村司令官の沈着果敢、死中に活を求めた決断、決行によって成功した。

アッツ島では、山崎陸軍少将以下2,683名全員玉砕。キスカ島および周辺海域では、玉木海軍少将以下2,280名の海没戦死。合計5,000名余の尊い犠牲者の御加護によって、キスカ島守備隊と北洋艦隊将兵あわせて10,000余名が北千島に無血転進することができた。

この部隊は、終戦まで４年有余、北辺の守りを固めて、朝鮮半島・ドイツのような〝分断国家〟になるのを許さず、挙国一致、戦後40余年で、〝経済大国日本〟を建設した蔭に、この雪・氷・霧におおわれた寒冷地で辛苦・健闘した〝北方部隊ー撤収作戦で生還して、戦後復興に尽力した勇士〟のあること、この北方部隊の貢献・功績を再認識すべきである。

Norman Dyhrenfurth and wife. –Courtesy The International Ski History Association

THE 87TH MOUNTAIN INFANTRY REGIMENT

The 87th Mountain Infantry Battalion was activated on Nov. 15, 1941 at Fort Lewis, WA. It was the first mountain infantry unit in the US Army and was expanded into a regiment in May 1942. It was part of the original units of the 10th Mountain Division at Camp Hale, CO and trained there in 1942-43. The 87th started it trip north to take part in the Kiska operation on July 25, 1943. After the invasion the regiment returned to Camp Hale and then took part in the Italian Campaign with the 10th from January to April 1945, It remained as part of the occupation force until August 1945 before returning to the United States. After the war many members of the 87th/10th would become involved in the ski and sporting goods business, and others would make a name for themselves in adventure related activities. One such individual was Norman Dyhrenfurth, son of well-known Himalayan explorers who would lead many climbing expeditions including the 1963 Everest Expedition that placed the first American on the top of Mount Everest.

87th Mountain Infantry Regiment

THE FIRST SPECIAL SERVICE FORCE

In the spring of 1942 the United States and Canadian governments agreed to establish Operation Plough and form a joint U.S./Canadian specialized commando unit trained in winter warfare and equipped with armored snow vehicles capable of either parachute or glider landings in the snow-covered regions of occupied Europe. The unit would conduct long-range sabotage operations against key industrial targets. Col. Robert T. Frederick was appointed its commander and the training base was a vacant National Guard post outside of Helena, Montana.

Operation Plough was canceled in early 1943 and the high command considered sending them to England or the Pacific but in April 1943 they were shipped to Camp Bradford, VA for amphibious training and then to Fort Ethan Allan in Vermont for more training. It was decided to use them as the first landing force in the invasion of Kiska. On June 26 they traveled by train to Angel Island, San Francisco and on July 9 they boarded two Liberty ships bound for Adak. They were instructed to remove all insignia from their clothing and not to mention where they were going to. After the successful occupation of the island the force was sent to Italy and then to the invasion of Southern France in September 1944. Set against a background of success in the field, the difficulties arising from cooperation between the two armies, and to the high number of Canadian casualties, led to a gradual erosion of the force's unique character and to its disbandment in December 1944. The force's museum and archives are located in The Montana Military Museum at Fort Harrison near Helena.

Monument at Helena, Montana

Landing on Kiska by William S. Story
former Executive Director of the First Special Service Force Assn.

I am one of the many members of the First Special Service Force who was delighted to find the Japanese had pulled out. After the experience of the 7th Infantry on Attu, we were not looking forward to a happy time on the larger and more heavenly- defended island. And because it was the Force that had the leading invasion role, we had reason to worry, especially when, on Amchitka, some of us picked up Tokyo Rose one day and heard her predict we would be landing on August 15!

Our first regiment came ashore in rubber boats with the goal of taking all the high ground to the west of the Japanese army barracks. There was no opposition on landing; all objectives were taken without a shot. Caves and huts had been searched, rice was found on the tables in the mess kits; one of our senior officers even reported a warm stove with still-live coals in the grate. But no Japanese. We passed the word back to the beaches for the incoming infantry to take it easy—we hadn't found any enemy yet, and while there was still a possibility of a surprise attack, they should keep their cool. But they came ashore looking for a fight. Meanwhile, we found more mess kitchens with fish and gobs of cooked rice on mess kits, but no soldiers. The last of them hadn't been gone long.

Our Third Regiment landed the next night, again in advance of the main body. And wouldn't you know—the wind blew the clouds away and the Third's boats were bathed in intense moonlight. Had there been any Japanese nearby, it would have been sheer slaughter.

Again, we passed the word—no enemy, take it easy. But the troops managed to shoot themselves up before starting souvenir hunting. Later, we had to set up a guard on the midget submarines because they were being pulled apart for souvenirs.

The problem with Kiska was poor intelligence all around. The Navy failed to keep proper tab on the Japanese vessel movements; the Army intelligence couldn't even extrapolate what was happening from the air photos at their command.

1st Special Service Force troopers ready for battle.

MAJOR GENERAL HARRY WICKWIRE FOSTER CBE, DSO

The commander of Canadian troops on the invasion of Kiska was born in Halifax, Nova Scotia in 1902. He was a senior Canadian Army officer who commanded two Canadian divisions in both the Pacific and European theaters during World War Two. He was the son of a Canadian World War One officer and educated at Kings College in Halifax as a cadet. He also attended schools in England, Quebec, McGill University in Montreal and the Royal Military College of Canada. He withdrew from RMC in 1924 and received the King's Commission and a posting with the Permanent Force (PF) with Lord Stathcona's Horse. In 1934 he obtained the rank of Captain and attended the Staff College at Camberly. From 1937-39 he was a Brigade Major at the start of the war.

In 1941 he was advanced to Lt. Colonel and commanded the 4th Reconnaissance Battalion (4th Princess Louise Dragoon Guards) and assigned to the 1st Canadian Infantry Division in England (1942). Then commanding officer of the 1st Battalion of the Highland Light Infantry of Canada. He led the Canadian contingent at Kiska and received the American Legion of Merit and other decorations. Later in 1943 he was promoted to Brig. General and took over the 4th Canadian (Armoured) Division and landed with them on Juno Beach on D-Day in France. He then led the 1st Canadian Infantry Division in Italy.

He retired in 1952 and took a civilian appointment of Chief Administrator of the Central European District, Imperial War Graves Commission. He died in 1964.

—Courtesy of David Foster, Pont Henry, Ontario

CANADIAN ARMY UNITS OF THE 13TH INFANTRY BRIGADE IN THE INVASION OF KISKA

24TH FIELD REGIMENT RCA

The 24th Field Regiment RCA was mobilized on March 18, 1942 as part of the 18th Brigade, 7th Division Home Defence. On July 15th the 18th Brigade was transferred to the 6th Division and in June 1943 the Regiment was selected to join the 13th Brigade of the division as part of the joint Canadian-U. S. Force for the attack on Kiska Island. The Battery disembarked on August 15 and 16 and preformed garrison duties until the end of the year. They along with the other units lived in "winterized" US Army 10' x 10' field tents with 4' walls, and were engaged in road and pier construction, transport fatigues, building and manning defenses and carrying on such training as condition permitted. A trooper recalled "I remember bulldozers and trucks being run constantly until they broke down. Then they were just abandoned and new ones took their place. I became very much aware of the depth, power and ability of the United States-far greater than anything I would ever see in Canada or Britain as the war progressed." Two tents were always placed together and placed in 4' bulldozed evacuations. Each tent had a coal fired stove in the center since wood was non-existent on the island. Double sleeping bags on camp cots provided individual bedding. Fog, rain and wind made the island an acutely unpleasant residence, and the troops were heartily glad when they left.

At the end of 1943 the regiment returned to Canada and a reorganized 6th Division as during the months that the 13th Brigade was on Kiska, the 7th and 8th Divisions were phased out. The 13th Brigade, intact resumed its defence role with the 6th Division until May 1944 when the infantry components of the Brigade were used to provide manpower for overseas battalions.

46TH LAA BATTERY RCA

The 46th LAA Battery RCA was from Simcoe, Ontario and was mobilized on March 18,1942 as part of the 9th LAA Regiment, 6th Division, Home Defence. The regiment trained in Ontario and then proceeded to Vancouver, BC in October 1942 to provide Anti-Aircraft support for the three Brigades of the 6th Division in Pacific Command.

On 12 July 1943 the Battery sailed for Adak, en route to Kiska for further training and acclimatization. The battery disembarked at Kiska on August 15 and 16, 1943 and preformed garrison duties until the end of the year. On 31 December the battery sailed for Vancouver to resume its Home Defence role with the 13th Brigade, 6th Division.

All of the following photos were obtained from Ed Storey of Nepean, Ontario and the Candian National Archives in Ottawa. There are many photos of the ordinary Canadian soldier of the invasion force. The magnitude of supplies, equipment and weapons the Japanese had to bring by ship and submarine after the occupation of the island on June 4 and the intensity of labor required to haul the guns into place, the huts and structures that had to be dug into the tundra and the work done on the airfield is quite mystifying how all this was done on the backs of the ordinary Japanese soldier or sailor.

A heavily laden Canadian trooper with Canadian and American equipment getting instructions before boarding the troop ship.
–Courtesy of the Ackerman Collection

Canadian troops bound for the Kiska operation boarding a troop ship in British Columbia.

A trooper with a vast assortment of gear loading aboard a landing craft, ready to hit the beaches. Notice his Kiska patch on his left sleeve, worn by both US and Canadian troops.

Unloading a Landing Ship Tank (LST), which could carry tanks and other mechanized equipment. These ships were the backbone of amphibious landing all over the world during the war. –Courtesy of the Holomoy Collection

A US Army Signal Corps cameraman films Canadian troops coming ashore from Landing Craft Tank (LST) and Higgins personnel boats.

Troops wading ashore from LCI (L) 82 (Landing Craft Infantry). The LCIs got close to shore so the water was only knee deep. And, of course, there was no opposition to the landing. —342-26

13th Infantry Brigade Patch

Members of the Canadian 25th Field Ambulance Corps. 341-4

Members of the 2nd Battalion Winnipeg Grenadiers band with newly issued American gear. The trooper in the foreground is still wearing Canadian GS Militia boots, with web anklets as opposed to the newly issued 'High Top' invasion boots. —220-10

Troopers sitting outside a crude Japanese hut.
–Courtesy of the Ackerman Collection

Canadian Fusliers (City of London) in front of a Japanese shelter. –341-9

Waiting in formation in the snow. Living conditions were sparse, especially in the large wall tents. –341-21

Another view of the living conditions. Troops on the right are digging a path to their tents in the deep snow. –341-27

Abandoned Japanese equipment.

Members of the24th Field Regiment line up for a photo behind the rock and concrete carin constructed by its members. It is still intact on Kiska Island. –Courtesy of the Holomay Collection

The Nozima Maru *beached at Trout Lagoon was found intact by the Allied invasion force. After a tough but unique salvage operation most of the ship was towed away. Until 1941 the Nozima Maru was operated by the NYK Line of Japan, but was taken over by the navy and converted to a 7,190-ton troop transport. On Sept. 15, 1942, after unloading supplies it came under intensive air attack and it was beached off of Trout Lagoon. It was further attacked and remained there until salvage operations took place in 1956. The bow section was left beached and can be seen today. (see report on page 250).* –341-18

Ocean Gale Sinks Tow

After nearly five months of effort, Fred Devine, owner of the salvage tug Salvage Chief, lost the refloated hull of the former Japanese motorship Nozima Maru in a storm off the northern coast of Japan, according to reports received here.

Devine and his crew were said to have had the 450-foot ship hull within a day's steaming of shelter Tuesday when extremely heavy seas caused the vessel to sink. Two or three men who were riding the vessel were said to have been removed before the hull went down.

The Canadian tug Sudbury, of Vancouver, B. C., which was accompanying the Salvage Chief, sent the report to its Vancouver office, and the report was relayed to Portland.

Month Taken to Prepare

The Salvage Chief left Portland in July, after a month's preparation which included construction of heavy lifting apparatus and loading of much material, for Kiska island, in the Aleutians, to refloat the Nozima Maru, which had been stranded there during World War II after it was hit by U. S. bombs.

Devine bought the hull as it lay and proposed to tow it to Japan for sale after refloating it. At that time, he commented that the project was a gamble but he was confident he could salvage the vessel.

The salvage work started in August and continued until early last month when the refloated hull was ready to be towed away. The Sudbury joined the tow a few days after the Salvage Chief left Kiska.

The loss was said to be partly covered by insurance.

The Salvage Chief was reported to have proceeded to Japan for refueling before it returns to Astoria, where it stands by during the winter months to assist ships in need.

Bomb-Hit Ship Floats

Devine Towing Vessel to Japan

Fred Devine, Portland's ship salvager and owner of the shipretriever, Salvage Chief, has succeeded in refloating the Japanese freighter Nozima Maru in Kiska harbor and will tow the vessel to a Yokohama shipyard.

A spokesman for Devine said here Saturday that the hull—minus a section of the bow cut off in the refloating—was in such good shape that the freighter may be reconditioned instead of being scrapped.

Devine's representative here said that the ship, which was new when it was bombed by American airmen in 1942, will be drydocked in Yokohama to permit thorough survey by shipping interests.

DEVINE WILL make no effort to pick up and carry the scrap from the bow section in towing the Nozima Maru to Japan. The vessel was damaged in the bow and run aground. Devine sliced off the ship at No. 3 hold and the stern then refloated.

Devine is to begin the 18-day tow from Kiska to Yokohama on or before October 15 with the Salvage Chief. His crew of 18 left Portland more than a month ago and plan to continue on to Japan aboard the salvage vessel.

Originally Devine was uncertain in what shape the bombed ship was and indicated it might be suited only for scrap.

Morris Schnitzer, president of the Steel Products company of Portland, conferred with Devine at Kiska before proceeding to Japan, it was learned here Saturday. The spokesman for Devine said that the vessel would definitely be towed to Yokohama and not to any Pacific Northwest port.

TURDAY, NOVEMBER 3, 1956

Tug Tows Ship Hull

Devine Telephones Progress Report

The Portland tug Salvage Chief was en route Thursday from Kiska Island, in the Aleutians, to Yokohama, towing the salvaged hull of the ex-Japanese motorship Nozima Maru and making 4.8 knots, Fred Devine, owner, told his wife, Lena, by radio telephone.

Devine said two drag chains which had been attached to the freighter hull to stabilize it during stormy weather, had been cut off because they apparently had hooked to something on the bottom of the ocean and had slowed the convoy to only two knots.

Devine said he enlisted the tug Sudbury of Victoria, B. C., returning light from Japan to Victoria, to help tow the freighter, but after the chains had been cut away he no longer needed the Canadian boat and was about to release it.

Sale to Follow Delivery

The Salvage Chief left Kiska October 24 and expected to make the run to Yokohama in 21 days. The hull will be offered for sale, Devine said.

Another salvage operation in the Aleutians is being undertaken by General Metals, of Seattle, which is recovering thousands of tons of scrap from naval stations at Attu, Amchitka Shemya and Adak. A converted landing ship recently brought 320 tons of scrap metal to Tacoma.

The Borneo Maru, *visible after being beached at Gertrude Cove after an air attack on Oct.6, 1942. It was a passenger ship built in 1917 but requisitioned by the Japanese army in 1941. It was bound for Kiska with food, construction supplies, ammunition and troops when it was spotted by air off of Attu and three B-24s attacked it but were driven off by the ship's anti-aircraft fire, but the ship was slightly damaged. It was again attacked by air unloading its cargo at Kiska and the captain beached it to prevent sinking. It was subsequently attacked by torpedoes but they failed to sink the ship. Below is a view of the interior.*

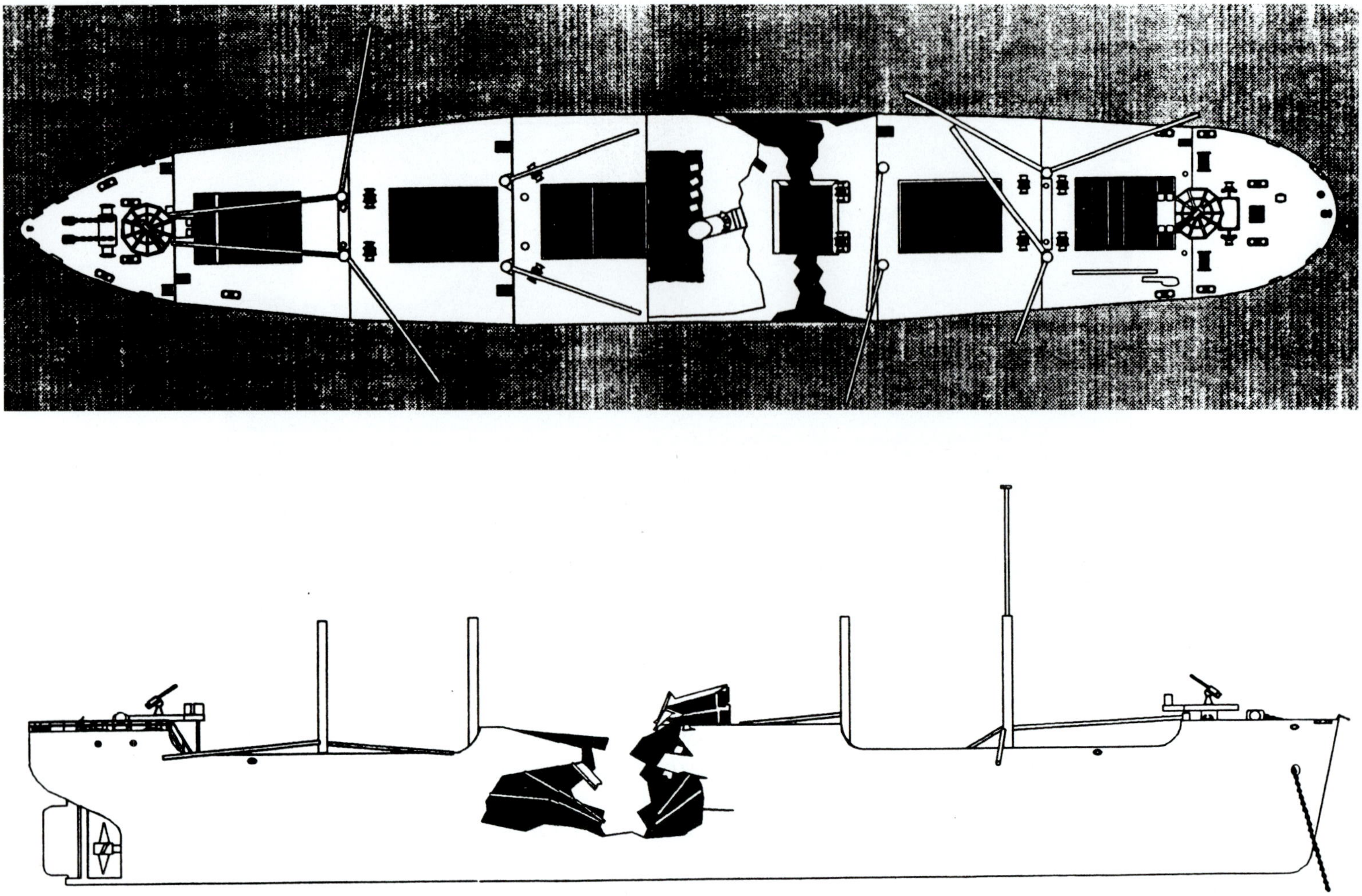

The Borneo Maru.

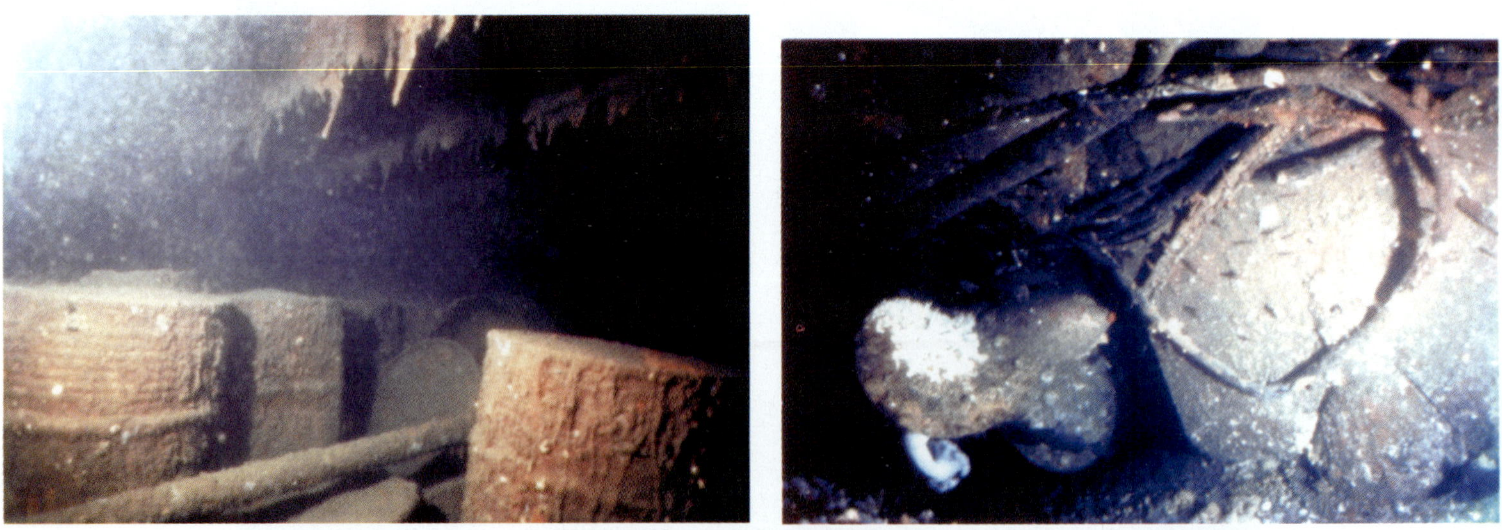

Underwater scenes from the ship.

A Japanese encampment showing the huts dug into the tundra to reduce the damage from bomb blasts.

When the Allies occupied Kiska they also had to dig in because of severe weather conditions.

Piers built by the Americans. Remnants are still visible today. –Courtesy of AC

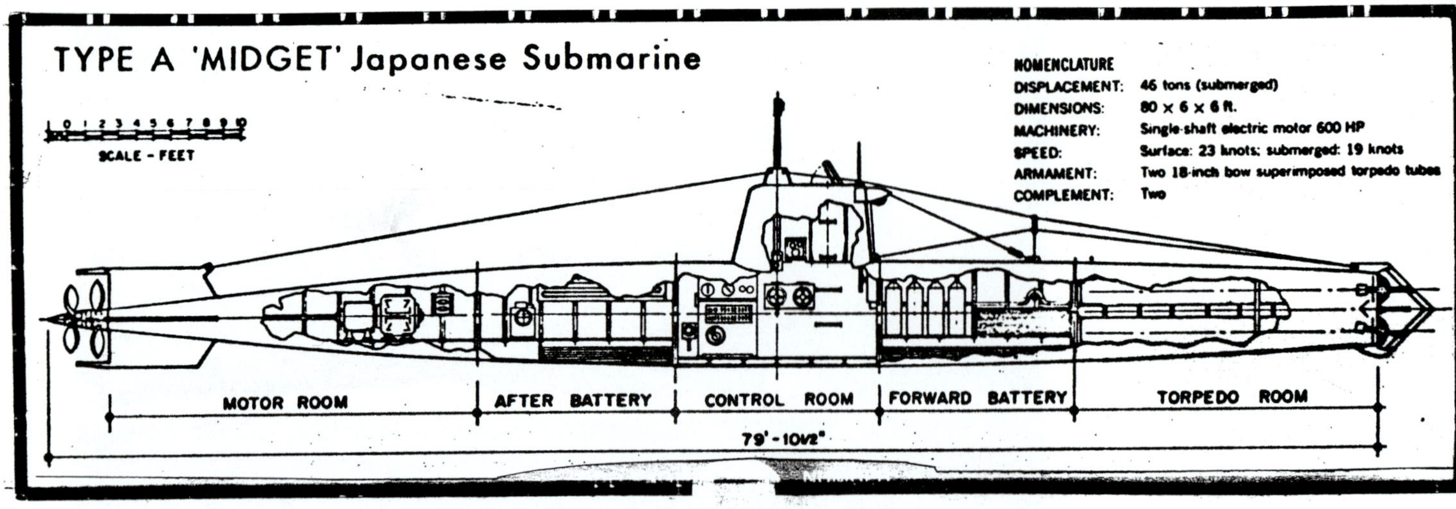

A drawing of the TYPE A 'Midget" submarine, which the Japanese brought three to Kiska and built a pen for them. Remnants of one complete, but highly damaged hull is still visible where it was abandoned when the island was evacuated. The Japanese Navy had experimented with midget submarines since the 1930s. They used five of them during the attack on Pearl Harbor with limited success, except one has been credited with a torpedo attack on the battleship West Virginia. Since the subs were driven by small electric motors with short-lived batteries they had to be launched close to their targets from large I-Class submarines. Eighty feet long, six feet in diameter at their widest point and displacing 46 tons, each sub carried two 18-inch torpedoes and was controlled by a two-man crew. Top speed was 23 knots on the surface, 19 knots submerged. They turned out to be of no use to the defense of the island.

The author is standing by the semi-intact Japanese midget submarine at the sub base on Kiska on his trip in 1989 with the US National Park Service, US Fish & Wildlife Service and the US Navy dive team. The sub was used as target practice and stripped for souveniers.

Parts of another destroyed midget submarine are scattered on the beach.

KISKA HARBOR INVESTIGATIONS AND WRECKS

Compiled by Larry Murphy of the NPS Submerged Cultural Resources Unit in 1990 after the Seamark Expedition

1. Possible sinking of I-9 submarine thought to be located in various sites around Kiska. This submarine was also used in the attack on Pearl Harbor and probably used to launch one of the midget submarines.

2. Sinking of I-7 submarine It was beached and sunk near Twin Rocks, which is offshore of South Head on June 23, 1943. It was carrying a load of railroad iron and estimates were made that the I-Class subs could carry 50 tons of cargo or 100 men.

3. RO-65 submarine was sunk by a B-24 on Sept. 28, 1942 in Kiska Harbor although the Japanese claimed it was sunk by accident.

4. RO-61 submarine is recorded sunk by depth charges by the *USS Reid* on Aug. 31, 1942 and strafed by PBYs just before its loss. The sub had torpedoed the seaplane tender *Casco* in Nazan Bay, Atka Island.

5. The destroyer *Oboro* was sunk off North Kiska land during a six-plane B-26 raid on Oct. 17, 1942. One B-26 was shot down.

6. The destroyer *Arare* was sunk by a torpedo from the *USS Growler* on July 5, 1942.

7. The cargo and transport ships *Nissan Maru, Nozima Maru, Borneo Maru, Kano Mar*u, and *Urajio Maru* were sunk around Kiska Island. The *Montreal Maru, Kotohira Maru* and *Akagane Maru* were sunk in the vicinity of the island.

8. Several sub chasers, gun boats, barges, mine-sweepers, a destroyer-mine layer and additional small craft varing in size from net tenders and patrol craft were sunk.

RO-65

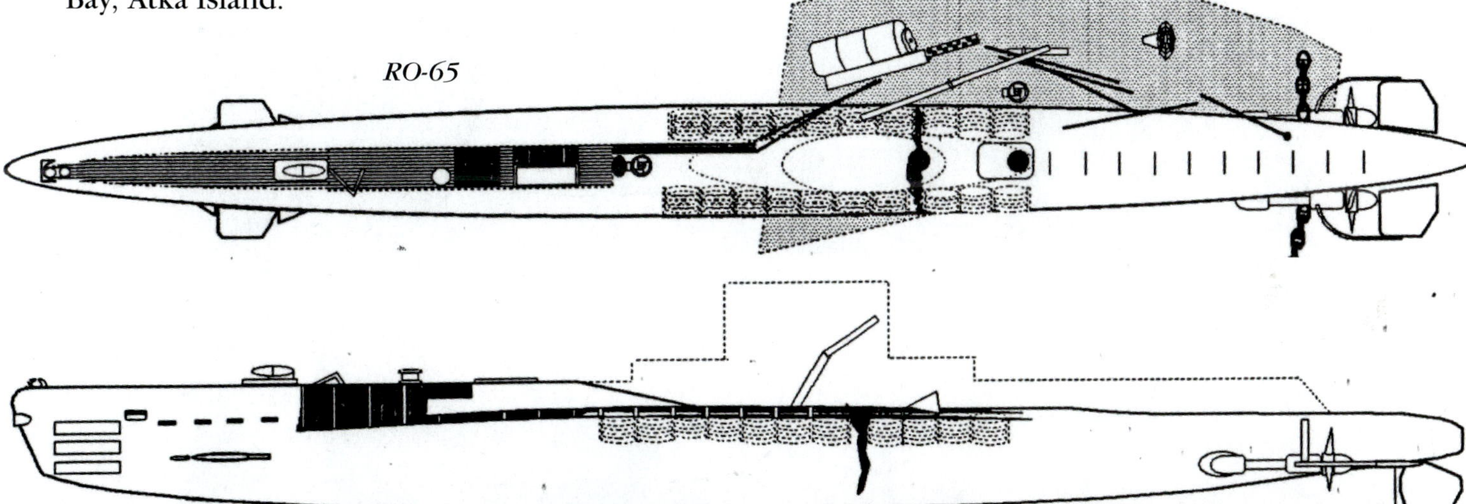

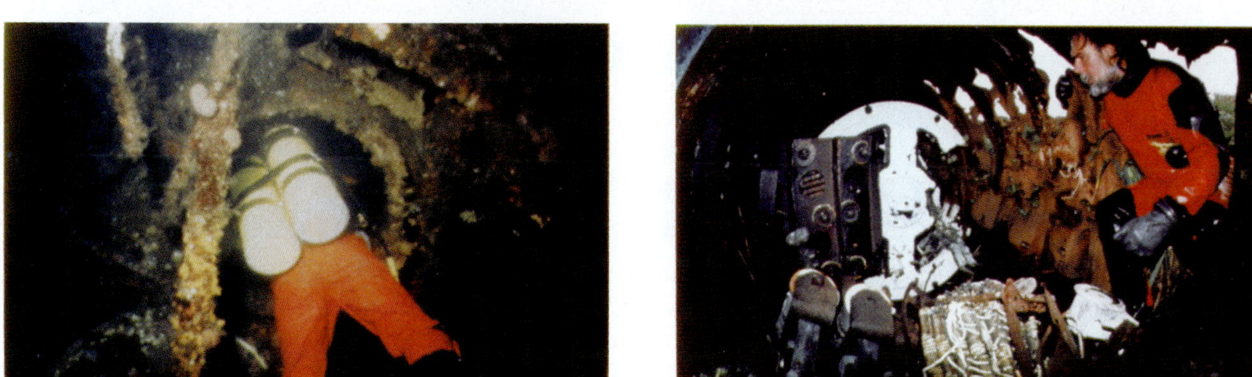

Interior views.

The first Kiska Harbor investigation took place in 1985. Two expeditions were organized and directed by marine biologist-photographer Rick Rosenthal. In January side-scan sonar was used to located shipwrecks. In July Rosenthal returned to produce a documentary on the island. He believed that the harbor could be another Truk Lagoon (with dozens of sunken Japanese ships) but found fewer underwater objects and noted" many of the ships known to have have sunk there are probably too deep for scuba divers." Rosenthal and his crew dove on the *Nissan Maru*, RO-65 and a nearly 40-foot landing craft, *Kano Maru* and a 200-foot upside-down boat hull. He reported "hundreds of barrels of diesel oil" on board Nissan Maru along with compartments filled with doorknobs and beer bottles. Divers recovered dishes, empty brass from a deck gun and a Japanese sake server. Rosenthal also investigated *Borneo Mar*u in Gertrude Harbor, and unsuccessfully searched for Japanese destroyer *Arare*. In addition to the sonar runs within Kiska Harbor, the area between Little Kiska and Kiska Island was surveyed with negative results.

In September 1989, a second harbor and land expedition named Seamark was conducted by the US Navy and National Park Service divers and historians (the author was one of the historians on this trip) to again look for sunken ships and to document Japanese remains on Kiska and Little Kiska islands. An RO submarine, a possible destroyer and remains of a B-17 were found in the harbor. Many types of small and very large guns were found along with ammunition, destroyed huts, outdoor cooking pots, underground caves and a Shinto shrine, in good condition. There have also been several private tourists parties visiting the island, but it is extremely difficult to reach the island, and very hard to walk on the tundra, except on the roads, especially for people not use to this type of environment.

This Japanese gun, salvaged from Kiska by the Canadian 24th Field Artillery Regiment is on display at the Vernon, British Columbia Vernon Military Camp (Vernon Training Camp). It is a 4. 7" CD gun (model 1905) used by the Japanese as a coastal defense gun. It is in Vernon because the 24th trained there before transferring to Vancouver, BC and then north for the Kiska invasion. The camp today is used as a training center for Canadian Army cadets. –Courtesy of Bob Spring, Maple Ridge, BC

— CHAPTER TWELVE—

THE KURILE ISLANDS OPERATION

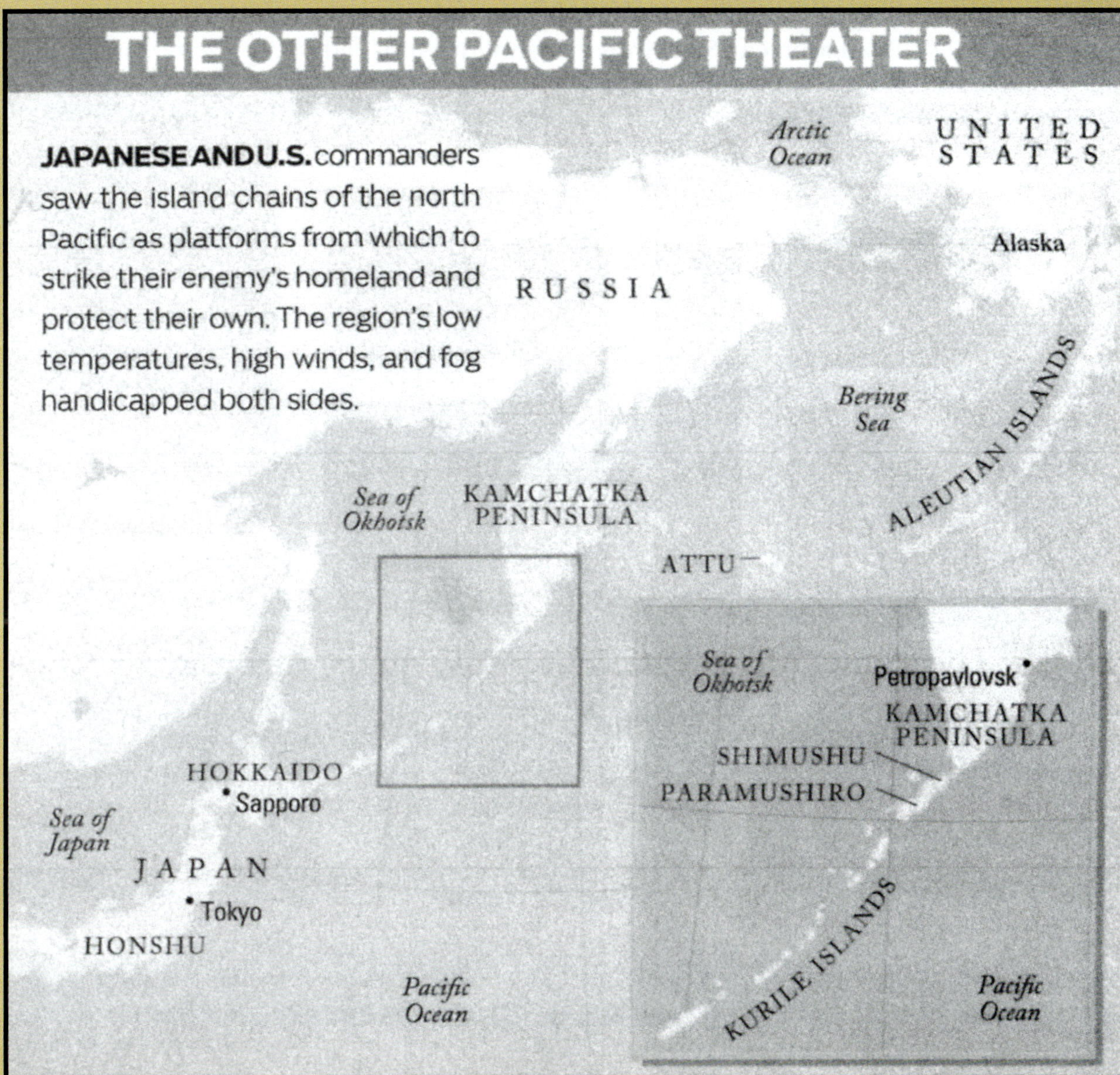

After the end of the Aleutian Campaign in August 1943 Allied forces focused their attention on the Northern Kurile Islands, which stretch from the Japanese mainland to the tip of the Russian Kamchatka Peninsula. There were naval and air bases on several of the islands and there were the northern most land area protecting the Japanese homeland. It also had valuable fishing grounds. A concentrated air and naval campaign commenced from late 1943 to 1945 from air bases on Attu and Shyema. The 11th Army Air Force's 77th Bombardment Squadron and 404th Bombardment Squadron and Fleet Air Wing Four participated in the air actions with B-25s, B-24s, PV-1 Venturas, PV-2 Harpoons, PB4Y-2s, PBYs, P-38s and OS2U Kingfishers. There were causalities; 83 11th Air Force and 20 Fleet Air Wing Four were killed. Some were shot down and captured by the Japanese and some planes crashed or were forced to land in Russia where they were interned by the Russians for many months (this was because of the Russian-Japanese Non-Aggression Pact that kept the Japanese from attacking Russia throughout the war, until the very end of the Pacific Campaign.

B-25s at Attu and in the air. Notice the 75mm cannon placed in the nose of the planes, which gave the B-25s increased fire power. –Courtesy of the James Rickey Collection

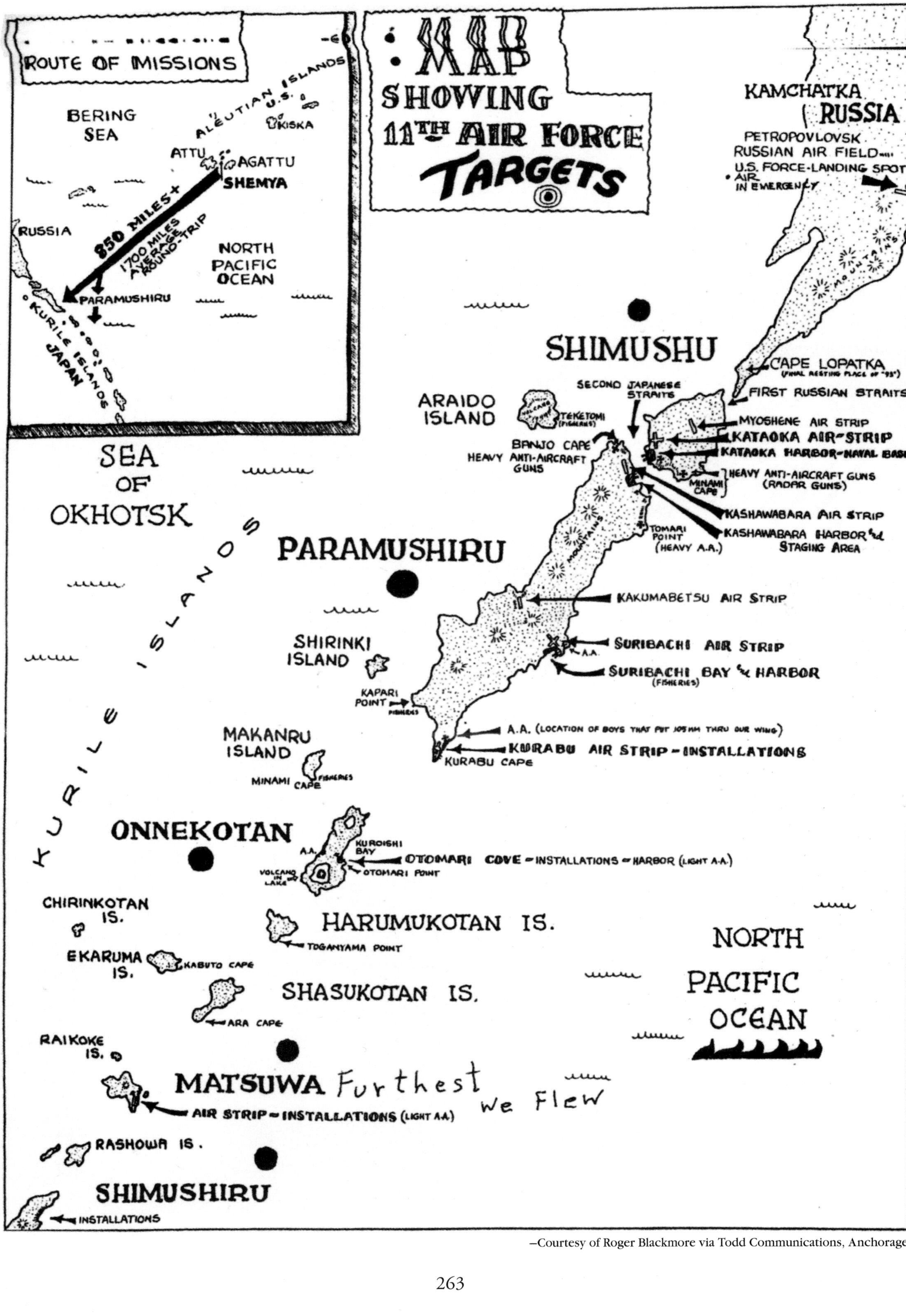

—Courtesy of Roger Blackmore via Todd Communications, Anchorage

Showing the bombing campaign on ships and land installations.
—Courtesy of the Glen Hiersche Collection

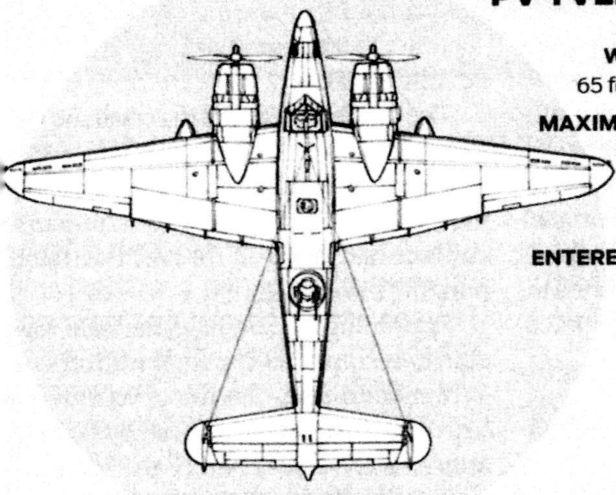

PV-1 VENTURA	PV-2 HARPOON
WING SPAN 65 feet 6 inches	**WING SPAN** 75 feet 11 inches
MAXIMUM SPEED 300 mph	**MAXIMUM SPEED** 280 mph
RANGE 1,600 miles	**RANGE** 1,800 miles
ENTERED SERVICE 1940	**ENTERED SERVICE** 1944

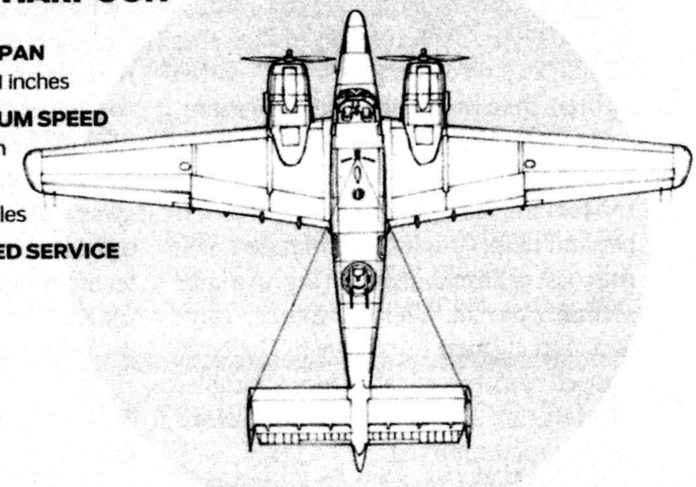

The PV-1 Ventura was derived from the Lockheed Model 18, a two-engine commercial plane which first flew in 1940. It was a land-based bomber-reconnaissance plane used mainly by the US Navy. It was used in the long-distance bombing campaign over the Kuriles but gas consumption was very high. The PV-2 Harpoon was derived from the PV-1 and gave greater fuel capacity, better armament and performance. It came into production in 1944.

ATTU SUN EXTRA

SATURDAY, 25 NOVEMBER

FLEET SMASHES MATSUWA
KURILE BASE BELIEVED KO'D

SURPRISE ATTACK CARRIED OUT IN ROUGH WATERS

(WITH THE NORTH PACIFIC FLEET OFF MATSUWA, 22 NOVEMBER - (SPECIAL) BY FRANK STURDY TO THE CHICAGO TRIBUNE, CHICAGO)

"NOW, HEAR THIS," A BRASSY VOICE CAME OVER THIS CRUISER'S LOUD SPEAKER SYSTEM IN THE NAVY'S TRADITIONAL COMMAND FOR ATTENTION TO AN IMPORTANT ANNOUNCEMENT. "NOW, HEAR THIS - THIS TASK FORCE WILL SET A COURSE FOR MATSUWA, AND IF WEATHER CONDITIONS ARE FAVORABLE, WILL CARRY OUT A BOMBARDMENT" THE JOB SET THIS TASK FORCE OF THE NORTH PACIFIC FLEET, WHILE CRUISING IN MID-PACIFIC THREE DAYS AGO WAS COMPLETED TONIGHT. MATSUWA WAS TROUNCED WITH MORE THAN 300,000 POUNDS OF SHELLS. HUGE FIRES WERE SET IN THE TWO-MILES SQUARE TARGET AREA. AS THE FORCE TURNED TAIL AND SPED SWIFTLY TO SEA WHEN BOMBARDMENT ENDED, NUMEROUS EXPLOSIONS SENT FLAMES KNIFING HIGH INTO THE SKY, AND AT LEAST FOUR BIG FIRES BURNED STEADILY, STILL VISIBLE WHEN THE FLEET HAD LEFT THE ISLAND AN HOUR BEHIND.

AS FAR AS COULD BE TOLD, THE ATTACK TOOK THE JAPS BY SURPRISE. THERE WAS ONLY WEAK AND INEFFECTIVE RETURN FIRE FROM THE BEACH. THE SHIP'S RADAR PICKED UP SURFACE TARGETS APPROACHING FROM THE REAR, PRESUMABLY TORPEDO BOATS, BUT TOWERING SEAS AND A SIXTY KNOT WIND PREVENTED THEM FROM CLOSING TO SHOOTING RANGE. THE FLEET ESCAPED WITHOUT BATTLE DAMAGE.

THE RAID WAS A DARING THRUST ACROSS THE NORTH PACIFIC FROM THE FLEETS ALEUTIAN ISLAND'S BASE, CARRIED OUT WITHOUT AIR COVER EXCEPT FOR PROTECTION DURING THE FIRST HALF OF THE DISTANCE BY LIBERATOR BOMBERS OF THE ELEVENTH AIR FORCE. WEATHER WAS THE FLEETS ONLY PROTECTION, WEATHER BAD ENOUGH TO PREVENT DISCOVERY BY JAP BOMBERS.

MATSUWA LIES AT ABOUT HE MIDDLE OF THE KURILE ISLANDS, 450 MILES NORTH OF THE TIP OF THE JAPANESE HOME LAND AND 950 MILES FROM TOKYO. THE JAPS HAVE USED IT AS A MAIN STAGING BASE FOR AIRCRAFT TO PARAMUSHIRO AT THE NORTH END OF THE CHAIN.

FOR TWENTY FOUR HOURS BEFORE STRIKING AT THE ISLAND'S RUNWAYS, HEAVY HOARD FUEL AND AMMUNITION DUMPS, THE TASK FORCE ZIG-ZAGGED IN ROUGH WATER 150 MILES OFF SHORE WAITING FOR LOWERING SKIES. WHEN REAR ADMIRAL JOHN MCCREA, COMMANDING THE FORCE FROM ANOTHER CRUISER SIGNALLED THE DECISION TO RUN IN, THE HEAVIER SHIPS AND THE PROTECTING SCREEN OF DESTROYERS HEADED FAST FOR THE TARGET FROM THE SOUTHEAST.

SEVERAL HOURS AFTER DARK THE FLEET BEGAN ITS BOMBARDMENT RUN, PARALLELING THE SHORE AT A DISTANCE OF ABOUT SEVEN MILES, UNDER A LOW CEILING BUT WITH VISIBILITY THAT WAS ALMOST TOO GOOD. FROM AN OBSERVATION POST HIGH ON THE FOREMAST OF THIS CRUISER, I COULD SEE THE SALVOS OF SHELLS ARCHING RED-TAILED TO THE BEACH BURSTING ON THE BLACKED-OUT TARGET.

WITHIN A FEW MINUTES THE FIRST FIRE FLOWERED IN A GREAT BALL THAT GREW STEADILY THROUGHOUT THE TWENTY MINUTE BOMBARDMENT, APPARENTLY A FUEL TANK FARM. BELOW DECKS, SWEATING GUN CREWS HEARD A DESCRIPTION OF THE BLASTING FROM TALKERS ON DECK AND CHEERED AS THEY HEAVED SHELLS AND POWDER BAGS.

An eye witness report by George McWilliams of the International News Service (I.N.S.) of a later raid on Matsuwa by the US North Pacific Fleet, Task Force 92

A hard-hiting task force of cruisers and destroyers blasted a hole in Japan's Northern flank tonight. They shelled Matsuwa Island in the Central Kuriles, 960 miles from Tokyo. It was the most damaging blow thus far to the string of island bases guarding the Empires back door. Huge fires kindled in fuel and ammunition dumps spending pillars of flames skyward, setting off explosions visible an hour after our ships headed home.

Return fire from shore batteries was weak and ineffective. Jap surface and aircraft did not attempt to intercept, and our ships suffered no causalities and no battle damage. The Task Force which hit the Jap homeland in the war's closest surface strike to Tokyo composed units of Vice Admiral Frank Jack Flecther's North Pacific Fleet. It was commanded by Rear Admiral John L. McCrea. The raid was also the longest surface strike without full air cover. Warships had an umbrella of Eleventh Army Air Force Liberators (B-24s) part way, but penetrated deep into enemy waters alone. They caught the Japs by surprise several hours after sundown.

Steaming past Tagan Point, the southeast tip of the island, cruisers and destroyers poured 150 tons of destruction into a two mile square target area in twenty minutes of furious salvos. From a box seat high in a cruiser's foremast, I saw heavy shells rocket shore ward, and heard the crew cheer as target after target uplift like knobs in pinball machines. One minute the Jap island was dark as a tomb, the next it was lighted by at least four big fires. And many smaller ones which mushroomed hundreds of feet air wards. This indicated direct hits on fuel storage tanks. As the task force swung from their target, Matsuwa's mile high Mount Fugo silhouetted a blow of flames, fanned by a fifty knot gale.

This bombardment was the fourth against the Kuriles since 4 February and the second against Matsuwa, which first was shelled 13 June. In all four strikes the Japs never succeeded scoring a hit on a single American ship. Matsuwa lies midway in the Kurile Chain, 350 miles north of Hokkaido, and though only six miles long by a half as wide it is the key bastion of Japan's northern defenses. It is believed the destruction resulting from the shelling may have naturalized this base for sometime and disrupted air operation in the North Pacific.

JAPANESE D.E. UNDER ATTACK BY B-25's OF 11TH A.F.

TARGET PARAMUSHIRO !

The jabbering little sons of the Rising Sun have suffered consequential losses in Pacific waters from the heavy guns of the task force now located temporarily at Dutch Harbor. A colorful history of courageous ocean fighting has been earned by the brave men who man the ships of this hard-hitting American force.

In the first naval bombardment of the Kurile Islands conducted in daylight, Pacific Fleet units under the command of Rear Admiral John L. McCrea smashed Japanese coastal defenses, fish canneries, shore installations and an airfield at Suribach Wan on Paramushiro's coast early in January 1945. A total weight of 181 tons of shells were hurled at the Nip station during the 20-minute bombardment. Admiral McCrea disclosed this result upon the task force's return to Attu.

Although the evidences of damage as seen from the bombarding warships were difficult to assess, a number of fires could be seen gathering headway among the blasted Suribachi installations as the task force withdrew. Return fire from the Japanese coastal batteries was ineffective and none of our ships suffered any damage.

By approaching Suribach Wan and conducting its bombardment in full daylight, the task force risked early discovery and possible attack by Jap aircraft based on Paramushiro and other nearby islands of the Kurile chain. However, complete surprise apparently was achieved, the task force steaming to within range of the shore line and opening fire before there was any indication that the Japanese defenders were aware of the attackers' presence.

American naval commanders were themselves 'surprised,' and pleasantly so!, by the comparative ease with which their warships were able to make their undetected approach, especially so since they were in range of Japanese radar stations on the island's east coast. Darkness soon cloaked American ships as they turned from the islands at the end of the bombardment and withdrew eastward at high speed. If any Japanese aircraft took off in pursuit, they were unable to find our ships. Daylight on the following day found the task force well off the enemy shore and the weather, which had favored our forces during the approach, again produced frequent snow and rain to hide the American ships from searching Jap aircraft.

As yet there has been no report from the photo reconnaisance planes, and until one is received it will be difficult to determine the extent of all damages, but Tokyo Radio broadcasts intercepted indicated it had been considerable. Tokyo Rose charged U.S. forces with killing 410 'innocent civilians' and rendering hundreds of others homeless. She indicated that damage to food processing factories was extensive and claimed that the American task force had been 'driven off by superior shore defense batteries and aircraft.'

We salute these heroic fighting men who are blotting out the symbol of the Rising Sun and bid them a warm welcome to Dutch Harbor.

— CHAPTER THIRTEEN—

LEGACY OF THE WAR

Japanese Memorial, 18 feet, 7 ton titanium star-shaped structure was placed on Engineer Hill, Attu on July 1, 1987 by the Japanese government with components flown in by the Alaska Air National Guard. In 2003 it was repaired after a storm damaged it. The "Peace Memorial" honors all who lost their lives in the North Pacific during the war. –Courtesy of Blaine Corneilson

This monument on Kiska reads:

TO THE MEN
OF
AMPHIBIOUS TASK FORCE 9
WHO FELL HERE AUGUST 1943
PLACED HERE AUGUST 1983
BY
87TH MOUNTAIN INFANTRY REGIMENT

Plaque placed on the grounds of the US Air Force Museum, Dayton, Ohio by veterans of the 11th Air Force.

This plaque about Colonel Yamasaki (Japanese Commander) was placed by the Americans on the lower slopes of Clevesy Pass on Engineer Hill in 1950 where he supposedly was killed in action, sword in hand in 1943.

–Courtesy of Blaine Cornelison

—Courtesy of Blaine Cornelison

The *USS St. Mihiel* brought the first Matanuska Valley settlers to the Palmer area in 1935 and the bell from the ship was acquired by the Palmer Historical Society and placed in the city park on the sixty-fifth reunion of the Matanuska Colony Project in 2000.

USS St. Mihiel (AP-32 was launched in October 1920 by the United States Shipping Board and operated by the US Army Transportation Corps from 1922 until mid-1940 as *USAT St. Mihiel*. It was then transferred to the Navy and commissioned as *USS St. Mihiel* (AP-32) on July 22, 1941. In November 1943, she was transferred back to the Army and made a hospital ship *USAHS St. Mihiel*. Having operated as a transport between the west coast and Alaska, with occasional runs to Hawaii prior to her transfer to the Navy, she preformed the same duty after commissioning. In July 1942, she transported the wreckage of the Akutan Zero to San Diego. In 1943, she called regularly at ports on mainland Alaska and in the eastern Aleutians. In May 1943, she participated in the occupation of Attu; then resumed more routine transport duties. On Sept 9, 1943 she headed south to San Francisco and on the 23rd headed west to Hawaii and from there began her last voyage for the Navy. Steaming to Boston where she was decommissioned in November 1943 and returned to the Army which used her as a hospital ship for the remainder of the war. Decommissioned again in 1946 she was scrapped in 1957.

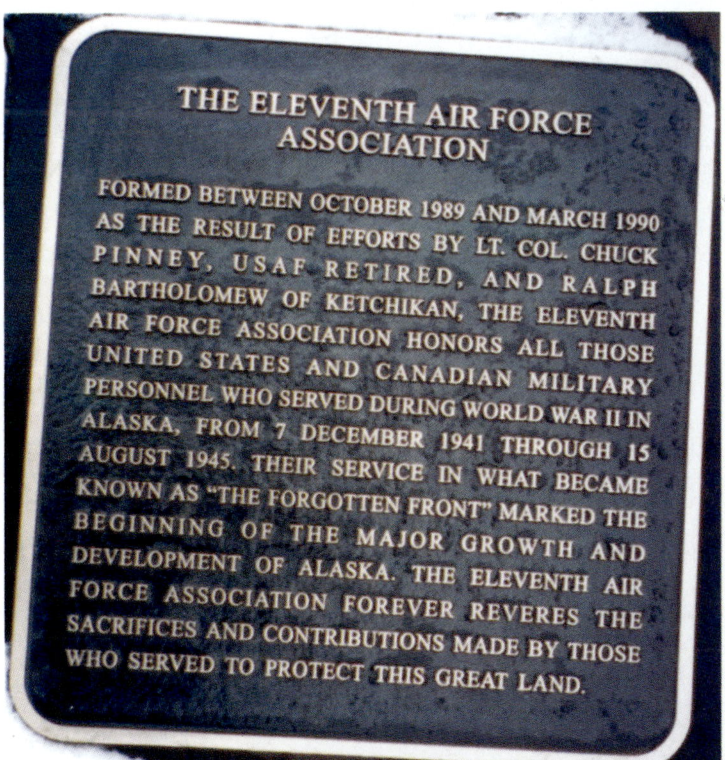

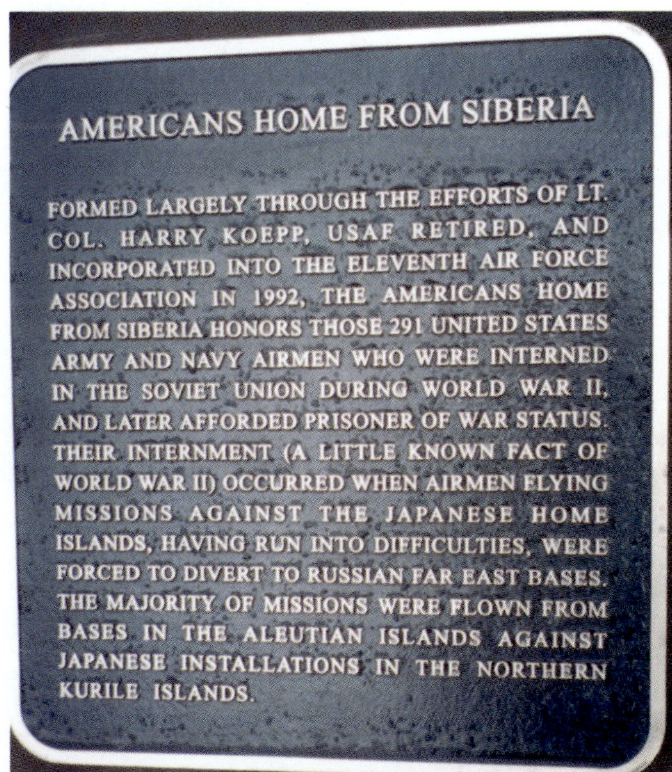

11th Air Force Memorial Dedication at Merrill Field, Anchorage, Alaska on October 6, 2001.
–Courtesy of Blaine Cornelison

11th Air Force/Americans Home From Siberia veterans' reunion, taken in front of the McCloud Memorial at Elmendorf Field on Oct. 5. 2001.

In 2017 and 2018 three 75th anniversary ceremonies were held in Alaska. One to commemorate the June 1942 bombing of Dutch Harbor and occupation of Attu and Kiska; One on the opening of the Alaska highway in November 1942 (a very primitive road at the time) and one to commemorate The Battle of Attu in May 1943.

Veterans of the Attu battle returned to Anchorage in June, 2018 for the 75th anniversary of the battle. Front row left to right; Gerry Russello, Bob Brocklehurst Sr., Paul Schaughency, Alan Seroll and Clint Goodwin. Back row left to right; Roy Dover, Bill Greene, Bob Hinsdale and Joe Sasser Jr. –Courtesy Suellyn Wright Novak

Japanese soldier descendants visited Anchorage for the 75th anniversary. Back row: Motoaki Asano, Blaine Cornelison, Ron Winkleman (Alaska Scouts), Hiroko Asano (Motoaki's mother), Kiyoko Takada. Front row: Kiyotaka Nemoto, Nobuyuki Yamazaki. –Courtesy Blaine Cornelison

A restored P-40 Curtiss Warhawk 42-10256, is now on display at the Warhawk Inc Museum in Granite Falls, MN. It displays the colors and markings of an 11th Air Force fighter commanded by Jack Chennault, son of Claire Chennault, the leader of the famed Flying Tigers of the CBI Theater. The aircraft design was a means of honoring his father. It is a K-model, one of the short fuselage early models built by Curtiss in Buffalo, NY. It was sent to Murmansk, Russia under the lend-lease program, and in September 1943 tangled with four Luftwaffe Bf-109 fighters and it was forced to crash land in a dry lake bed near Murmansk along with another P-40 42-10083. In the 1980s the planes were salvaged and placed in a Russian museum. Ken Hake from Tipton, Kansas bought both planes in 1992 and shipped them to his restoration facility in Tipton were he spent 15 years restoring the airframe of 42-10256. In 2003 Ken Fagen bought the plane and finished the restoration at his P-40 restoration facility in Granite Falls after three years. Many parts had to be hand-made or searched for worldwide. The plane took it's first flight on June 5, 2006 and brought home the coveted Phoenix Award from AirVenture at Oshkosh that year. The other P-40 from Russia is also being restored at Hagen's facility.

Another P-40N from Alaska is restored and on display at the Michael King Smith Memorial Museum (Evergreen Air and Space Museum) in McMinnville, OR. The plane crashed, due to engine failure, into a fresh water marsh near Port Hayden. It was recovered by Al Redick of Reno and sold a number of times before Evergreen bought it in 1990.

The look of Jack Chennault's P-40 of the 11th Air Force fighter command.

Hill Aero Space Museum in Ogden, UT. P-38 restoration is on display. It is a composite of two P38s in Alaska, one that crashed on Buldir Island and one at Cold Bay. One was delivered to Alaska in July 1943 and flown by the 11th Fighter Squadron until crashing in February 1945 and scraped.

Display at the Hill Aero Space Museum.

Two more Alaska aircraft are on display at the Hill Aero Space Museum, Ogden, UT. A P-38J Lighting 42-67638 was assigned to the 11th Air Force, 343rd Fighter Group, 54th Fighter Squadron. In May 1944. It operated from Alexai Point Airfield on Attu. On Feb. 2, 1945 Lt. Arthur Kidder took off on a test flight but lost track of land and running low on fuel crashed landed on the tiny island of Buldir. He was rescued but the plane remained on the island for nearly 50 years, being used for target practice by passing planes. The Air Force Heritage Foundation of Utah recovered the plane, under tough conditions in August 1994. It was sent to California for restoration, using portions of another crashed P-38 from Cold Bay. It was delivered, restored, to Hill in August 1996.

On Jan. 1, 1945, 2nd Lt. Robert Nesmith, on a training flight, crashed his P-38 42-13400 at Temnac Bay at Attu. He was not hurt and part of the plane was salvaged. But the rest stayed "in Situ" for over 50 years, being used as gunnery practice for other pilots. A group-Project Lighting Save, was a group of volunteers who were to bring the plane back to Anchorage for possible restoration. At the last minute the U.S. Air Force Museum decided not to accept it for display and only due to the persistence of John Cloe, historian of the Alaskan Air Command and its commander Lt. Gen. David McCloud did the plane finally make it to Elemendorf AFB, after a very difficult recovery effort in 1999. After eight months of very detailed and amazing work by a group of volunteers it was rolled out and put on display, with other aircraft in front of the Operations Building at Elemendorf. General McCloud died in an airplane crash in July 1998 and the outdoor museum is named after him.

Temnac Bay, Attu. —Courtesy of Steve Levi

The restored P-38 at Elmendorf Air Force Base. —Courtesy of Blaine Cornelison

Japanese gun mount.

Remains, monument and airport "terminal" on Attu. Much of Attu and other islands have had massive clean-ups through the years to the present day. –Courtesy of Blaine Cornelison

Remains on Little Kiska and Kiska of mostly Japanese guns, collapsed huts, shrines, underground caves and other miscellaneous items plus a few Allied structures.

Dutch Harbor wartime remains.

Mt. Ballyhoo has an amazing amount of American constructed bunkers, caves and quonset hut remains.

The Natioanl Park Service's World War Two visitor center.

More wartime remains around Dutch Harbor. The observation bunker is on a prominent point on Mount Ballyoo. To the left is a gun emplacement.

Remains of Quonset and other huts are scattered around the mountian.

The propeller of the USS Northwestern.

The museum was founded in 2001 to honor veterans of all wars and especially ones that fought in Alaska during World War Two. There are artifacts and displays from the American Civil War to recent conflicts. The bronze statue faces the front of the museum (there are eight more statues scattered around Alaska towns) and depicts a member of the Alaska Territorial Guard which was formed in 1941 under the leadership of Maj. "Muktuk" Marston. The Guard eventually consisted of 20,000 volunteers from seven Native ethnic groups and other Alaskans, whose collective ages ranged from 12-80 years old, including some 30 women. They watched the northern coast for enemy movements, aided in rescue missions and would help in any enemy attack. They disbanded in 1947.

The museum is located at:
333 W 4th Avenue, Suite 227, Anchorage
Phone number, 907-677-8802
www.alaskaveteran.org

—Courtesy of Jann Sherill

Interior display.
—Courtesy of Jann Sherill

The Alaska Territorial Cavalry Motorized ATC (M) is a group of Alaskans who have organized a club that supports activities and legislation helpful to the preservation and use of historic military vehicles by responsible owners and other interested persons. The ATC (M) was created in 1990 and is a 501C-3 non profit organization. We are an affiliate of the Military Vehicle Preservation Association (MVPA). The ATC (M) meets once a month and publishes a monthly newsletter in which members can exchange information relative to the collection and use of military vehicles. We regulary participate in car shows, air shows, parades, Veteran's ceremonies, memorial services and other events. We currently have 125 members, including many service and ex-service members. We are willing to share our experiences in the recovery, restoration, maintenance and safe operation of these vehicles. We also enjoy sharing our common interest in military vehicles, military memorabilia and military history with others. Contact Mark Strumsky at m.strumsky@mooseak.com

—Courtesy of Mark Strumsky

ALASKA TERRITORIAL CAVALRY
(MOTORIZED)

TRUCK
TRACKS

3250 N Brockton Ave.
Wasilla, AK 99645

An Affiliated Chapter of the Military Vehicle Preservation Association

Monthly Newsletter
www.akmvpa.com

Volume 14, Issue 4 April 2018

Karen Abel and daughter, Alexandra Texidor-Abel . —Courtesy of Karen Abel

An RCAF (P-40E) AK 875, named Hope's Lope is on display in the Smithsonian's Udvar Hazy Center in Chantilly, Virginia. Karen Abel, a Canadian living in Florida discovered the plane on display was flown by her grandfather in the Aleutian Campaign as part of the RCAF 11(F) "Thunderbird" Squadron. His life was spared on a mission by a ground loop at a refueling stop while en route to Umnak Island. The crash put the plane out of service and put him on a transport. The rest of his formation would fly on with a majority of them fatally crashing into a mountain side when they got disoriented in the ever dense and unforgiving Aleutian fog. It is planned to eventually redo te plane to its original RCAF look.For more information and the story of the B-24D Liberator bomber that crashed on Atka Island in 1942, go to her blog–Florida Beaches to the Bering Sea.

Alaska Aviation Museum is located on the Lake Hood Seaplane Base in Anchorage. Its mission since 1988 is to preserve, display, and honor Alaska's aviation heritage, by preserving and displaying historic aircrafts, artifacts and memoriabillia, and to foster public interest in aviation and its history. The museum has over 30 aircrafts on display, some of World War Two vintage, a restoration hangar, flight simulators, two theaters and a Hall of Fame. It includes a PBY-5A Catalina and 1940 Curtiss P-40E Aleutian Tiger #241.

4721 Aircraft Drive, Anchorage, AK 99502 • 907-248-5325 • www.alaskaairmuseum.org

Pioneer Air Museum is located in the old Alaskaland Complex, now Pioneer Park. It has 20 aircraft, including several of World War Two vintage.

Airport Way, Fairbanks, AK 99707 • 907-451-0037• www.pionerairmuseum.org

The Stinson L-1 is a single engine high wing military observation plane that was manufacture in December 1941 and was assigned to the 11th Air Force at Fairbanks and Anchorage. It is the sole survivor of approximately 400 L-1s manufactured during WWII. It was donated to the Museum by Karl S. Johnstonein in 2002.

This PBY-5A crashed into Dago Lake on the Alaska Pennisula in 1947 after the engine quite. It was retreived in 1984 by the museum and taken to King Salmon, and then in 1987 to the museum where it waits for restoration.

APPENDIX

Museums in the United States and Canada that have World War II items and displays

1. The History Museum, Great Falls, MT
2. The Nanton Lancaster Museum, Nanton, AB
3. The Hangar Flight Museum, Calgary, AB
4. Alberta Aviation Museum, Edmonton, AB
5. Bomber Museum of Canada, Edmonton, AB
6. BC Aviation Museum, Sidney, BC
7. Greater Vernon Museum and Archives, Vernon, BC
8. Rock Mountain Rangers Museum, Kamloops, BC
9. Comox Air Force Museum, Comox, BC
10. CFB Esquimalt Naval & Military Museum, Esquimalt, BC
11. Okangan Military Museum, Kelowna, BC
12. The Dawson Creek Visitors Center, BC
13. Fort St John North Peace Museum. BC
14. The Fort Nelson Heritage Museum, BC
15. Watson Lake Interpretive Center, Yukon
16. Macbride Museum of Yukon History, Whitehorse, Yukon
17. The Yukon Transportation Museum, Whitehorse, Yukon
18. Alaska Veterans Museum, Anchorage
19. Anchorage Museum
20. Museum of the Aleutians, Unalaska
21. US National Park Service World War Two Museum, Dutch Harbor
22. Museum of Alaska Transportation and Industry, Wasilla
23. Alaska Aviation Heritage Museum, Anchorage
24. Baranov Museum, Kodiak
25. Kodiak Military History Museum
26. Big Delta State Historical Park, Big Delta
27. Pioneer Aviation Museum, Fairbanks
28. University of Alaska Museum, Fairbanks

A 1942 Gum, Inc. bubble gum card depicting scenes of World War Two.

BIBLIOGRAPY

1. Arnold, Rhodes, *Foul Weather Front, A History of Air Operations in the North Pacific*, Pina Paisano Publications, Metairie, LA, 1995.
2. Benedict, H. Bradley, *Ski Troops in the Mud, Kiska Island Recaptured,* Littleton, CO, 1990.
3. Breu, Mary, *Last Letters From Attu, The True Story of Etta Jones, Alaska Pioneer and Japanese P.O.W.*, Alaska Northwest Books, Anchorage, AK, 2009.
4. Chandonnet, Fran, *Alaska At War*, Alaska Humanities Forum, Anchorage, AK , 1993.
5. Cloe, John H. Mission to the Kurils, Todd Communications, Anchorage, AK, 2016.
6. _________, *The Aleutians Warriors, A History of the 11th Air Force & Fleet Air Wing 4*, Pictorial Histories Publishing Co., Missoula, MT, 1991.
7. _________, Attu, *The Forgotten Battle*, National Park Service, Anchorage, AK, 2017.
8. Coats, Ken, *To Alaska, Fifty Years On The World's Most Remarkable Highway*, McClelland & Stewart Inc., Toronto, Ontario, 1992.
9. Cohen, Stan B., *Alcan & Canol, A Pictorial History of the Alaska Highway*, Pictorial Histories Publishing Co., Missoula, MT, 1979.
10. _________, *Trail of 42*, A Pictorial History of World War II in Alaska and Northwestern Canada, Pictorial Histories Publishing Co., Missoula, MT, 1979.
11. _________, *The Forgotten War, A Pictorial History of the Alaska Highwa*y, Pictorial Histories Publishing Co., Missoula, MT, four volumes.
12. Coyle, Brenden, Kiska, *The Japanese Occupation of an Alaska Island*, University of Alaska Press, Fairbanks, AK, 2014.
13. Duesenberg, H. *Alaska Highway Expeditionary Force, A Roadbuilders Story*, H & M Industries, Cedar Lake, Iowa, 1984.
14. Freeman, Elmer, *Those Navy Guys and their PBYs, The Aleutian Solution*, Kedging Publishing, Spokane, WA, 1984.
15. Garfield, Brian, *The Thousand Mile War, World War II in Alaska and the Aleutians*, Ballantine Books, New York, NY, 1969.
16. Goldstein, Donald M. and Katherine Dillon, *The Williwaw War, The Arkansas National Guard in the Aleutian Islands, Alaska, and American Military Strategy, 1867–1945*, Naval Institute Press, Annapolis, MD, 2003.
17. Grainger, John H., *World War II In The Defense of Alaska*, Tongress Publishing Co., Ketchican, AK, 2003.
18. Hammett, Dashiell and Robert Colodny, *The Capture of Attu, The Infantry Journal*, Washington DC, 1944.
19. Hays, Otis, Jr. *Alaska Hidden Wars, Secret Campaigns on the North Pacific Rim*, University of Alaska Press, Fairbanks, AK, 2004.
20. _________, *Home From Siberia, The Secret Odysseys of Interned American Airmen in World War II*, Texas A & M University Press, College Station, TX 1990.
21. Long, Everett and Ivan Y. Heganblyn, *Cobras Over The Tundra*, Arktika Publishing Co., Fairbanks,AK, 1992.
22. Marston, Muktuk, *Men of the Tundra*, October House, New York, NY, 1969.
23. Mills, Stephens E., *Arctic War birds, Alaska Aviation of World War II*, Superior Publishing Co., Seattle, WA, 1971.

24. Mobley, Charles H., *World War II Aleut Relocation Camps in Southeast Alaska*, National Park Service, Anchorage, AK, 2015.

25. Morgan, Lael, *The Aleutians*, Vol. 7, Number 3, Alaska Geographic, Edmonds, WA, 1980.

26. Morgan, Murray, *Bridge to Russia, Those Amazing Aleutians*, E. P. Dutton & Co., New York, NY, 1947.

27. Murphy, Brian, *81 Days Below Zero*, De Capo Press, Boston, MA, 2015.

28. Naval Historical Center, *The Aleutian Campaign, June 1942–August 1943*, Department of the Navy, Washington, DC, 1993.

29. Perras, Galen Roger, *Stepping Stones to Nowhere, The Aleutian Islands, Alaska, and Military Strategy, 1867–1945*, Naval Institute Press, Annapolis, MD, 2003

30. Potter, Jean, *Alaska Under Arms*, The MacMillan Co., New York, NY, 1942

31. Rearden, Jim, *Forgotten Warriors of the Aleutian Campaign*, Pictorial Histories Publishing Co., Missoula, MT, 2005.

32. _________, *Koga's Zero, The Fighter That Changed World War II*, Pictorial Histories Publishing Co., Missoula, MT, 1995.

33. _________, Castner's Cutthroats, *Saga of the Alaska Scouts*, Pictorial Histories Publishing Co., Missoula, MT, 1990.

34. Remley, David, *Crooked Roads, The Story of the Alaska Highway*, McGraw Hill Co., New York, NY, 1976.

35. Routhier, Ray, *The Back Devils, A Pictorial History of the First Special Service Force*, Advanced Litho Printing, Great Falls, MT 1982.

36. Rourke, Norman Edward, *War Comes to Alaska, The Dutch Harbor Attack, June 3-4, 1942*, Burd Street Press, Shippingburg, PA, 1997.

37. Salsbury, Cliff, *Soldiers of the Mist, Minutemen of the Alaska Frontier*, Pictorial Histories Publishing Co., Missoula, MT, 1992.

38. Scrivner, Charles L., *The Empire Express, Historical Aviation Album*, Temple City, CA, 1976.

39. Spenneman, Dirk, *The Cultural Landscape of the World War II Battlefield of Kiska, Aleutian Islands, Land, Water and Society*, Sturt University, Abbury, NSW Australia, 2011.

40. Stevens, Peter F., *Fatal Drive, Solving the World War II Mystery of the USS Grunion*, Regnerg Publishing Co., Houston, TX, 2012.

41. The Infantry Journal, *The Capture of Attu, As Told by the Men Who Fought There*, The War Department, Washington, DC, 1944.

The author with Zenji Abe who participated in both the Pearl Harbor and Dutch Harbor attacks.

Stan Cohen was born and raised in Charleston, West Virginia and is a geology graduate of West Virginia University. After working in the oil fields in his native state he moved to Misssoula, Montana in 1961 to work for the US Forest Service. In the summers of 1962 and 1963 he worked for the service in southeast Alaska and the Kenai Peninsula. In 1963 he entered into a ski business in Missoula at the local ski area and between that and a downtown ski shop, spent 11 years in the business. He founded Pictorial Histories Publishing Company in 1976 and since 1980 has been a full time writer and publisher, authoring or coauthoring 72 books and publishing about 350. And for 15 years had his own geology consulting business in Missoula. He has traveled extensively in Alaska and the Yukon. He has been to the Aleutians and Priblof islands five times and has written fifteen photo history books on Alaska and the Yukon, including four volumes of the Forgotten War series. In 2008 he was awarded the Contributing to Alaska History award. He lives, writes, and publishes from his home in Missoula with his wife, Anne.

Blaine Cornelison is a Native of Idaho, but has lived in Alaska since 1977. He has been involved in both Military and Western history the majority of his life and stems from a major military and western pioneer family in Idaho.

Baine has been involved with all phases of DOD projects throughout Alaska and the lower 48 for over 40 years, most specifically living and working the entire length of the Aleutian Chain. He is heavily involved with Alaska Historical Aviation and Alaska Military museums.

He continues to consult on all phases of DOD projects in Alaska, the lower 48, and the central Pacific. He lives in Wasilla, Alaska with his wife, Dianna

Blaine posing with a Japanese glass ball and bamboo rod in front of an abandoned Japanese landing craft at Attu while working on the island.